STRATEGIES FOR WORD IDENTIFICATION

Phonics from a New Perspective

BARBARA J. FOX
North Carolina State University

Merrill,
an imprint of Prentice Hall
Englewood Cliffs, New Jersey   *Columbus, Ohio*

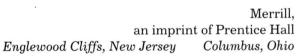

Library of Congress Cataloging-in-Publication Data

Fox, Barbara J.
    Strategies for word identification : phonics from a new perspective / Barbara J. Fox
        p. cm.
    Includes bibliographical references and index.
    ISBN 0-02-339191-X
    1. Reading—Phonetic method—Study and teaching (Higher)
  I. Title.
  LB1050.3.F69   1996   95-15688
  372.4' 145—dc20   CIP

Editor: Bradley J. Potthoff
Production Editor: Christine M. Harrington
Photo Editor: Anne Vega
Text/Cover Design: Jill E. Bonar
Production Manager: Laura Messerly
Electronic Text Management: Marilyn Wilson Phelps, Matthew Williams, Karen L. Bretz
Illustrations: Steve Botts

© 1996 by Prentice-Hall, Inc.
A Simon & Schuster Company
Englewood Cliffs, New Jersey 07632

Photo credits: Scott Cunningham, Cunningham/Feinkopf Photography, p. 44

Printed in the United States of America

10 9 8 7 6 5 4 3

ISBN: 0-02-339191-X

Prentice-Hall International (UK) Limited, *London*
Prentice-Hall of Australia Pty. Limited, *Sydney*
Prentice-Hall of Canada, Inc., *Toronto*
Prentice-Hall Hispanoamericana, S. A., *Mexico*
Prentice-Hall of India Private Limited, *New Delhi*
Prentice-Hall of Japan, Inc., *Tokyo*
Simon & Schuster Asia Pte. Ltd., *Singapore*
Editora Prentice-Hall do Brasil, Ltda., *Rio de Janeiro*

*To Floss Cogburn Le Coq for her dedication to excellence,
her unflinching belief in the value of knowledge,
her lifelong habit of reading for pleasure and information,
and her robust love of learning.*

PREFACE

This book is an invitation to become a teacher who supports readers as they develop and use many different word identification strategies. The perspective of the book is that word identification is a group of strategies that children develop as they learn to read, not a single letter-sound by letter-sound pathway to pronunciation.

Children use word identification strategies whenever they meet unfamiliar words in storybooks, poems, novels, articles in the popular press, or content area materials. Strategies support growth of learners' reading vocabulary, and these strategies develop in a relatively predictable sequence. The development of word identification strategies is enhanced when teachers provide opportunities for learners to explore the alphabetic writing code in many different ways, and when the learning of strategies is an integral part of learners' everyday reading and writing experiences.

For a good many years, we have been caught up in a debate between those who champion a great deal of letter-sound instruction and those who do not. The type of decoding at the center of this debate is sounding out words letter-sound by letter-sound. This is how many people define phonics. The ability to work out pronunciation letter-sound by letter-sound is certainly important for children who learn to read a language written in an alphabet. However, this type of decoding is only one of several word identification strategies that readers use. What's more, word identification strategies are successful only when the words readers identify make sense in the reading context.

In the chapters that follow, you will discover how readers reach out for new word identification strategies when they feel the need for better ways to identify the unfamiliar words they see in books, poems, plays, and articles. You will find out how learners first depend on strategies that bypass our alphabetic writing system. Then you will learn how readers, as they have more and more reading and writing experiences, gradually pay greater and greater attention to the words authors write and to the letters inside words. And you will find out how readers' word identification strategies become increasingly sophisticated as their familiarity with our alphabetic code increases.

When you read Chapter 1, you will learn what strategic word identification is all about and how readers use cues in the reading context to identify unfamiliar words. In Chapter 2, you will learn how emergent readers and writers gain insight into the form and function of written language, and you will discover the special insight into spoken language, called phonological awareness. As you read Chapters 3 through 6, you will learn what readers need to know and be able to do to use strategies. Additionally, you will find in these chapters implications for teaching and descriptions of learning activities that support readers in becoming accomplished strategy users. Finally, in Chapter 7, you will gain insight into why some learners have difficulty developing word identification strategies and what you can do to help them.

Should you decide to become a teacher who focuses on strategies, you will set aside memorization and drill-and-kill practice. You will use your knowledge of the sequence in which strategies develop to guide learners toward the development and use of more streamlined strategies. And you will make the development and use of word identification strategies an integral part of all sorts of students' experiences with print and language that go on in your classroom every day. I invite you to use this book to become this kind of teacher.

ACKNOWLEDGMENTS

I am indebted to the many teachers who welcomed me into their classrooms, to the children who were willing learners and eager participants in the activities their teachers shared, and to the principals who encouraged and supported their teachers. Without them this book could not have been written. Of the teachers I visited and who shared their classrooms with me, I would like to especially thank: Judy Skroch of Effie Green; Joan Perry of Emma Conn; Sarah Rodgers of Fox Road School; Denise Rhodes, principal, and David Wall of Franklinton Elementary; William Abel, principal, and Amy Stone of Immaculata Catholic School; Donna Dysert, Donna Kocur, and Karen Royall of Lacy Elementary; Helen Collier, principal, Gail Ace, and Marilyn Gray of Penny Road School; Moria O'Connor, principal, Carolyn Banks, Diana Callaghan, Debbie Faulkner, Pat Lemmons, and Gail Walker of Poe International Magnet School; Pam Bridges, principal, Judy Honeycutt and Patricia Gonzales of Willow Springs; JoAnn Everson; and Ronald Honeycutt. A special thanks to Catherine Clements for her good advice, to Celia Jolley for her helpful words and to Elizabeth Beecher for her wise counsel. Thanks also goes to the reviewers of this text: Ann Hall, Univeristy of South Florida; Patricia P. Kelly, Virginia Tech; John J. Pikulski, University of Delaware; Timothy Rasinski, Kent State University; Melissa J. Rickey, Eastern Montana College; Leo Schell, Kansas State University; Sam L. Sebesta, University of Washington; and Gail Tompkins, California State University, Fresno. Finally, thanks to Linda Scharp and Brad Potthoff, my editors at Merrill, for their guidance and vision.

CONTENTS

CHAPTER

USING THE ALPHABETIC CODE STRATEGICALLY

This chapter explains a strategy approach to word identification. You will

learn how readers strategically use the reading context to identify unfamiliar

words and why teachers explore the English alphabetic writing system with

the learners they teach.

K E Y   I D E A S

✳ Written language and spoken language are codes used to send and receive messages.

✳ The alphabet is a special type of written code that uses letters to represent sounds.

✳ Word identification strategies are organized ways to identify unfamiliar words in the sentences authors write.

✳ Word identification strategies help readers add words to their reading vocabularies and develop the abilities to automatically recognize words and to read independently.

As a good reader, you automatically recognize the words that you commonly encounter when reading. Instead of figuring out words, you focus on comprehension. This is exactly as it should be. But consider what it is like for readers who do not have a vast reservoir of written words in memory and who come across many unfamiliar words in their day-to-day surroundings and in the books they read. Meeting a large number of new words is a major impediment to comprehension, and so it is not surprising that those who are learning to read concentrate on developing their reading vocabularies. One way learners do this is to use the cues in the reading context, including the alphabetic writing system of English, to figure out the identity of words they do not automatically recognize.

CODES, CODE USERS, AND OUR ALPHABET

Consider the note Maria wrote (see Figure 1–1). If you speak and read Spanish, Maria's message is crystal clear. The words are easy to recognize, the sentences are well formed, and you know why the picture and the message are a perfect match.

On the other hand, even if you can speak Spanish but cannot read it, the format of the note and Maria's drawing are the only reliable clues to meaning. Hence, you can use information gleaned from the picture and your own background knowledge to make an educated guess about the content. In fact, from the heart-shaped illustration, you might logically infer that this is either a Valentine or a love letter. But unless you recognize the words Maria wrote, your grasp of the meaning is limited, and your comprehension is only a gross approximation of Maria's message. To go beyond supposition, you must learn the same thing that beginning readers learn: how to strategically use an alphabetic writing system to identify unfamiliar words in the reading contexts in which they appear. However, saying the words is not enough. You

FIGURE 1–1
Maria's note: Can you get the message?

must know the meaning of the words Maria has written. Added to this, you must understand the sentence structure and the words Maria uses, have a specific purpose for reading, and appreciate the social context in which notes such as this are written and read. (See the translation of Maria's note at the end of this chapter.)

Many languages use an alphabetic code to represent speech, among them Spanish, English, Arabic, Russian, French, and Icelandic. The alphabet is only one type of code, however. In fact, the learners whom you teach, regardless of their age, are experienced code users—whether or not they know anything about the alphabetic code in English or any other language. You and the learners in your classroom are quite literally immersed in a sea of codes: Spoken language is a code of speech sounds; mathematics, a set of numbers; the Morse Code, a combination of dots and dashes; semaphore, a system of flag positions. The alphabet is just one of many codes: It is a group of written letters.

People who send messages translate their ideas into all sorts of coded signals—speech sounds, numbers, dots and dashes, flag positions, or letters—that are understood by others. People who receive messages decode, or translate, the signals they see or hear into understandable words and ideas. For example, to decode the dots and dashes of Morse Code, listeners must know two things: (1) what letters of the alphabet that the dots and dashes stand for and (2) the meaning of the words that dots and dashes spell. Suppose, for the sake of illustration, that a listener hears the following tapped out in Morse Code:

    .... .– –

If the listener knows that .... stands for **h**, that .– represents **a**, and that – is used for the letter **t**, then it is a relatively simple matter to translate the signal into **h-a-t**. And if the listener also knows the meaning of **hat**, decoding is complete.

The alphabet works on the same principle, only letters are used as the coded signals for speech, instead of the dots and dashes in Morse Code. Just like Morse Code users, readers who successfully decode **hat** must know two things: (1) how letters represent speech sounds and (2) the meaning of the written word that letters spell. That is, in order to be successful, the words readers identify must already be in the readers' speaking vocabularies. For the reader who knows that **h** represents the sound "h," that **a** represents "a," and that **t** stands for "t," all that remains is to blend these sounds together to pronounce **hat**.* And when readers also know the meaning of the spoken word **hat**, decoding is complete. Though figuring out pronunciation letter-sound by letter-sound is the common perception of what decoding means, this is only one of several word identification strategies you will learn about in this book.

Readers use word identification strategies to support comprehension: They use the strategies to remove the ambiguity that occurs when they cannot automatically recognize the words authors write. For any word identification strategy to be effective, the words readers identify must make sense in the messages authors write. When readers identify unfamiliar words, they consider the reading context in which unfamiliar words appear, the alphabetic writing system of English, their own reasons for reading, and what they already know about the subject they are reading about. All of these considerations are explored in the next section.

THE USE OF STRATEGIES AND CUES IN IDENTIFYING WORDS

Readers interpret storybooks, novels, textbooks, magazine articles, newspaper editorials—virtually all written material—within their unique framework of personal knowledge and experience. For instance, the tongue-in-cheek humor of Scieszka's (1989) book *The True Story of the Three Little Pigs!* is fully appreciated only when readers know the original version of the story. In addi-

---

*In this book, for simplicity, rather than using a standard system of phonetic symbols, letters that typically stand for the sounds are used and are placed within quotation marks.

FIGURE 1–2
Readers use their unique background knowledge and cues from the reading context to construct authors' messages.

tion, readers must bring to this storybook social-cultural knowledge and an understanding of point of view and current practices of reporting the news. The author counts on his readers knowing all these things when he writes about the first little pig thinking "It seemed like a shame to leave a perfectly good ham dinner lying there in the straw" and when he compares the first little pig to "a big cheeseburger" (p. 15).

Along with social-cultural background knowledge, readers use the cues in spoken and written language. Readers bring to print a deep understanding of the word order, meaning, and sounds of the spoken language. Knowing a great deal about spoken language is a tremendous asset, for the predictable patterns of speech are also present in written language. Information about grammar, meaning, and the written code represent three types of information, or cueing systems, that support readers as they make sense of authors' messages.

Syntax is the grammatical arrangement of words in phrases, sentences, and paragraphs. It is important because the grammatical structure of language helps readers interpret the meaning of authors' messages. **Syntactic context cues** are the basis on which readers decide whether an author's word order is consistent with English grammar. Readers use syntactic context cues to predict words in phrases and sentences. For instance, in **The little _ chewed on a bone,** readers know that the word following **little** is a person or an animal (a noun). Likewise, readers know that the word following **dog** in **The little dog _ on a bone** is an action word (a verb). Syntactic context cues also give readers insight into the meaning of sentences. Readers who use syntactic context cues know that the meaning of phrases, sentences, and paragraphs may change when words are sequenced in different ways, for example, **The little dog chewed on a bone** versus **The dog chewed on a little bone.** While the first sentence refers to a small dog and the other to a small bone, the word sequence of both conforms to the structure of English. But the sentence **The chewed on a dog bone little** makes no sense at all. The word order is not consistent with the structure of English, and so the sentence is not meaningful language. Hence, when readers use syntactic cues, they ask themselves, "Does this seem like language?"

Semantic context cues, a second source of information, are the meaningful relationships among words in phrases, sentences, and paragraphs. This is the basis on which readers decide if an author's message is logical and represents real world events, relationships, and phenomena. Readers draw on their knowledge of the meaningful relationships among words and on their prior knowledge of the topic they are reading about. In so doing, readers look for meaning that is consistent with both the text and their experiences. For example, readers use semantic context cues to determine that the relationship among words in **The little dog chewed on the bone** is meaningful and that the relationship among the words in **The little bone chewed on the dog** is not. Hence, when readers use semantic context cues, they ask themselves, "Does this make sense?"

From a broader perspective, the reading context also includes the overall conditions under which materials are read and readers' reasons for reading. As a consequence, when readers consider syntactic context cues and semantic context cues, they do so in light of reading environment (such as noisy or quiet, shared reading or reading independently, with time limits or without time limits) and reasons for reading (such as for pleasure or for study, to get the gist or to locate facts).

Syntactic and semantic context cues, together with the overall conditions under which materials are read, create a rich base on which word identification and reading comprehension rest. When readers use the reading context, they draw upon all the cues available to them, selecting and combining information in order to construct authors' messages. Brian's note (Figure 1-3) illustrates how syntactic context cues and semantic context cues can work together in reading a text. You can automatically recognize all the words as belonging to your reading vocabulary except one: **spreencler.** If you were to try to decode this word without thinking about context, it would be difficult to figure out just what Brian meant to say. However, **spreencler** is surrounded by other words that contribute valuable clues to its meaning.

From syntactic context cues, you infer that **spreencler** is a noun, not a verb, adverb, or adjective. From semantic context cues, you surmise that this unknown object is something children play with, which rules out such things as spoons or sprockets. If you know the types of activities Brian and Mike enjoy, and if you also know the types of things Mike has to play with, you can use this background knowledge to narrow down your choices even further. For many readers, this is enough information to deduce the identity of **spreencler.**

Though the syntactic context cues and semantic context cues are rich, if you want to be absolutely certain about the word, you will turn your attention to alphabetic code cues. **Code cues** are the associations among letters and

FIGURE 1–3
Brian's note: How do you
figure out the meaning?

I am

playing

in Mikes

spreencler

sounds that are the backbone of our alphabetic writing system. The contribution of code cues is to help you further narrow down the field of possible words. When readers use code cues, they ask themselves, "Does this word sound and look right? Does the word I identify fit the context?"

When using syntactic context cues, semantic context cues, and code cues to identify words, readers need to keep the focus on meaning since they need to think about words that make sense in passages. The easiest way to combine code cues with syntactic context cues and semantic context cues is to ask yourself, "What word begins with **spr**, ends with **er**, and makes sense in Brian's message?" With this combination of cues, your chance of making a good educated guess increases substantially because code cues help you narrow the field of possible words. If the guess you make is sensible, you discontinue decoding, confident that you understand Brian's message.

If the beginning and ending code cues in **spreencler**, syntactic context cues, and semantic context cues are not enough to figure out this word's identity, then you consider all the letters in spelling. Should you choose to do this, you would probably sound out **spreencler** letter-sound by letter-sound. But, having sounded out **spreencler**, you still have not pronounced a recognizable word. Brian's spelling is unconventional, and so the outcome of sounding out is a nonsense word. Yet this nonsense word is quite similar in sound to a meaningful word in your speaking vocabulary that fits nicely into the overall reading context.

There is a curious and very interesting phenomenon at work here: In using code cues, readers do not always have to arrive at pronunciations that are absolutely perfect spoken renditions of the words authors intend to write. Pronunciations need only sound enough like real words to trigger recognition. By combining information from different cues, you know without a shadow of a doubt that Brian intended to write that he is playing in Mike's **sprinkler.**

While use of all types of cues contribute to understanding messages like the one Brian wrote, this does not imply that every cue is equally helpful in every reading situation. Learners' reasons for reading affect the importance learners assign to accurate word identification. For example, a fifth grader who reads her science textbook for information needs to pay close attention to the words the author wrote. A second grader who is reading an article in the children's magazine *Ranger Rick* for pleasure is more likely to be concerned with the overall ideas in the article, not with detailed information. Correct identification of nearly all words is far more important for understanding the information in science textbooks than it is for enjoying articles in *Ranger Rick.*

Insofar as Brian's note is concerned, if your reason for reading is to find out who Brian is playing with, you might make an educated guess for **spreen- cler,** using only syntactic context cues and semantic context cues, having found out that Brian is in Mike's company. Conversely, if you are concerned with knowing precisely what Brian is doing, you will analyze **spreencler** to determine exactly what type of play Brian is engaged in. All in all, the amount of mental attention you allot to word identification depends on how concerned you are about absolute understanding. Your concern for under- standing is, in turn, determined in part by the reason you decided to read Brian's note in the first place.

Overreliance on any one cue is inefficient, time-consuming, and likely to result in poor comprehension. Good readers know this and hence balance syntactic context cues, semantic context cues, and code cues with the type of text they are reading, the reading environment, their own reasons for read- ing, and their own background knowledge. Though it is not necessary to dis- tribute attention equally to all cues, it is necessary to be able to take maxi- mum advantage of the information cues provide, should reading situations call for it. When all is said and done, the strategic use of the reading context hinges on taking advantage of syntactic context cues, semantic context cues, and code cues. And, of course, the reasons for reading and the background knowledge readers bring to text help determine how much attention readers choose to pay to the cues available to them.

WHAT IS PHONICS, WHO TEACHES IT, AND WHY?

Phonics is the study of the relationship between the letters in written words and the sounds in spoken words. You teach phonics whenever you help read- ers decipher our alphabetic writing system: When you help readers figure out that **bone** begins with the same letter and the same sound as **banana, boat,** and **bubble**, you are teaching phonics. When you support learners as they compare and contrast words spelled with a double **e**, such as **green, seed, free,** and **street,** you are a phonics teacher. When you help readers think about a word that begins with **c**, ends with **t**, and makes sense in the sentence, **Mark's _ eats tuna fish,** you are teaching phonics. When you encourage writers to spell "the way words sound," you help writers think about and analyze our alphabetic writing system, which is what you do when you teach phonics.

Every teacher, whether an advocate of whole language, literature-based, basal or skills instruction, explores the alphabetic writing system with learners of English. There are three reasons teachers do this.

First, by strategically using a relatively small amount of code knowledge, readers can identify a large number of words. For instance, readers who know the sounds that **t** and **ur** represent in words like **turn** and **turkey** can figure out the pronunciation of words that share these letters, such as **turban** and **turmoil**. Readers then can add words to their reading vocabularies by connecting written words with words in their speaking vocabularies. This is crucial if learners are to build a vast reading vocabulary in a relatively short period of time.

Second, knowing phonics enhances automatic word recognition (Stahl, 1992). Words that are recognized automatically are "on the tip of the tongue." These words seem to leap off the pages and into readers' minds without so much as a conscious thought. Some attention is needed, of course, but the level is minimal in comparison with the mental resources readers have available to them. Automatic recognition frees readers—mature readers like you and me, as well as readers in grades 1 through 8—to concentrate their mental energy on comprehension (LeBerge & Samuels, 1985).

On the one hand, when readers automatically recognize words, they can pay more attention to the meaning of authors' messages because their attention is not occupied with word identification. On the other hand, when readers do not automatically recognize words, they divert their attention away from comprehension and allocate it instead to word identification. In the latter situation, word identification syphons off the mental attention that readers need to understand authors' messages. As a consequence, comprehension is robbed of attention, and understanding may be compromised (Samuels, 1988).

Third and last, readers who strategically use our alphabetic writing system have a tool to identify unfamiliar words on their own without any help from others. This gives readers a great deal of independence because their ability to read is not held hostage by a great many words that they do not automatically recognize. Because readers do not have to depend on their teachers or other people to tell them words, they are free to read any book at any time in any place. This means that readers can enjoy all sorts of books and magazines on their own, at home, in the car, in the library. This brings us to the question of how you, the teacher, can help learners become strategic users of our alphabetic code.

SUPPORTING READERS AS THEY BECOME STRATEGIC CODE USERS

Unlike the Greek goddess Athena who sprang fully grown from Zeus's head, word identification strategies do not emerge fully formed from a few incidental experiences with print. Strategies require careful nurturing and a supportive environment in which to develop. This does not mean a drill-and-kill approach to learning in which readers memorize isolated letter-sound combinations. Rather, it means giving readers many opportunities to understand how our alphabetic writing system works and many chances to strategically use this information as they read and write every day. Your role as the teacher is to guide learners, to model strategies, and to talk with learners about the strategies they use.

To develop and use word identification strategies, readers need to know how, when, and why to use strategies (Graves, Watts, & Graves, 1994). You will find descriptions of learning activities that support strategy development in Chapters 2 through 6. The learning activities follow this model: Readers are guided to (1) explore different word identification strategies with their teachers, (2) then move to practice with teacher guidance, and (3) end by transferring learning to reading and writing tasks.

1. **Exploration** gives readers opportunities (1) to observe how a particular strategy works, (2) to gain insight into how to use a strategy, and (3) to develop enough understanding of the strategy to try it under supervision. This is the time when teachers explain and model and when learners and their teachers join together to explore the code and to use strategies to identify unfamiliar written words in all sorts of contexts.

2. **Guided practice** gives readers a chance to try strategies, make inferences, draw conclusions, and cement understanding with the guidance of their teacher. Guided practice includes the thoughtful correction of mistakes and misapplications. It ensures that readers get knowledge of results, immediate feedback, and reinforcement.

Some of the readers in your classroom will need relatively minimal practice, while others will require a good deal more. For readers who need more practice than is included in the activities in Chapters 2 through 6, use the practice and reinforcement activities described in Appendix A. These activities are especially helpful for readers whose lack of code knowledge prevents them from effectively using word identification strategies. So, save the practice and reinforcement activities for readers who will definitely benefit from more code knowledge. Do not use the practice and reinforcement activities in Appendix A with readers who already have the information they need to strategically use the alphabetic code.

3. **Transfer** is the time when readers apply word identification strategies to various reading, writing, and problem-solving activities. Readers might work cooperatively and collaboratively to write poetry, create imagina-

tive cartoons, solve riddles and crossword puzzles, make up tongue twisters, write descriptions of favorite fiction characters, and so on.

The readers whom I teach benefit immensely from lots of opportunities to explain in their own words what they know, how they know it, and why they choose different word identification strategies. When readers explain their reasons for using the strategies they do, they take control of their own learning, develop a self-conscious awareness of their own code knowledge, as well as an appreciation of why and when to use different strategies. To support readers as they reflect on their use of word identification strategies, ask questions such as these:

1. Does what you just read sound like a real word?
2. Does what you just read seem like language?
3. Does the word make sense in the passage?
4. How did you figure out that word?
5. What other kinds of words can be figured out just the way that you figured out this one?
6. When would you use this same way to figure out another word?
7. What did you learn today that will help you be a better reader?

As readers answer questions like these, they organize observations, form generalizations, change or alter information and ideas, and, perhaps most important, become sensitive to how the strategic use of code cues supports comprehension.

FIGURE 1–4
Discussing strategies with readers gives them opportunities to develop insight into how, when, and why to use strategies.

LOOKING AHEAD

Word identification strategies are organized, systematic ways to determine the identity of unfamiliar words. The strategies are developed over time in a reasonably predictable sequence that begins long before children read story-books and long before they go to school. Though the exact order in which word identification strategies develop is not completely understood, we do know that learners use some strategies before others. We also know that awareness of written and spoken language is an important part of learning to read a language written in an alphabet. So, we begin in Chapter 2 by explor-ing the form and function of written language, as well as phonological aware-ness, which is the understanding that spoken language is made up of words, syllables, rhymes, and sounds.

Chapter 3 explains four strategies that develop early—the environmental cue strategy, the picture cue strategy, the incidental cue strategy, and the sin-gle code cue strategy. These strategies are important for readers to under-stand because they pave the way for the development of the analogy, letter-sound, and chunk strategies, which are described in Chapters 4, 5, and 6, respectively.

The analogy strategy and the letter-sound strategy develop at about the same time, usually during first grade. When learners who use the analogy strategy encounter an unfamiliar word, they look for groups of letters that are present in words they already know how to read. They then use this informa-tion to figure out pronunciation of the unfamiliar word. Next, readers cross-check to decide whether a word makes sense in the reading context. The strategy of cross-checking (Chapter 4) is the last step in word identification, regardless of the word identification strategy used.

If there is a stereotype for decoding, surely it has to be the letter-sound strategy (Chapter 5). Readers who use the letter-sound strategy connect the sounds represented by the letters in the written words with the sounds of spoken words. The chunk strategy (Chapter 6) is the most streamlined word identification strategy described in this book, the last to develop, and a more advanced strategy than either the analogy or letter-sound strategies. Readers who use the chunk strategy recognize many different-size chunks, or groups of letters, in words. Many of these chunks are meaningful (as the **aqua** in **aquarium**), which gives readers information about pronunciation, as well as word meaning. Though readers in grades 1 through 3 use chunks, it is not until about the fourth grade that the chunk strategy really begins to mature. And, as readers move into higher grades, they continue to refine their ability to use this strategy. Though accomplished readers prefer to use more effi-cient strategies, readers keep less efficient strategies in reserve just in case sophisticated strategies fail. Thus, in a very real sense, every word identifica-tion strategy that readers develop is always available, should a situation call for it.

Translation of Figure 1–1, Maria's Valentine

Dear Mrs. Saracho,

You are a great teacher. I am learning new things every day. I hope that you will be able to teach here next year. You are the nicest teacher in fifth grade.

Love,

Maria

REFERENCES

Graves, M. F., Watts, S., & Graves, B. (1994). *Essentials of classroom teaching: Elementary methods.* Boston: Allyn & Bacon.

LeBerge, D., & Samuels, S. J. (1985). Toward a theory of automatic information processing in reading. In H. Singer & R. B. Ruddell (Eds.), *Theoretical models and processes of reading* (3rd ed., pp. 813–840). Newark, DE: International Reading Association.

Samuels, S. J. (1988). Decoding and automaticity: Helping poor readers become automatic at word recognition. *The Reading Teacher, 41,* 756–760.

Scieszka, J. (1989). *The true story of the three little pigs!* New York: Viking Penguin.

Stahl, S. A. (1992). Saying the "p" word: Nine guidelines for exemplary phonics instruction. *The Reading Teacher, 45,* 618–625.

BECOMING AWARE OF LANGUAGE

Insights into Print and Phonological Awareness

This chapter describes how emergent readers and writers develop insights into the form and function of written language and into the words, rhymes, and sounds of spoken language. Also included in this chapter are learning activities to increase learners' abilities to detect rhyme, to separate spoken words into sounds, and to blend sounds into words.

K E Y   I D E A S

----

* ❊ As emergent readers and writers explore written language, they become aware of the form and function of writing. They learn the conventional ways that print is arranged on pages, the features of words and letters, and the purpose of written messages.
* ❊ As emergent readers and writers explore spoken language, they develop phonological awareness, which is awareness of the words, rhymes, and sounds in language.
* ❊ Phonological awareness develops sequentially, beginning with word awareness, then progressing to rhyme awareness, and finally to sound awareness (which refers to the abilities to separate words into sounds and to blend sounds into words).

James' writing (Figure 2–1) shows that he is discovering how writing is arranged on pages and that he is learning how written language is made up of words and letters. His writing includes letters, two words (**at** and **no**) copied from the print in his kindergarten classroom, a large form that looks somewhat like a letter, and two smiley faces. He writes **at** and **no** on a line he has drawn. From his writing, we can infer that James knows that letters are important for authors' messages, that the words in his classroom are significant, and that writing is positioned on lines. James will continue to develop awareness of written and spoken language as he writes, listens to stories that are read aloud, watches his teacher write, dictates stories, and watches his teacher point to words (or sweep a hand under words) while reading.

FIGURE 2–1
By experimenting with writing, emergent readers and writers, like James, have opportunities to discover the conventions of written language.

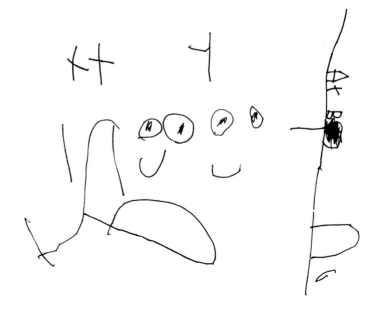

One of the greatest challenges facing emergent readers and writers is sorting out which pieces, or segments, of written language represent which pieces (segments) of spoken language. This is somewhat like putting together a jigsaw puzzle. Whereas the pieces of a jigsaw puzzle are colorful cardboard segments, the pieces of spoken language are words, rhymes, and sounds, and the pieces of written language are words, groups of letters, and single letters. Just as a jigsaw puzzle solver sorts cardboard puzzle pieces by color to decide which are blue sky and which are white snow, a reader sorts spoken and written language pieces to determine which are words, which are rhymes, which are individual sounds, and which are letters. Once the pieces (segments) of spoken and written language are identified, readers and writers have a basis on which to connect one segment (a spoken word or sound) with another segment (a written word or letter). Whereas a jigsaw puzzle solver fastens cardboard pieces together to construct a recognizable picture, readers and writers associate pieces of spoken and written language to identify words and construct authors' messages.

DEVELOPING AWARENESS OF WRITTEN LANGUAGE

As emergent readers and writers have reading and writing experiences, they develop awareness of the form and function of written language. Written language is based on certain conventions of print and on certain concepts of print. When emergent readers and writers develop awareness of the conventions of print, they come to understand how writing is arranged on pages. They learn that print goes from left to right and from top to bottom on the page, that white spaces separate words, and that punctuation—capitals, periods, commas, and so on—is an important aspect of writing.

When learners develop an understanding of the concepts of print, they learn that words are made up of letters and that writing, not pictures, is the medium through which authors communicate with readers. Children come to understand that each letter has a unique shape and that words are differentiated by their unique pattern of letters.

When learners develop awareness of the function of writing, they discover that writing is a meaning-driven activity, that authors' purpose in writing is to send messages, that written messages take many forms, that different forms serve different purposes, and that messages are written and read in social contexts.

One of the ways emergent readers and writers explore written language is through their own writing. Clay (1979) likens writing to a building-up process in which writers construct words by thinking about letter shapes, letter sequences in words, and the spatial relationships among words. Learners develop insight into the form and function of written language as they construct written messages by scribbling, drawing, repeatedly writing the same letter, copying words, and thinking about the letters and sounds of words they want to write.

It takes time and experimentation with written language for learners to write (Ferreiro & Teberosky, 1982). Scribbling that has connected wavy lines, resembles cursive, and goes from left to right on the page is an early form of experimentation. So, too, is the use of drawing. Sometimes emergent readers and writers retell stories, recall events, give descriptions, and share ideas using their illustrations. As these learners begin to develop insight into the concepts of print, they write mock letters (letterlike forms) or real letters with mistakes (Schickedanz, York, Stewart, & White, 1990). Sometimes learners use several forms at once, as we see in Marty's writing (Figure 2–2). Marty uses a connected scribble (wavy line), mock letters, and real letters when he writes. Marty's writing shows top-to-bottom and left-to-right orientation, though he writes on a decidedly downward slant.

As children move toward conventional writing, they experiment with letters, sometimes writing the same letter over and over again, as in Michelle's writing (Figure 2–3). Not only does Michelle repeatedly write the same let-

FIGURE 2–2
Marty, a kindergartener, uses connected scribbles, mock letters, and real letters when he experiments with writing.

ters, she uses capital (uppercase) and lowercase letters, and she copies several words from the print in her kindergarten classroom. She writes some words by themselves, while others are part of continuous strings of letters with no space separating one word from another. From Michelle's writing, we can infer that she is developing insight into the form of written language: She is sorting out in her own mind the properties that make letters and words unique. She already knows writing is arranged from top to bottom and from left to right on pages. However, Michelle does not fully appreciate the concepts of word and letters, for she neither used white spaces to separate the words she copied nor combined letters to write her own words.

Emergent readers and writers like Michelle and Marty must learn to pay attention to the distinctive features, or physical properties, that distinguish one letter from another (Rayner & Pollatsek, 1989). Differentiating letters is particularly challenging when letters share the same distinctive features, such as **b** and **d**; **p** and **q**; **m** and **n**; **E** and **F**; **m** and **w**. This is also true for words that share many of the same letters, such as **was** and **saw**; **then** and **when**; **were** and **where**. With so many relatively similar-looking letters and so many words that have several letters in common, word reversals and letter confusions are a normal part of learning to read (Dechant, 1991). Consequently, it is typical for kindergartners, first graders, and sometimes even second graders to reverse words and confuse letters.

As learners develop greater awareness of words and letters, they separate words with spaces and use letters to represent sounds. Emergent writers use their knowledge of the sounds in words and the letters in the alphabet to

FIGURE 2–3

Through pieces of writing like this, learners like Michelle have opportunities to discover the ways that words and letters are formed.

invent spelling. For instance, learners invent spelling by using a few consonant letters to represent words, as **wn** for **went** and **rn** for **run**. When the
concepts of word and letter develop even further, learners begin to use more
letters to write words and the words include vowels. For example, **bites** might
be written as **bis** and **could** as **cod**. Words written like this are called semiphonetic because letters that represent important sounds are left out (Gentry,
1987). Nadia (Figure 2–4), for instance, invents her own spelling by using letters to represent some, but not all, of the sounds in words, as in **pazz** for
pizza, **eut** for **ate**, and **suy** for **Sue's**.

Words that can be figured out by associating sounds with letters are
called phonetic (Gentry, 1987). Examples of this type of invented spelling are
noc for **knock, varry** for **very, tern** for **turn,** and **bekus** for **because**. Rashid,
whose story is shown in Figure 2–5, uses a mixture of semiphonetic (the word
wen for **when**), phonetic (**stichis** for **stitches**; **hert** for **hurt**), and conventional spelling (the words **like** and **my,** for example). Rashid is developing
insight into punctuation, as illustrated by his use of some capitals and periods. He has developed word and letter concepts and hence appreciates the
importance of using letters that represent sounds in words. He also knows
that writing is purposeful, is intended to be shared, and can tell something
important about the writer.

Writing and reading depend on awareness of the segments of speech and
print. For instance, Rashid could not write **stichis** (**stitches**) if he did not

FIGURE 2–4
Nadia uses semiphonetic
spelling to write nearly all the
words in her story: **I went to
Sue's and ate pizza.**

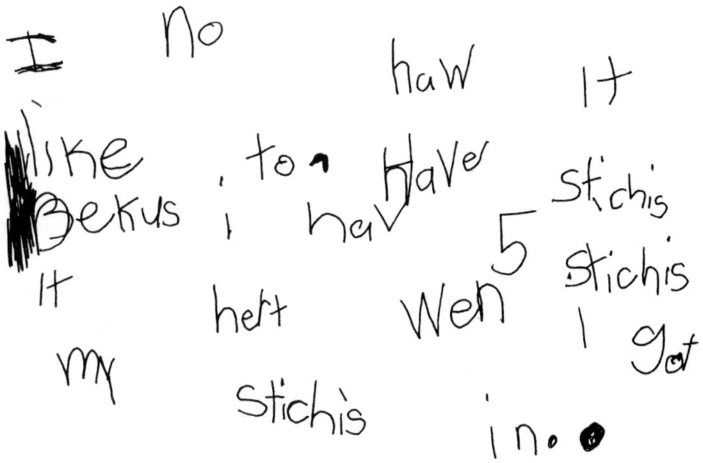

FIGURE 2–5
Rashid's story includes a combination of phonetic and conventional spelling: **I know how it's like to have stitches because I have five stitches. It hurt when I got my stitches in.**

know that: (1) spoken language is made up of words, (2) written words correspond to spoken words, (3) spoken words are made up of sounds, and (4) letters represent the sounds in spoken words. Thinking analytically about the segments of written and spoken language is essential, and this is especially so for children who learn to read a language that uses an alphabetic writing system.

DEVELOPING PHONOLOGICAL AWARENESS

The language that children bring to school serves many purposes. First and foremost, it gives them a way to interact with others so as to exert some measure of control over their lives and their environment. So long as children carry on everyday conversations, they concentrate on communication, not on words, syllables, rhymes, and sounds. This changes when children learn to read. As children move toward literacy, they begin to think about spoken language in a different way. Children stand back from the meaning of language in order to analyze speech. And, as they do this, emergent readers and writers discover that spoken language is composed of words, syllables, rhymes, and sounds. The learners in your classroom who are aware of the words, syllables, rhymes, and sounds in language have developed **phonological awareness**.

Phonological awareness is the ability to think analytically about the word, syllable, rhyme, and sound segments of language and the ability to act on the basis of this analysis. Children who are phonologically aware can (1) separate spoken language into words, syllables, rhymes, and sounds, and (2) blend sounds together to pronounce words. These learners deliberately arrange, rearrange, add, and delete language segments. What's more, learners use their awareness of the segments to connect spoken language with written language.

In the absence of phonological awareness, learners perceive speech as a continuous, undivided stream and therefore lack insight into the basic premise of written language—that print represents speech.

Awareness of the segments of spoken language develops in a predictable sequence: Awareness of the words in everyday conversations develops first. Some children may make this discovery when they are as young as three years old, but most certainly do so by the beginning of kindergarten (Fox & Routh, 1975). When children are aware of words and have opportunities to explore language, they develop syllable awareness. And, as emergent readers and writers explore nursery rhymes and poetry in day-care centers, preschool, and kindergarten, they develop awareness of rhyme in language. Later, when kindergartners and first graders have lots of opportunities to explore spoken and written language, they discover that words and rhymes are made up of individual speech sounds.

It has been suggested that syllables should be the first segment children learn to read, since syllables are easier than individual sounds to separate from words (Gleitman & Rozin, 1973). But written English is not suited to a system of writing in syllables (called a syllabary). For one thing, our language represents speech at the sound (or phoneme) level, not at the syllable level. Furthermore, because of the way consonants are combined with vowels, there are many different syllables in English. In fact, there are so many different syllables that it is not worthwhile to memorize the sounds associated with them. Unlike syllables, some rhymes recur quite frequently in English, as the rhyme in **cascade, brigade, parade**, and **marinade.** Paying attention to rhymes, then, is more beneficial than paying attention to syllables. For this reason, the focus here is on word awareness, rhyme awareness, and sound awareness, rather than on syllables.

Word Awareness

Children show that they conceive of spoken language as a series of word-length segments when they can tap a pencil for every word in a sentence such as **The frog jumped into the puddle,** clap for each spoken word, or move a block for every word. These children are consciously aware that spoken messages are put together by stringing one word after another. These learners are, therefore, prepared to search for meaningful word-length segments in print that match the meaningful word-length segments they identify in speech.

Words are large segments of spoken language and hence are the easiest segments to separate from speech. There are two reasons this is so: First, the words in everyday messages are meaningful, which is a distinct advantage to learners when listening for them in spoken language. And second, words are large bundles of sound and, as a result, are more obvious than rhymes or individual sounds in language.

Word awareness develops gradually as a natural consequence of experiences with language and is enhanced by reading and writing (Roberts, 1992). Reading contributes to word awareness inasmuch as written words are concrete referents, which can help emergent readers form and then crystallize the abstract concept of word-length language segments. Writing experiences contribute to word awareness in that the writing process encourages learners to think about the spoken word-length segments they would like to include in their messages.

One way to heighten word awareness is to point—and have learners point—to each word as it is read. Pointing to words as they are read in big books, storybooks, poems, and stories on wall charts has two advantages: First, this helps learners discover the match between voice (spoken words) and print (written words). And second, pointing to words gives learners opportunities to discover the word-length segments in spoken language that are represented by the word-length segments in written language. Other ways to enhance word awareness are to draw attention to interesting words by framing words (cupping hands around words), drawing clouds around words (drawing lacy bubbles around words), and using a word window to highlight words (using tagboard strips cut so as to reveal one word at a time).

Rhyme Awareness

Traditional nursery rhymes, jump-rope jingles, clapping games, and counting verses, such as "One Potato, Two Potato," are jam-packed with rhyme. Children tune into rhyme quite early in their lives, so it is no coincidence that the kind of language play that capitalizes on rhyme comes into its own during the elementary school years (Reich, 1986). In fact, children as young as three are sensitive to rhyming words (MacLean, Bryant, & Bradley, 1987) and, when given a chance to tell a friendly puppet which words sound alike, kindergartners are generally quite good at deciding whether two words rhyme (Treiman & Zukowski, 1991). What's more, kindergartners who are aware of rhyme are better readers later in school than kindergartners who are not sensitive to rhyme (Bradley & Bryant, 1978).

Rhyme awareness is a middle ground between awareness of words and awareness of individual speech sounds. Emergent readers and writers who detect rhyme have enough phonological awareness to connect speech with print at a level that is smaller than whole words but larger than single sounds. Rhyme awareness primes learners to look for the letters in written words that represent the rhyme in spoken words. This, in turn, paves the way for the use of rhyme to identify unfamiliar words by analogy, which is explained in Chapter 4. Additionally, the concept of rhyme gives writers insight into ways to spell words that rhyme and into ways to use rhyming language.

The four-year-old who says that **muffet** and **tuffet** sound alike is aware of rhyming language. The first grader who gives examples of rhyming words, such as **car, star,** and **jar,** is paying attention to rhyming sounds. Children also show rhyme awareness when they make lists of rhyming words or when they clap for rhyming words in poetry. Likewise, children can demonstrate awareness of rhyme in their writing.

Justin (Figure 2–6) has developed considerable awareness of rhyme. He wrote this poem after he and his first grade classmates had shared a good number of books about apples. *Ten Apples Up On Top!* (LeSieg, 1961), which tells the rhyming story of animals balancing apples and being chased by an angry bear with a mop, clearly influenced Justin's thinking as he composed. Notice how Justin uses two of the rhyming words from the storybook—**top** and **mop**—to create his own special poetic mood, message, and expression.

While most learners develop rhyme awareness early, it is quite possible that some of the kindergartners and first graders in your classroom are not aware of rhyming sounds in language. When these learners increase their awareness of rhyme, their reading ability will also improve (Bradley & Bryant, 1983). Awareness of rhyme helps reading ability regardless of how old learners are, how smart they are, or how many years of education their mothers have (Bradley, Maclean, Crossland, & Bryant, 1989, reported in Bradley & Bryant, 1991). So if some of the learners whom you teach are unaware of the rhyming sounds in language, it will be beneficial for them to develop this awareness.

Activities to Increase Rhyme Awareness

Bookstores and libraries offer a cornucopia of poetry collections for all ages, not to mention excellent books written in verse, such as *Drummer Hoff* (Emberly, 1967) and *In the Tall Tall Grass* (Fleming, 1991) for younger learners, and *Heartland* (Siebert, 1989) and *Half a Moon and One Whole Star* (Dragonwagon, 1990) for older learners.

FIGURE 2–6
Justin's rhyming poem, "Apples," shows that he has developed an awareness of rhyming sounds in language.

Apples

APPLES ON THE BOTTOM
APPLES ON TOP
APPLES ON THE CEILING
AND AN APPLE MOP!

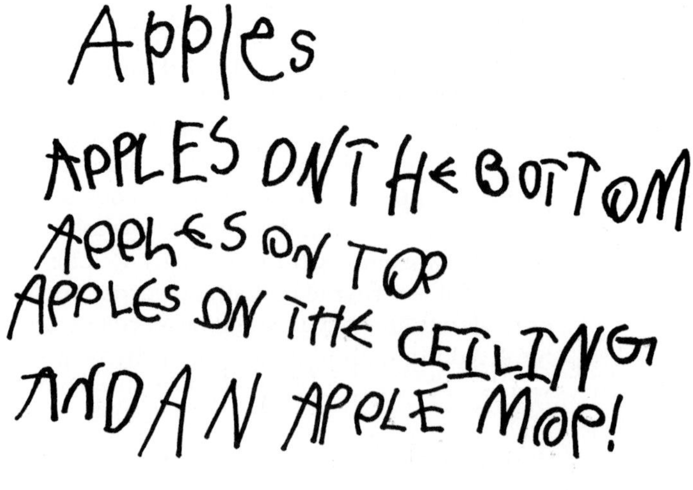

As you explore rhyming words with learners, make up rhymes for holidays, seasons, numbers, children's names, the names of teachers in your school, the names of things children are studying in science and social studies, and the names of characters in favorite books. Write the rhymes with learners and have them write them on their own. Put the children's poems on bulletin boards; hang them from the ceiling; tape them to the door; write them on the chalkboard. Frame rhyming words; encourage learners to think of rhyming examples; talk about why some words rhyme and others do not; make lists of rhymes; create games with rhyme.

✳ Hands Up for Rhyme

This easy, effective activity capitalizes on the poems learners enjoy everyday in your classroom. What's more, it uses a whole-group response format that gives everyone a chance to participate.

Things You'll Need: Good poems with lots of rhyming words; colorful pieces of construction paper.

Exploration: Seat learners comfortably on the floor, give each a colorful piece of paper, and ask learners to hold up the paper every time they hear two words that rhyme. For example, you might say **"mop—top"; "peach—each"; "plum—top."** As learners hold up paper, you quickly discover who is aware of rhyme and who is not.

Guided Practice: Now, ask learners to hold up a paper every time they hear a word that rhymes with a certain word in a poem or a book written in verse. For example, the words **sleep** and **deep** appear on page 3 of Crescent Dragonwagon's book *Half a Moon and One Whole Star* (1990). So you might challenge learners to listen for rhyme by saying something like, "Listen while I read. When you hear a word that rhymes with **keep,** hold up a colored square." Or learners might listen for words that rhyme with **jump** in the sentence **We have a Wump with just one hump** (page 18) from *One Fish, Two Fish, Red Fish, Blue Fish* (Dr. Seuss, 1960). Write rhyming poems or rhyming verse from books on the chalkboard (or on a large piece of chart paper), talk about rhyme, point out rhyming words, and then use the poems for the next activity.

✳ Inventing Rhyme

In this activity, emergent readers and writers listen to familiar rhyming poetry or books written in verse and predict rhyming words.

Things You'll Need: Familiar and unfamiliar poems with lots of rhyming words.

Exploration: Say a familiar poem while learners listen. Then invite learners to say the poem in chorus with you. Talk about rhyming words. Next say several lines, leaving out the last rhyming word in a line. Ask listeners to say the rhyming word that is left out. For example, you might recite a familiar nursery rhyme, such as Wee Willie Winkie, but leave out the word **o'clock**, which rhymes with **lock**. When you get to the end of the line with **o'clock**, pause and ask learners to say the rhyming word. When learners can anticipate rhyming words in familiar poems, it is time for guided practice.

Guided Practice: Now say a poem that learners have not heard before. Explain that listeners are to say the rhyming words that you leave out. Follow the same procedure just used, pausing at the end of a line that has a rhyming word and giving learners time to offer their own rhyming words. Of course, some of the words learners offer will not be the same ones the authors wrote. But so long as words rhyme, listeners are demonstrating that they are gaining insight into rhyme. Conclude by saying the whole poem, emphasizing the melodic cadence of the rhyming language. (This activity draws on spoken language. However, if you wish to include print, I suggest that you use the exploration and guided practice portions of the activity Predicting and Writing Rhyme, explained in Chapter 4.)

✳ Picture-Rhyme Matching

In this activity, learners match pictures of objects that rhyme and then draw their own pictures of rhyming objects.

Things You'll Need: Lots of pictures of things that rhyme; crayons, paper, a pocket chart (use the chalk tray if you do not have a pocket chart).

Exploration: After many rhyming poems and stories written in verse have been shared with learners, put three pictures in a pocket chart—two that represent words that rhyme and one that represents a word that does not. Ask learners which two words rhyme. Take away the picture for the nonrhyming word. After learners understand that they are to find pictures of words that rhyme, put several pictures in the pocket chart. Challenge learners to find rhyming pairs and to put pairs next to each other. Move to guided practice when learners can match pictures of things whose names rhyme.

Guided Practice: Explain that learners are to draw pictures of two things whose names rhyme. Fold pieces of paper in half and pass out one piece to each learner. Then, challenge learners to draw two pictures of rhyming objects. Ask learners to draw one picture on one side of the sheet, the second picture on the opposite side. Share the finished rhyming pictures with the whole group. Additionally, you may want to label the pictures learners draw.

As an extension activity, you might invite learners to work collaboratively to cut out pictures from magazines and catalogs and to then make rhyming collages by pasting all the pictures whose names have the same rhyming sound on the same large sheet of paper. When rhyming collages are finished, work with the learners to write captions for each picture.

Sound Awareness

Learners with sound awareness can do two things: First, they can separate words into sounds. They can, for instance, separate a word such as **lamp** into four sounds—"l," "a," "m," "p." To do this, learners disassemble words—they literally break words apart into individual sounds. Second, learners blend individual sounds together to form meaningful words. When learners blend, they assemble sounds into words. For example, the sounds "l" + "a" + "m" + "p" would be blended together into "lamp."

At six years old, Melanie (Figure 2–7) already knows something that every reader of a language written in an alphabet must learn: She knows which spoken sounds to connect with which written letters. Look at the clever way she writes **ch-ch-ch-chilly, sn-snowballs, ch-chillier,** and **ah ah ah ahchooooo!** She literally separates language into sounds before her readers' eyes. Melanie has a highly developed awareness of the sounds in spoken words. This is an example of the type of sound awareness that children develop as they explore written and spoken language.

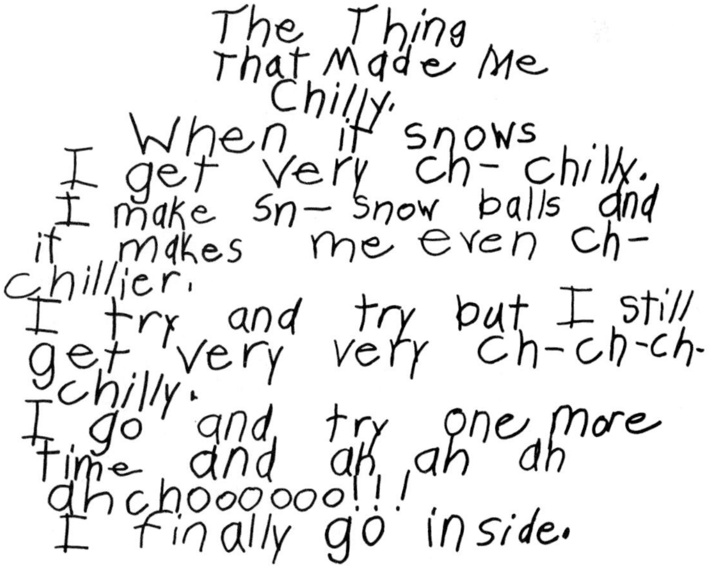

FIGURE 2–7
Melanie demonstrates sound awareness when she separates the beginning sounds from words in her story to help her readers experience the sensation of being cold.

The Thing That Made Me Chilly.
When it snows I get very ch- chilly.
I make sn- snow balls and it makes me even ch-chillier.
I try and try but I still get very very ch-ch-ch-chilly.
I go and try one more time and ah ah ah ahchoooooo!!!
I finally go inside.

The individual sounds in spoken language are much more challenging to identify than whole words and rhymes. For this reason, I can say with certainty that if learners are aware of sounds in words, they are also aware of rhyme. The reverse is not true: Learners who are aware of rhyme are not necessarily aware of individual sounds. Over the years, I have taught many children who are keenly sensitive to rhyme, but who cannot separate words into sounds and blend sounds into words.

The individual sounds, or phonemes, in words are not single sounds at all. Rather, they are a whole collection of slightly different sounds, called allophones. For instance, the "**p**" in **pig** is not exactly the same sound as that heard in **strap,** nor is it the same as that heard in **leopard, suspicion, disprove,** or **lamp**. Even though these sounds are not identical, listeners perceive them to be the same and hence group all these allophones into one phonemic category—"**p.**"

Sound awareness is essential to reading and writing because alphabetic writing is a code for individual speech sounds, not for whole words or rhymes. If readers are to strategically use our alphabetic writing code, they must understand that (1) sounds are strung together to form the words of language, (2) words can be separated into sounds, and (3) the letters in written words correspond to the sounds in spoken words. It is not surprising, then, that learners with low sound awareness do poorly on tasks in which they must use the alphabetic code (Juel, Griffith, & Gough, 1986). Yet, when given opportunities to increase sound awareness, these learners successfully use the alphabetic code to identify words (Fox & Routh, 1984).

Though separating words into sounds is important, learners must also be able to blend sounds together to form words. It makes sense, then, that the combination of helping children learn to separate words into sounds and to blend sounds into words has a highly beneficial effect. Children who are taught to separate words into sounds and to blend sounds into words are better at reading words (Torgesen, Morgan, & Davis, 1992). What's more, these children are better readers throughout the early grades (Ball & Blachman, 1991; Lie, 1991).

Not only are learners with sound awareness better readers, but they are better spellers, too. The words that first and second graders correctly separate into sounds are spelled with greater accuracy than the words that learners incorrectly separate into sounds (Foorman, Jenkins, & Francis, 1993). Hence, phonological awareness at the sound level is linked to both reading and spelling.

The positive effect of sound awareness is also observed in whole language classrooms. First graders in whole language classrooms who were taught to separate words into sounds read real words, nonsense words, and passages aloud better than their classmates who were not taught to separate word into sounds (Uhry & Shepherd, 1993). All things considered, if some of the learners whom you teach have not discovered the sounds in language, they will benefit from activities that increase sound awareness, becoming better readers as a consequence.

In the sections that follow, you will find six activities I have used to increase learners' ability to separate words into sounds and to blend sounds. These activities are helpful, to be sure, but so too are opportunities to read, to write, and to share books in which authors play with language. Authors who play with language open up all sorts of wonderful opportunities for learners to gain insight into language segments. For instance, in *There's a Wocket in My Pocket* (Dr. Seuss, 1974), beginning sounds are changed to create engaging nonsense words, such as **wasket** for **basket, nink** for **sink, zamp** for **lamp,** and **yottle** for **bottle.** Another example of this type of book is *The Cow That Went Oink* (Most, 1990). In this fanciful story, a cow who says "oink" and a pig who says "moo" teach other the proper words for their species, changing language in intriguing and mind-engaging ways. By sharing books such as these, emergent readers and writers have opportunities to make inferences and draw conclusions about the manner in which sounds are arranged, rearranged, and sequenced in language.

Learning to separate and blend sounds is not particularly effective without some letter-sound knowledge (Ball & Blachman, 1988; Lundberg, Frost, & Petersen, 1988). My recommendation is that you combine activities to separate and blend sounds with opportunities to explore our alphabetic writing code. This combination—learning to separate and blend sounds while also learning how the alphabetic code represents sound—is a powerful union and the most likely to result in the greatest learning.

Activities to Increase the Ability to Separate Words into Sounds

Generally speaking, emergent readers and writers first develop the ability to isolate beginning sounds from words, such as the **"b"** in **bat,** then learn to separate ending sounds, like the **"t"** in **bat,** and last become able to isolate medial sounds, like the **"a"** in **bat** (Foorman et al., 1993). Hence, you will probably find that the learners whom you teach find it easier to separate beginning and ending sounds from words than to separate medial sounds from words.

When you share sound awareness activities with learners, say the words slowly, keeping the sounds connected while at the same stretching them out, much like you pull a rubber band from a small to a large size. "Rubber banding" highlights individual sounds without actually breaking words apart. "Rubber banding" words is especially helpful for emergent writers like Nadia (Figure 2-4) and Rashid (Figure 2-5) who use invented spelling to write words. "Rubber banding" calls learners' attention to the sounds in words. In so doing, "rubber banding" helps emergent writers identify the sounds in words that they do not know how to spell (Reutzel & Cooter, 1992).

Should you decide not to "rubber band" but to pronounce sounds separately, be careful not to add extra sounds unless it is absolutely necessary. For example, "s" can be pronounced all by itself; it need not be pronounced as "**suh.**" Some sounds require that we add an extra vowel, the "**uh.**" For example, the sound represented by the letter **b** in **bunny** sounds like "**buh**" when said alone. This, however, is not the case with "**f,**" "**m,**" and "**l.**" So, be aware of how you pronounce sounds in isolation, and add an extra vowel only when necessary. Remember, too, that the number of sounds in words is not always equal to the number of letters in spelling. For example, **sheep** has three sounds "**sh,**" "**ee**" (long **e**), and "**p,**" but five letters. It is the number of sounds, not the number of letters, that is important.

✳ Tapping Sounds

Tapping sounds is fun for learners, requires very little time, takes virtually no preparation or materials on your part, and is effective. All you do is say learners' names, words from themes studied in your classroom, words from content area subjects, words from familiar storybooks, or words on wall charts. All learners do is listen to words and tap for each sound heard (Figure 2–8).

Things You'll Need: Pencils and a hard surface to tap them on. Or if learners tap fingers to palms, nothing is needed at all.

Exploration: Use familiar words from poems, storybooks, and wall charts, as well as learners' names, the names of characters from books, and important words from themes and content subjects studied in your classroom. Since short words are easier to separate into sounds than long words, demonstrate

FIGURE 2–8
Tapping sounds helps learners develop awareness of the individual sounds in words.

how to tap by saying a short word slowly, **see** for instance. As you "rubber band" this word, tap a pencil for each sound as it is heard or tap fingers to palm for each sound heard. In this example, you would tap twice because **see** has two sounds ("**s**" and "**ee**" [long **e**]).

Guided Practice: Now it is time for learners to do the tapping. Give each learner a pencil or ask learners to use their fingers and palms to tap. Say a word slowly, making sure that you stretch out the sound, and ask learners to tap for each sound heard. I have found that repeating this process with the same word two or three times is beneficial at the beginning. Later, when learners gain some proficiency at tapping, saying a word once is enough. And, of course, once learners can tap words with two sounds, introduce words with more sounds.

✳ Listening for Sounds

Variations of this activity have been used since the 1970s when a Soviet researcher, Elkonin, developed a method in which children move tokens for sounds in words. Today, a similar technique is used in Reading Recovery lessons (Clay, 1985) and recommended by many authors (Bolton & Snowball, 1993; Griffith & Olson, 1992). The version I describe can be used successfully with groups of up to about four learners.

Things You'll Need: Lots of colored one-inch tiles (explained in Appendix B); words from books shared many times.

Exploration: Use words from books that have been read and reread many times. Suppose, for the sake of illustration, that **cat** is a word in often-shared books. Say "**cat**" slowly, "rubber banding" it so that all sounds are pronounced clearly. Next, show learners how to move one tile as each sound is heard. Ask learners to line up the tiles in a row from left to right. Last, say "**cat**" slowly again, pointing to a tile as each sound is pronounced. Talk about the idea that words are made up of sounds, and that each tile represents one sound. After learners understand that one tile is to be moved for each sound heard, it is time for guided practice.

Guided Practice: Give each learner a few colored tiles, say a word slowly ("rubber banding" it), and ask learners to move one tile for each sound heard. (I suggest that you begin with very short, familiar words, such as **be** and **my**. Later, when learners are able to separate short words into sounds, introduce longer words.) Say the word slowly and ask learners to move one tile for every sound heard. Once all tiles are in place, ask learners to tell the order of sounds.

When learners can move a tile for every sound heard and have some knowledge of the alphabetic code, write letters on the tiles. This helps increase awareness of the connections between the sounds in spoken words and the letters in written words. Writing letters on tiles means, of course, that you will need to make lots of different tiles. (Look in Appendix B for tips for preparing materials.)

✳ Counting Sounds

In this activity, learners choose a card that has the same number of boxes written on it as the number of sounds heard in a word. I have found counting to be a little more challenging than tapping or moving tiles, so I recommend that you use this activity after learners are successful moving tiles for the sounds heard in words.

Things You'll Need: Sound Box Cards on which two, three, four or more boxes have been drawn (cards with boxes that represent the sounds in words, as described by Clay [1985] and explained in Appendix B).

Exploration: Draw two rectangles on the chalkboard. Divide one rectangle into two boxes, the other into three. Pronounce a word slowly ("rubber banding" it), for example, **"cat."** Then help learners discover that one of the rectangles has as many boxes as the word **"cat"** has sounds. To do this, count the sounds in **"cat"** and count the boxes in each rectangle. In this example, **"cat"** has three sounds, so learners would look for a rectangle that has three boxes. Once learners understand what they are to do, they are ready for guided practice.

Guided Practice: Pass out two (or more) cards, each with a different number of boxes. Then slowly say a word, "rubber banding" it so that each sound is clearly heard. Ask learners to count the number of sounds they hear, to find the card that has the same number of boxes as the word has sounds, and to hold up the card. As you use this activity, carefully watch learners to see who responds quickly, who hesitates overly long, and who waits for a neighbor to select a card. Any learner who hesitates or who copies from a neighbor needs more practice.

Activities to Increase the Ability to Blend Sounds

Blending requires that learners remember the correct order of sounds in words. When you listen to children blend, you may observe that poor blenders delete sounds, reverse sounds, or add sounds. Additionally, when children blend, they must manage the distortions that occur when some sounds are pronounced in isolation. For example, the **"j"** in **"jam"** is really something like **"juh"** when said by itself. To blend the sounds **"j" + "a" + "m"** into **"jam,"** learners need to drop the extra **"uh"** sound from **"juh."** You may well find, as I have, that the extra **"uh"** confuses many would-be blenders. And finally, I have found that seeing letters helps learners develop the concept that the sounds represented by letters are supposed to be combined into words. Hence, two of the following activities use letters. I suggest that you begin with Arm Blending. Then when learners have developed some ability to blend this way, introduce the two activities that use letters along with auditory blending.

✳ Arm Blending

Arm blending is a simple, effective technique in which learners place their hands in different positions on their arms as they blend. Year after year I successfully teach beginning readers and disabled readers to blend this way. You and the learners whom you teach will be impressed with the results!

Things You'll Need: No special material is needed.

Exploration: Explain that learners are to line up sounds on their arms in an imaginary blending pathway. For the sounds **"b," "a,"** and **"t,"** demonstrate by saying the first sound (**"b"**) as you place your right hand on your left shoulder (reverse for left-handed children), the second sound (**"a"**) as you put your hand in the crook of your arm, and the third sound (**"t"**) as you place your hand near your wrist. Now slide your right hand down your left arm from shoulder to wrist blending the sounds together as your arm moves (Figure 2–9). Repeat several times and invite learners to join you.

Guided Practice: Say the individual sounds in a word and ask learners to place their hands on their arms, beginning at the shoulder and ending near the wrist. Next learners blend sounds together as they slide their hands down their arms. When finished, ask learners what word they pronounced. Later, when learners are comfortable with Arm Blending, ask them to blend silently and then call on someone to say the whole word.

✳ Walking Sounds Together

In this simple, engaging activity, learners walk underneath large letters on a chalkboard, say the sounds associated with the letters, and blend the sounds as they walk. Walking Sounds Together requires knowledge of letter-sound correspondences, so it is best reserved for learners who have some code knowledge.

FIGURE 2–9
Arm blending is a simple,
effective technique that
learners can use with the
guidance of their teacher or on
their own.

Things You'll Need: No special material is needed.

Exploration: Write a word on the top half of the chalkboard. Make letters extra large, and space letters about one foot apart. For this activity, choose words that are spelled the way they sound. Put a line next to the last letter. To demonstrate, walk underneath letters, saying the sound each letter represents and folding sounds together so that one sound blends with another. Ask learners to say the word that was blended. You then write the word on the line. Demonstrate several times with different words and then move to guided practice.

Guided Practice: Invite volunteers to walk slowly underneath the letters in a word written on the chalkboard while everyone in the group blends one sound with another until the whole word is pronounced. Ask learners what word they pronounced, and then write the word on the line. Though Walking Sounds Together is intended to be shared with a group, this activity can be modified for use with one or two learners. To do this, exchange the chalkboard for a piece of paper on which different words are written. Make letters in words about one inch apart; put a line at the end of each word. Then, for each word, ask each learner to draw a loop from one letter to the next when blending.

✳ Sliding Sounds Together

The younger learners whom I teach enjoy this activity a great deal, perhaps because it uses a picture of a slide to graphically depict the blending process (Figure 2–10). Like the process of Walking Sounds Together, sliding requires some knowledge of our alphabetic code.

Things You'll Need: No special material is needed.

Exploration: Draw a large slide on the chalkboard. Write a word on the slide, spreading out letters so that they go from the top to near the bottom. To demonstrate blending, pronounce each sound as you slide your hand under each letter, adding sounds one after the other until you reach the bottom of the slide. Ask learners to tell you the word, and then write the word at the bottom of the slide. Be sure to slide in a fluid motion and to keep your voice aligned with your sliding hand.

Guided Practice: Write a word on the slide that learners have seen in storybooks or on wall charts and that is spelled with letter-sound combinations learners already know. Now, invite a volunteer to be the slider—the person who moves his or her hand down the slide. Ask the whole group to blend the sounds as the "slider" slides toward the bottom. Ask the slider to pronounce the whole word when he or she gets to the bottom.

FINAL OBSERVATIONS

Finally, it must be stressed that for the best results phonological awareness activities need to be combined with in-depth experiences in reading, writing, speaking, and listening. Use tape recorders, and read books aloud. Have learners write poems, repeat chants and raps, listen for sounds in learners' names, and find pictures of things that begin or end with the same sounds.

FIGURE 2–10
The slide in the activity Sliding Sounds Together gives learners a visual cue for blending. After sounds are blended, the whole word is written at the bottom the slide.

Enjoy literature with learners, and in the process draw learners' attention to the sounds in language that make up words and that add to the pleasure of reading and writing stories and poetry. Talk about the important words learners see around them everyday. Use nursery rhymes, language games, and jump-rope jingles. Give learners plenty of opportunities to experiment with written language, and encourage learners to write and to pay attention to the print they see around them everyday in their environment—in magazines and newspapers, in books, in poems, and in your classroom.

REFERENCES

Ball, E. W., & Blachman, B. A. (1988). Phoneme segmentation training: Effect on reading readiness. *Annals of Dyslexia, 38,* 220-225.

Ball, E. W., & Blachman, B. A. (1991). Does phoneme segmentation training in kindergarten make a difference in early word recognition and developmental spelling? *Reading Research Quarterly, 26,* 49–66.

Bolton, F., & Snowball, D. (1993). *Teaching spelling: A practical resource.* Portsmouth, NH: Heinemann.

Bradley, L., & Bryant, P. E. (1978). Difficulties in auditory organization as a possible cause of reading backwardness. *Nature, 271,* 746–747.

Bradley, L., & Bryant, P. E. (1983). Categorizing sounds and learning to read: A causal connection. *Nature, 301,* 419–421.

Bradley, L., & Bryant, P. E. (1991). Phonological skills before and after learning to read. In S. A. Brady & D. P. Shankweiler (Eds.), *Phonological processes in literacy* (pp. 85–96). Hillsdale, NJ: Lawrence Erlbaum Associates.

Clay, M. M. (1979). *Reading: The patterning of complex behavior.* Portsmouth, NH: Heinemann.

Clay, M. M. (1985). *The early detection of reading difficulties* (3rd ed.). Portsmouth, NH: Heinemann.

Dechant, E. (1991). *Understanding and teaching reading: An interactive model.* Hillsdale, NJ: Lawrence Erlbaum Associates.

Dragonwagon, C. (1990). *Half a moon and one whole star.* New York: Alladin Books.

Emberly, B. (1967). *Drummer hoff.* New York: Simon and Schuster.

Ferreiro, E., & Teberosky, A. (1982). *Literacy before schooling.* Portsmouth, NH: Heinemann.

Fleming, D. (1991). *In the tall, tall grass.* New York: Henry Holt.

Foorman, B. R., Jenkins, L., & Francis, D. J. (1993). Links among segmenting, spelling, and reading words in first and second grades. *Reading and Writing: An Interdisciplinary Journal, 5,* 1–15.

Fox, B., & Routh, D. K. (1984). Phonemic analysis and synthesis as word attack skills: Revisited. *Journal of Educational Psychology, 76,* 1059–1064.

Gentry, J. R. (1987). Spel . . . is a four-letter word. Portsmouth, NH: Heinemann.

Gleitman, L., & Rozin, P. (1973). Teaching reading by use of a syllabary. *Reading Research Quarterly, 8,* 447-483.

Griffith, P. L., & Olson, M. W. (1992). Phonemic awareness helps beginning readers break the code. *The Reading Teacher, 45,* 516–523.

Juel, C., Griffith, P. L., & Gough, P. B. (1986). Acquisition of literacy: A longitudinal study of children in first and second grade. *Journal of Educational Psychology, 78,* 243–255.

LeSieg, T. (1961). *Ten apples on top!* New York: Random House.

Lie, A. (1991). Effects of a training program for stimulating skills in word analysis in first-grade children. *Reading Research Quarterly, 26,* 234–250.

Lundberg, I., Frost, J., & Petersen, O. (1988). Effects of an extensive program for stimulating phonological awareness in preschool children. *Reading Research Quarterly, 23,* 263–284.

MacLean, M., Bryant, P., & Bradley, L. (1987). Rhymes, nursery rhymes, and reading in early childhood. *Merrill-Palmer Quarterly, 33,* 255–282.

Most, B. (1990). *The Cow That Went Oink.* San Diego, CA: Harcourt Brace Jovanovich.

Rayner, K., & Pollatsek, A. (1989). *The psychology of reading.* Englewood Cliffs, NJ: Prentice Hall.

Reich, P. A. (1986). *Language development.* Englewood Cliffs, NJ: Prentice Hall.

Reutzel, D. R., & Cooter, R. B. (1992). *Teaching children to read: From basals to books.* Englewood Cliffs, NJ: Merrill/Prentice Hall.

Roberts, B. (1992). The evolution of the young child's concept of word as a unit of spoken and written language. *Reading Research Quarterly, 27,* 124–138.

Schickedanz, J. A., York, M. E., Stewart, I. S., & White, D. A. (1990). *Strategies for teaching young children* (3rd ed). Englewood Cliffs, NJ: Prentice Hall.

Seuss, Dr. (1960). *One fish, two fish, red fish, blue fish.* New York: Random House.

Seuss, Dr. (1974). *There's a wocket in my pocket.* New York: Random House.

Siebert, D. (1989). *The heartland.* New York: Harper Trophy.

Torgesen, J. K., Morgan, S. T., & Davis, C. (1992). Effects of two types of phonological awareness training on word learning in kindergarten children. *Journal of Educational Psychology, 84,* 364–370.

Treiman, R., & Zukowski, A. (1991). Levels of phonological awareness. In S. A. Brady & D. P. Shankweiler (Eds.), *Phonological processes in literacy* (pp. 85–96). Hillsdale, NJ: Lawrence Erlbaum Associates.

Uhry, J. K., & Shepherd, M. J. (1993). Segmentation/spelling instruction as part of a first-grade reading program: Effects on several measures of reading. *Reading Research Quarterly, 28,* 218–233.

EARLY STRATEGIES

Using Logos, Pictures, Smudges, and Single Code Cues to Identify Words

This chapter explores four early word identification strategies. You will learn how emergent readers and writers use cues in the environment and in pictures to make sense of print. You will also find out how learners use incidental cues like colored ink and word shape to identify words. Then you will discover the way that emergent readers and writers use single code cues to identify words and why this is an important step toward the development of reliable word identification strategies. Finally, you will learn about activities to help learners who are using these strategies.

K E Y   I D E A S

---

* The earliest word identification strategies develop long before children go to school and long before children actually learn to read.
* Emergent readers and writers often associate meaning with cues in the environment, such as logos and the designs of product packages. In doing this, they are using the environmental cue strategy.
* Learners who use the picture cue strategy infer meaning from illustrations.
* Emergent readers and writers who use the incidental cue strategy rely on colored ink, word shape, letter shape, and other visual reminders like smudges to identify words.
* When learners turn their attention to the alphabetic code and remember an association between a letter-sound or a letter name and a written word, they are using the single code cue strategy.

The four word identification strategies explained in this chapter develop early, either before children go to school or when they start school. Three of the strategies do not use alphabetic code cues, and the fourth takes only minimal advantage of our alphabetic writing system. As a consequence, these early strategies are not reliable ways to figure out the identity of unfamiliar words. Nevertheless, emergent readers and writers use them, and hence it is important that you understand how they work. With insight into these early strategies, you are in a position to guide learners so that they move beyond dependence on these unreliable pathways to word identification and toward the use of more dependable routes to word identification.

EARLY STRATEGIES

When learners first notice print in their everyday lives, they make sense of written messages by using information gleaned from the things they see every day in their surroundings and from information depicted in illustrations. Learners who associate the meaning of print with familiar features in the environment use the **environmental cue strategy**; learners who infer the meaning of written messages from illustrations use the **picture cue strategy**. Neither strategy requires that learners think about the segments of spoken language or carefully observe written language. To use these two strategies, learners do not need phonological awareness, knowledge of the alphabetic code, or the ability to identify individual written words or letters in written messages.

So long as environmental cues and picture cues satisfy learners' needs to make sense of the print in their surroundings and in books, learners may continue to use the two strategies. However, environmental and picture cues do not provide enough information when learners want to read different messages in all sorts of books and magazines or want to write their own messages. When learners realize this, they begin to search for other ways to identify the words authors write.

In their search for more trustworthy word identification strategies, emergent readers look beyond cues in the environment and in pictures. In so doing, learners discover a group of cues that include colored ink, word shape, letter shape, and visual reminders like smudges and dog-eared pages. These cues are incidental to the alphabetic code inasmuch as they do not reveal information about the way that the alphabetic code signals words. The use of these cues, called the **incidental cue strategy**, is another step toward the development of code-based word identification strategies. And, as you will find out in a later section of this chapter, the use of word shape and letter shape, though they are not alphabetic code cues per se, do require some conscious inspection of print.

Learners next turn to the use of one, or perhaps two, letter- and sound-based cues in words. Learners who use this strategy, known as the **single code cue strategy**, have some phonological awareness and some code knowledge, though at a minimal level. Readers who use one (maybe two) code cues fix their attention on a single letter (or two) and then use the sound associated with that letter to remember a word. Though this takes only minimal advantage of code cues, it is the beginning of the strategic use of alphabetic code cues.

THE ENVIRONMENTAL CUE STRATEGY: MAKING SENSE OF THE WRITING IN EVERYDAY SURROUNDINGS

Five-year-old John copied **California, October, no, stop,** and **soap** from the wall chart in his kindergarten classroom (Figure 3–1). At three years old, Vitterica already knows she can find hamburger, drink, fries, and a small toy at every fast food restaurant with golden arches on the sign. Why do these young children connect meaning with the print and illustrations they see on signs, product labels, billboards, and food packages? The answer, say Harste, Burke, and Woodward (1982), lies in learners' need to make sense of their environment.

Making sense of print in the environment gives preschoolers a measure of control over their lives. The preschooler who can recognize the box of Raisin Yum Yum cereal on the grocery shelf might be able to talk her mother into buying that particular breakfast food. Though she quickly recognizes the cereal box, this same child cannot read the word **raisin** on the package of raisins her mother buys for midday snacks. While this preschooler might not be able to tell what the writing **Raisin Yum Yum** actually "says," in all likeli-

FIGURE 3–1
John enjoys copying the words
he sees displayed in his
kindergarten classroom.

hood she can give an approximation that is both meaningful and contextually acceptable. Shown a box of Raisin Yum Yum, she might say something like "cereal," "breakfast," or "eat breakfast." The reason emergent readers give feasible approximations is that they connect meaning with the everyday settings in which print appears, not with the specific words in written messages.

Instead of remembering words by their spellings, emergent readers use the environmental context to trigger memory—the proximity of golden arches and a fast food restaurant, the color of the drink container on the grocery shelf, the red octagon shape for Stop signs on street corners (Ehri, 1992). Children literally "read" the environment in which print occurs, not the print itself (Mason, 1980). What's more, to connect meaning with environmental cues, emergent readers do not have to analyze spoken or written language into word-length segments.

It is not surprising, then, that preschoolers who use the environmental cue strategy generally do not notice misspellings, like **Xepi** for **Pepsi,** nor do they recognize words when logos are removed or when the words are written outside their normal environmental contexts (Masonheimer, Drum, & Ehri, 1984). However, by associating meaning with the environmental context in which print appears, learners are taking an important step toward developing the concept that writing is supposed to make sense.

Environmental cues are a truly universal experience and virtually everyone knows how to read environmental print. This makes print in the environment a medium through which learners' families, whatever their educational or language background, can help their children develop their first reading strategies. What's more, when teachers value young children's ability to read environmental print, children are encouraged to build a positive image of themselves as successful readers.

THE PICTURE CUE STRATEGY: SHARING IDEAS THROUGH ILLUSTRATIONS

Long before children know enough words to read storybooks on their own and well before going to school, many can read their favorite books by inferring and predicting meaning from pictures. Emergent readers who connect illustrations with meaning use a picture cue strategy. These learners expect writing to label pictures and therefore look for cues to meaning in illustrations.

Preschoolers routinely infer the meaning of print from pictures. For instance, four-year-old Thomas used the picture cue strategy when he proudly held up a poster of a race car his father brought from a business trip to Detroit and announced that the poster said: "Gentlemen, start your engines." The fact that the words on the poster bore not the slightest resemblance to the message Thomas read was of little consequence to him; Thomas focused entirely on the rich picture context.

Like the print in our everyday surroundings, the pictures in storybooks are an avenue to meaning that does not call for knowing specific words, remembering letters, or understanding the principle of alphabetic writing. It follows, then, that emergent readers who use cues from the environment to read signs and labels are also likely to use pictures to read storybooks. To successfully use the environmental cue and picture cue strategies, emergent readers need only associate meaning with easy-to-recognize features like the McDonald's® golden arches and the illustrations in books. And, of course, neither strategy calls for phonological awareness, understanding of concepts of print, or code knowledge. Still, the picture cue strategy is a step forward. Emergent readers who know how stories are sequenced can use the pictures they see in their storybooks to tell stories as they turn pages, which brings learners closer to written language and enhances their insight into the way that stories are structured.

The artistic illustrations in picture books extend and elaborate the meaning of authors' messages. Picture books actually invite emergent readers to construct their own versions of stories, based on the pictures. Learners who expect pictures to signal meaning often imitate the fluent reading they hear when adults read aloud to them. These children use pictures to give a coherent rendition of a meaningful story. Turning the pages and cueing on pictures, learners say words that could have been written by the author but that are not necessarily on the page.

After hearing a story read and reread many times, children learn the combination of text and illustrations so well they can "read" by heart, com-

FIGURE 3–2
Before children recognize the
words authors write, they may
create sensible stories by
inferring meaning from the
illustrations on pages.

bining memory for written text with picture cues. These learners "read" picture books such as *Where the Wild Things Are* (Sendak, 1963) without so much as looking at the words Sendak wrote. Learners who "read" the pictures in storybooks or who recite stories from memory are developing the idea that the writing inside books is meaningful and can be rendered into spoken language. Added to this, emergent readers are learning that reading is an enjoyable, rewarding activity that offers a great deal of pleasure.

Emergent readers who use the cues in pictures to "read" their favorite storybooks may also use pictures when they write stories on their own. Sometimes children's stories have only pictures; sometimes their stories include mock letters, real letters, and items from environmental print. Kesha, a beginning kindergartner who is five years old, drew the picture story in Figure 3–3 after hearing her teacher read and reread *Arthur's Halloween* (Brown, 1982). Notice that Kesha faithfully renders the big scary house that is prominent in *Arthur's Halloween,* including a smiley face on the door to show the house is not frightening. Kesha clearly understands the picture-meaning connection. She also knows that writing is an important feature of books, and therefore, in her picture story, she includes letters and a word copied from the print in her classroom. When Kesha read her picture story, she described the house that she drew, and she described events that she remembered from *Arthur's Halloween.*

Over the years, Kesha has had a great deal of experience with scribbling and drawing. The picture story she creates reflects these early experiences. In some ways, the **O**s are part of Kesha's picture story. If the learners whom you teach write stories like Kesha's, rest assured that such stories represent a normal stage in becoming literate. Including letters in pictures is, indeed, something emergent readers typically do on their way toward discovering the principle of alphabetic writing (Ferreiro & Teberosky, 1979). From Kesha's writing, you can infer that she is beginning to make the transition from thinking of pictures to express meaning to thinking of letters and written words to convey meaning. She is searching for a medium through which she might effectively communicate with her audience, as yet unaware of the manner in which our alphabetic writing system represents speech.

THE INCIDENTAL CUE STRATEGY: PAYING ATTENTION TO COLOR, SHAPE, AND SMUDGES

The small brownish smudge on the bottom of the page is all Sarah needs to know that the words in her storybook say, "Kittens like to curl up into soft round balls when they sleep." The funny tail on the **q** is enough for Durrell to identify the word **quick**; Mai Lee recognizes **pig** because it is written in red ink on the bulletin board; Latonya identifies **hippopotamus** by its unique shape:

FIGURE 3–3
As children like Kesha begin to pay attention to written language, they may draw pictures to represent the events in familiar storybooks, and they may include pictures, letters, and words copied from their classroom.

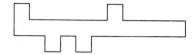

Each learner infers something different about the features that set one group of letters apart from another. Sarah uses a smudge on the page as the cue to word recognition, Durrell uses letter shape, Mai Lee colored ink, Latonya word shape.

Though the cues are very different, Sarah, Durrell, Mai Lee, and Latonya each use the same strategy: They select a cue that is completely incidental to the way that our alphabetic code represents speech, and they then connect that cue with meaning (Gough & Juel, 1991). This is a low-level, uncomplicated way to identify words. It requires no attention to letter sequence or to the cues in alphabetic writing. However, it does require that emergent readers understand the function of the white spaces that separate words and, if words are written in sentences, left-to-right and top-to-bottom progression. You can expect the emergent readers whom you teach to use incidental cues before they use alphabetic code cues. This is so regardless of how easy or difficult words are to identify in print (Gough, 1993).

You can safely assume that the learners in your classroom who use the incidental cue strategy also know how to use the environmental cue and picture cue strategies. The opposite is not necessarily true: Learners who use the environmental cue and picture cue strategies do not necessarily use incidental cues to identify words.

Jesse, whose story is shown in Figure 3-4, uses a combination of picture cues and incidental cues to read words in messages. Jesse looks for smudges, word shape, letter shape, and color cues. He uses picture cues to infer meaning. And, if he knows something about the story, he uses his background knowledge and picture cues to tell the story from memory. When he writes, Jesse puts one letter after another across the page. He writes his name and copies the words **yellow** and **me**, as well as the letters of the alphabet, from the print in his kindergarten classroom. He also includes numbers and a picture.

What Jesse does not do is to link the letters in written words to the sounds in spoken words. Jesse does not yet understand the basic premise upon which alphabetic writing rests, and therefore he writes strings of random letters (when he is not copying). Jesse is interested in print, however, for his careful copying suggests that he is aware of the importance of words in his classroom and that he is searching for ways to make sense of written language.

Because incidental cues are not tied to the alphabetic code, they have no predictable, logical association with the written language. Hence, four- and five-year-olds who use the incidental cue strategy may remember a word on a

FIGURE 3–4
Jesse knows that words and
letters are important, and he
explores written language by
copying the many different
types of print that he sees in
his classroom.

flash card when the card has a thumbprint, but not when there is no
thumbprint. When such learners are shown a card with only a thumbprint
(no word), they may say the word even though it is not there. What's more,
when a thumbprint appears on a card with a different word, learners may
read that word as though it were the first word they learned. It is the smudge,
not the spelling, that these learners select as a cue (Gough, Juel, & Griffith,
1992).

Even so, the learners in your classroom who look for incidental cues are
actively searching for ways to make sense of our writing system. They are
thinking about print, looking for features that set one group of letters apart
from another, and generating hypotheses about writing.

Color is the most obvious of the four types of incidental cues. I was
reminded of this one morning as I watched kindergarten children reading a
wall chart of daily activities. The wall chart had the following seven sentences
that learners read each morning at the beginning of the school day: "We will
read a book together. We will talk about the story. We will have centers. We
will have lunch. We will listen to a story. We will drop everything and read. We
will write." As one little boy read the familiar sentence, **We will write**, he
stopped when he came to the word **write**. Without a moment's hesitation his
friend, Jacob, lent a helping hand. "You know it's **write** because it's written in
green," Jacob announced helpfully. While **write** was written in green on the
chart, the other words in the sentence were in black. Jacob knew that colored
ink set **write** apart from other print on the wall chart and therefore he was
using color to identify this word.

COLORFUL WORDS

Writing in color . . .

gives your classroom lots of pizzazz, but it does not support word learning in any real sense. When words are written in cheery colors, it may take emergent readers more time to add words to their reading vocabularies. The reason is that emergent readers pick up on the most obvious cue, the cue that requires the least amount of effort and that is the easiest to discern. After all, why go to the trouble to use the letters to differentiate one word from another when color is so much easier to recall? In your classroom, use color wisely and be sensitive to the ways that learners approach unfamiliar words. Write in black ink if it appears that learners are using color rather than spelling as the cue to word identification.

Word shape, or configuration, is a second type of incidental cue. When emergent readers use word shape to identify unfamiliar words, they pay attention to the overall contour formed by letters. The word **hat**, for example, has two ascending letters separated by a letter that stays on the line, so its configuration looks like:

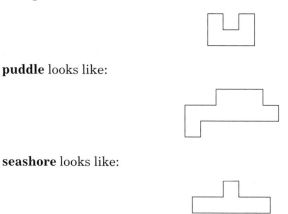

puddle looks like:

seashore looks like:

Unlike colored ink, word shape is not completely irrelevant to our writing system, since shape is determined by whether letters in a word are on the line or extend above and below the line. However, word shape (and letter shape, too) does not give emergent readers cues to sound. Word shape does, however, provide some information emergent readers can use to narrow down word choices, though this information is frequently unreliable.

If every word had a unique shape, configuration would be an excellent cue. But, because so many words have virtually identical patterns of upward and downward sloping letters, identifying words by their configuration alone makes reading more difficult than it should be. Learners who use configuration to recognize the word **hat** are bound to be confused when they try to generalize this information to other words with a similar shape, such as **bat, tub,** and **hot.** All this is to say that knowing a word's configuration has practically no transfer value to identify other words. In short, learners cannot use what they know about the configuration of one word to learn another word. For this reason, it makes no sense at all to ask learners to guess a word by its shape, draw an outline around a word to highlight its shape, or match a written word to its shape (Dechant, 1991).

Though configuration is unreliable, it can contribute to word identification when words are in sentences (Healy & Cunningham, 1992). Syntactic context cues, semantic context cues, alphabetic code cues, and word shape give readers overlapping, or redundant, information. The more overlap (the greater the redundancy), the easier it is to identify unfamiliar words. For instance, seeing the shape

is of little value in the sentence, **John grabbed his**

and ran out of the house, because both **bat** and **hat** fit nicely into the context (each is a noun and makes sense in the context). However, the sound associated with the letter **b** (code cue) combined with syntactic context cues, semantic context cues, and word configuration might be enough for a learner to correctly identify the word **bat.**

In addition to word shape, emergent readers may also use letter shape to identify words. It seems that emergent readers who use incidental cues do not think of individual letters as a special class of objects with constant shapes and forms (Adams, 1990). When these learners look at letters, they focus on such properties as circles, arcs, humps, and lines. Learners might, for instance, remember the word **nail** because the letter **n** has one "hump"; **took** because it has two circles in the middle that look like eyes; **banana** because it begins with a stick and ball (the lowercase **b**). Paying attention to circles, arcs, humps, and lines creates all sorts of confusion. Take **g** and **j,** as an example. Both **g** and **j** have "tails," so learners may not think of **g** and **j** as different letters. Emergent readers who identify the word **game** because it has a "tail" may misread **juice** because the letter **j** has a "tail" too.

A major drawback to the use of incidental cues is that the cues that are helpful under one reading condition are frequently not helpful under other reading conditions. So long as words are written in color, appear on pages with smudges, have unusual characteristics like a double **oo,** a distinctive letter, or a unique shape, learners may identify words with ease. But the use of these cues can lead to a great many misidentifications, as well as to confusion and frustration. Learners may recognize words when they are written in color or appear on a dog-eared page, but these same learners may not recognize these same words when they are written in other settings (no color and no dog-eared page). Learners may be baffled when asked to read words that have a similar feature, such as the double **oo** in **took, book,** and **food.**

Further, incidental cues work when emergent readers recognize a mere handful of words. However, as learners add more and more words to their reading vocabularies, incidental cues become less and less useful. The incidental cue strategy does not disappear, however. It stays in learners' word identification repertoire. What happens is that this early strategy becomes much less important in light of more reliable strategies that use a greater number of code cues (Alegria & Morais, 1991).

THE SINGLE CODE CUE STRATEGY

If environmental cues, picture cues, and incidental cues were reliable routes to the identification of many different words, emergent readers would have no reason whatsoever to develop other word identification strategies. As it turns out, these three early strategies do not give beginning readers enough information to identify the many unfamiliar words they come across in daily reading.

When emergent readers begin to use alphabetic code cues to identify unfamiliar words, they typically take a rather simplistic and marginally effective route to word learning, an approach called the single code cue strategy. With this strategy, they use a single letter-sound correspondence (maybe two) or a single sound (or two) to identify a word. As emergent readers listen to stories read aloud, share books in school, write stories, and participate in reading lessons, they form generalizations about how letters of the alphabet represent sounds in words. Learners notice, or are taught by their teachers, that letters in written words represent sounds in spoken words. From this, learners may conclude that the way to identify words is to connect a letter-sound, or a letter name, with pronunciation (Ehri & Wilce, 1985; Ehri, 1992).

A single code cue is a letter-sound correspondence or a letter name that emergent readers connect with the pronunciation of a word. For example, if a learner sees the word **sandwich** in a storybook and if that learner knows the sound associated with the letter **s**, the learners may then identify **sandwich** by associating the sound represented by the letter **s** with the **s** sound heard in **"sandwich."** A letter name may be used as a cue to identify a word if the name includes a portion of the sound that the letter represents. For instance, a learner who knows the name of the letter **s** may associate a portion of the sound heard in the letter name—the **"sss"** that is part of the name—with the **s** sound heard in **"sandwich."**

Once emergent readers link a code cue with a written word, they may assume that the same cue always represents the same word. As a consequence, if emergent readers use the sound represented by the letter **t** ("**t**") in **tuba** as a cue to identify this word, then every word that has a **t** in spelling is read as "**tuba**." Hence, **turtle, mitten, bat,** and **tree** are read as "**tuba**" because each shares the same code cue—the letter **t** that represents "**t**." Here are some characteristics of single code cue users.

What Single Code Cue Strategy Users Know about Phonological Awareness At a **minimum,** learners who use the single code strategy are aware of at least one sound in the spoken words they hear in everyday conversations, though their phonological awareness may well be greater than this. Complete knowledge of the way that sounds are arranged, rearranged, and sequenced in words develops later as learners have experiences writing, reading, speaking, and listening, and as learners become more proficient at the strategic use of our alphabetic code.

What Single Code Cue Strategy Users Know about Code Cues Learners who use the single code cue strategy know the features that distinguish one letter from another and therefore identify individual letters consistently and reliably. They know that words are made up of letters and know the sounds of a few letters or the names of a few letters. While code knowledge may not go beyond a handful of letter-sounds or letter names, this is all it takes to identify words with the single code cue strategy.

What Single Code Cue Strategy Users Do with Their Knowledge To better understand the single code cue strategy, consider how Estiban uses a single code cue to learn the word **potholder** in the storybook *Oma and BoBo* (Schwartz, 1987). On page 20 of the book, the author writes, "Oma looked at her old red potholder hanging on the wall." The picture on page 20 depicts other sentences on the page far better than the ideas in this sentence. Consequently, the picture cue strategy is not very helpful. Interestingly, the words **old red,** which always go along with **potholder,** could be a strong context clue. But this is just the second time the words **old red potholder** appear in the book. Any connections in Estiban's mind between the words **old red** and **potholder** are weak at best and probably nonexistent. Hence, Estiban turns to the single code cue strategy and here is how he uses it:

1. Estiban notices that **potholder** begins with a letter he recognizes—**p.**
2. Estiban associates the sound that **p** represents ("**p**") with the spoken word "**potholder.**"
3. The next time Estiban comes across **potholder** in the story, he thinks of the sound that the **p** represents ("**p**") and then uses this combination to identify the written word **potholder.**

Beginning and ending letters are easier to connect with sounds than letters in the middle of words (Treiman, 1985), which explains why children like Estiban most often use first and last letters as code cues (Ehri & Wilce, 1985; Ehri, 1992).

If Estiban did not know the sound associated with the letter **p** (or any other letter in **potholder**), he could still use the single code cue strategy, provided that he knew the name of such letters as **p, t, l,** or **d.** Many letter names include part of the sound that letters represent in words, which gives readers clues to letter-sound relationships (Ehri, 1983). For example, when Estiban says the name of the letter **p,** he also says part of the sound **p** represents in **potholder.** Most consonant letters give clues to letter sounds, and the names of the vowels (**a, e, i, o,** and **u**) are helpful when vowels represent long sounds, as in **came, sleep, tide, road,** and **tube.** The idea is that when letter names contain some of the sounds that letters represent in words, learners can use the letter names as clues to pronunciation. Therefore, even if the only thing Estiban knows about letters happens to be their names, he can link the sound cue in a letter name to pronunciation.

Learners who use the single code cue strategy frequently read the wrong words because a single code cue—the letter-sound association or the letter name—leads to the possibility of misidentifying the written word with any word that shares that cue. Since so many different words share letters, the strategy is obviously very ineffective. Still, the single code cue strategy does help ease learners into the strategic use of our alphabetic writing system. Perhaps the greatest advantage of the single code cue strategy is that it gives learners opportunities to develop, test, and revise hypotheses about our alphabetic writing system.

As emergent readers experiment with the code cues in words—even a single cue—they are refining their phonological awareness and extending their code knowledge. The more learners know about the segments of spoken and written language, the more learners absorb, internalize, and generalize information about the alphabetic code. Increased phonological awareness and greater code knowledge, in turn, provide a platform for developing more reliable and more streamlined word identification strategies. Though the single code cue strategy is relatively short-lived, it serves as a gateway to the use of the alphabetic code and as such is the precursor of more advanced word identification strategies.

TEACHING CODE CUES IN CONTEXT

In today's first grade classrooms, some learners may use picture and incidental cue strategies, some may use the single code cue strategy, and still others may use more reliable word identification strategies. The lesson I describe here is a good match for users of the single code cue strategy because it places relatively low demands on phonological awareness. Learners do not have to separate words into individual sounds, nor do they have to blend individual sounds together. It is also beneficial for emergent readers and writers who use incidental cues and picture cues because it gives them opportunities to observe connections between spoken and written language. And it can be helpful for readers who use more advanced word identification strategies in that these readers have opportunities to expand their reading vocabularies.

The lesson has three parts: (1) exploration of code cues, (2) guided practice in context, and (3) transfer to different reading contexts. To illustrate the lesson, I will describe how a first grade teacher supports readers as they learn about the beginning consonant **f.** Here is how the three parts fit together:

1. *Exploring Code Cues*   The teacher begins by reminding learners that the word **farm** is in the book *Old MacDonald Had a Farm* (Adams, 1975) and in the book *Skip to My Lou* (Westcott, 1989)—books with which the students are familiar. The first graders in this class know the meaning of **farm,** so the teacher need not define the word, though this would be necessary if learners had never heard **farm** before. (Only one word is used in this illustration, though more than one could be included in actual lessons.)

To explore the **f** in **farm,** the teacher writes **farm** on the chalkboard, saying each letter name as he writes it. Having written **farm,** he asks learners to read it along with him. He points out that the same sound heard at the beginning of "**farm**" is also heard at the beginning of "**fat,**" "**fox,**" and "**food.**" The teacher then focuses learners' attention on the beginning letter, **f.** To do this, the teacher covers up the **arm** and points to the **f** and talks about this letter. Then he uncovers **arm** to reveal the whole word. Next, he underlines the **f** in **farm.** He then writes **fat, fox,** and **food** on the chalkboard, spelling the words aloud as he writes them. He asks learners to think of other words that begin with the same sound heard in "**farm.**" Learners think of **father, Friday, funny,** and **five.** The teacher writes these words on the chalkboard, spelling words aloud as he writes them and calling attention to the beginning letter, **f.**

2. *Guided Practice*   The teacher writes several short sentences with **farm** that learners have seen in familiar books and stories. The teacher then invites the whole group to read each sentence in chorus with him. He points to words as they are read so as to demonstrate the connection between written and spoken words and to reinforce the concept that print is a medium through which messages are conveyed.

For example, one of the sentences the teacher writes on the chalkboard is **Take care of the farm,** which appears on page 8 of the Big Book *Skip to My Lou* (Westcott, 1989). "Who can find the word **farm** in this sentence?" he asks. Lots of eager hands fly into the air, and a volunteer then goes to the chalkboard to underline the word (Figure 3–5). In so doing, children learn that there is a one-to-one connection between written words and spoken words. Furthermore, finding words in sentences gives learners practice using code cues along with reading context and helps learners cement images of words in their minds.

3. *Transfer to Reading Contexts*   Learners write **farm** in their personal dictionaries. Then learners look for **farm** as they read a storybook with their teacher or with a partner. Finally, the teacher gives small groups of learners index cards on which a variety of words are written. Learners then work cooperatively to combine words to create their own sentences with **farm.**

And, for added enrichment, the teacher writes the text of *Skip to My Lou* (Westcott, 1989) on a long piece of chart paper. The chart paper is then spread on the floor. Learners work with partners to draw pictures illustrating meaning. Once the illustrated chart is complete, the teacher and learners read it together in chorus, talk about the meaning, the illustrations, and the ideas in the story. Then the teacher tapes the chart on a wall so that learners can reread the story at their leisure. In these ways, every child has an opportunity to successfully participate in the lesson, regardless of whether that child uses picture cues, incidental cues, one or two code cues, or all the code cues in words.

MOVING BEYOND EARLY STRATEGIES

Learners move beyond early strategies when they have opportunities to explore our alphabetic writing system, to read many different books, poems, and messages, and to write for many different purposes. One of the ways readers move beyond the early strategies is to look for code cues in unfamiliar words that are present in familiar words. When readers do this, they use

FIGURE 3–5
Finding words in sentences from often shared storybooks and poems helps readers learn that there is a one-to-one connection between written words and spoken words.

existing information to construct and acquire new knowledge by dividing words (or syllables) into sound and letter patterns. This is the key to identifying words with the analogy strategy, which is the topic of the next chapter.

REFERENCES

Adams, M. J. (1990). *Beginning to read: Thinking and learning about print.* Cambridge, MA: The MIT Press.

Adams, P. (1975). *Old MacDonald had a farm.* Singapore: Child's Play Ltd.

Alegria, J., & Morais J. (1991). Segmental analysis and reading acquisition. In L. Rieben & C. A. Perfetti (Eds.), *Learning to read* (pp. 135–148). Hillsdale, NJ: Lawrence Erlbaum Associates.

Brown, M. (1982). *Arthur's halloween.* Boston: Little, Brown.

Dechant, E. (1991). *Understanding and teaching reading: An interactive model.* Hillsdale, NJ: Lawrence Erlbaum Associates.

Ehri, L. C. (1983). A critique of five studies related to letter-name knowledge and learning to read. In L. Gentile, M. L. Kamil, & J. S. Blanchard (Eds.), *Reading research revisited* (pp. 143–153). Englewood Cliffs, NJ: Merrill/Prentice Hall.

Ehri, L. C. (1992). Reconceptualizing the development of sight word reading and its relationship to recoding. In P. B. Gough, L. C. Ehri, & R. Treiman (Eds.), *Reading acquisition* (pp. 107–143). Hillsdale, NJ: Lawrence Erlbaum Associates.

Ehri, L. C., & Wilce, L. S. (1985). Movement into reading: Is the first stage of printed word learning visual or phonetic? *Reading Research Quarterly, 20,* 163–179.

Ferreiro, E., & Teberosky A. (1979). *Literacy before schooling.* Portsmouth, NH: Heinemann.

Gough, P. B. (1993). The beginning of decoding. *Reading and Writing: An Interdisciplinary Journal, 5,* 181–192.

Gough, P. B., & Juel, C. (1991). The first stages of word recognition. In L. Rieben & C. A. Perfetti (Eds.), *Learning to read: Basic research and its implications* (pp. 47–56). Hillsdale, NJ: Lawrence Erlbaum Associates.

Gough, P. B., Juel, C., & Griffith, P. L. (1992). Reading, spelling and the orthographic cipher. In P. B. Gough, L. C. Ehri, & R. Treiman (Eds.), *Reading acquisition* (pp. 35–48). Hillsdale, NJ: Lawrence Erlbaum Associates.

Harste, J. C., Burke, C. L., & Woodward, V. A. (1982). Children's language and world: Initial encounters with print. In J. Langer & M. Smith-Burke (Eds.), *Bridging the gap: Reader meets author* (pp. 105–131). Newark, DE: International Reading Association.

Healy, A. F., & Cunningham, T. F. (1992). A developmental evaluation of the role of word shape in word recognition. *Memory and Cognition, 20,* 141–150.

Mason, J. M. (1980). When do children begin to read: An exploration of four-year-old children's letter and word reading competencies. *Reading Research Quarterly, 15,* 203–227.

Masonheimer, P. E., Drum, P. A., & Ehri, L. C. (1984). Does environmental print identification lead children into reading? *Journal of Reading Behavior, 16,* 257–271.

Schwartz, A. (1987). *Oma and BoBo.* New York: Harper & Row.

Sendak, M. (1963). *Where the wild things are.* New York: Harper & Row.

Treiman, R. (1985). Phonemic analysis, spelling, and reading. In T. Carr (Ed.), *New directions for child development: The development of reading skills* (Vol. 27, pp. 5–18). San Francisco, CA: Jossey-Bass.

Westcott, N. B. (1989). *Skip to my lou.* Glenview, IL: Scott, Foresman.

THE ANALOGY STRATEGY

Using Familiar Words to Identify Unfamiliar Words

This chapter describes two strategies: the analogy strategy and the cross-checking strategy. As you read this chapter, you will learn how syllables are made of onsets and rimes, how the analogy strategy—in which readers use word parts to read unfamiliar words—works, and how to help readers use familiar words to identify unfamiliar words. You will also discover how readers use the cross-checking strategy and why this strategy is important for word identification.

K E Y   I D E A S

✸ Syllables have a two-part structure, consisting of an onset, which is the consonant(s) at the beginning of syllables, and a rime, which is the vowel and any subsequent consonants at the end of syllables.

✸ Readers who use the analogy strategy connect an onset and a rime in words they already know how to read with the same onset and rime in a word they do not know.

✸ The cross-checking strategy helps readers make sure that the words they identify fit the reading context.

✸ Successful word identification depends on cross-checking, regardless of the strategy used to decode the word.

Look at the following sets of words:

rain	fish	more
train	swish	shore
obtain	finish	ignore
terrain	publish	explore
maintain	astonish	omnivore
constrain	embellish	commodore
bloodstain	accomplish	underscore

A quick glance is all it takes to recognize that the same patterns of letters and sounds occur in many different words. Once learners discover that the seven words in each of these three word mountains share a letter pattern, learners have a way to organize their thinking so as to use the code cues in known words to identify unknown words. The idea is to make analogies from words that are in learners' reading vocabularies to words that are not in reading vocabularies. Learners who use analogy as a strategy find a shared letter pattern in words, such as the **ain** in **rain** and **train**, and then use the similarity to identify unfamiliar words that have the same pattern, such as **maintain** and **constrain**.

LOOKING INSIDE SYLLABLES

Lucy sets a decidedly lighthearted tone as she ruminates about school in the poem in Figure 4–1. Lucy repeats words, rhymes words, and, what's more, all the words she uses have only one syllable.

FIGURE 4–1
Some of the one-syllable words
in Lucy's poem consist of an
onset and a rime; others
consist of a rime only.

School

I like school.
School is fun.
School is nete.
School is cool.

Every word, even the smallest, is made up of at least one syllable. Each syllable has just one vowel sound and so the number of syllables in a word is equal to the number of vowels heard during pronunciation. For instance, you hear one vowel when you pronounce **"train,"** which means that **"train"** has just one syllable. You hear two vowels in **"obtain,"** three vowels in **"astonish,"** and four in **"incarcerate."** Therefore, **obtain** has two syllables, **astonish** three, and **incarcerate** four syllables.

Looking inside the syllables in Lucy's poem reveals a two-part structure that consists of an **onset** and a **rime** (Fowler, Treiman, & Gross, 1993; Treiman, 1992). **Onsets** are the consonants that come at the beginning of syllables, as the **sch** in **school**. Likewise, the **s** in **sit**, the **sl** in **slit**, and the **spl** in **split** are onsets. Onsets are always consonants, and there can be several clustered together at once (**sch** and **spl**, for example). **Rimes** are made up of the vowel and consonants at the end of syllables. The rime in **school**, for example, is **ool**. Similarly, the **ent** in **tent** is a rime made of the vowel (**e**) and the consonants that follow (**nt**); the rime in **scream** is **eam**; in **black**, it is **ack**.

All syllables have a rime, which means that rime is everywhere in our language. Rhyming words like **school** and **cool** share a rime, in this case **ool**. When rime is common to two or more words, the words share a rhyming sound.

In rimes, consonants do not have to follow the vowel: sometimes the vowel ends the syllable, as in **my** (onset = **m** + rime = **y**) and **be** (onset = **b** + rime = **e**). Some syllables have only a rime, no onset, as in **an** and **it**. Table 4–1 shows the onset-rime structure of the one-syllable words in Lucy's poem. Words with more than one syllable are analyzed in just the same way. The only difference is that syllables are combined, as shown in Table 4–2.

TABLE 4-1
Onsets and Rimes in Lucy's
Poem

Onset	+	Rime	=	One-Syllable Word
sch	+	ool	=	school
c	+	ool	=	cool
	+	is	=	is
l	+	ike	=	like
f	+	un	=	fun
n	+	eat	=	neat

In Appendix C, you will find lists of rimes and examples of words in which rimes appear. Beginning readers and expert readers alike use onsets and rimes to identify words (Bowey, 1990). So Appendix C includes examples of one-syllable words, like **skate** and **late,** as well as longer words like **calculate, elevate,** and **mutate.** The onsets and rimes in syllables provide tremendous insight into our alphabetic writing system. And when readers develop knowledge of onsets and rimes, the stage is set to move beyond the single code cue strategy and into use of the analogy strategy.

USING THE ANALOGY STRATEGY

The analogy strategy is so worthwhile that all readers—from beginners to experts—use it (Baron, 1979; Goswami, 1986). Readers who use the analogy strategy connect onsets and rimes in words they already know how to read with the same onsets and rimes in words they do not know how to read. The basic premise is that if words share onsets or rimes, then words must also have similar pronunciations. This requires that learners think of shared letter patterns in words (Graves, Watts, & Graves, 1994). Thinking of shared letters and sounds calls for a good deal more phonological awareness and code knowledge than does the use of a single code cue, as you will learn in the next section.

TABLE 4–2
Onsets and Rimes in Multiple-Syllable Words

Onset	+	Rime	+	Onset	+	Rime	+	Onset	+	Rime	=	Word
p	+	ump	+	k	+	in					=	pumpkin
m	+	et	+		+	al					=	metal
p	+	oul	+	tr	+	y					=	poultry
c	+	al	+	c	+	u	+	l	+	ate	=	calculate
sk	+	el	+		+	e	+	t	+	on	=	skeleton
r	+	e	+	pl	+	en	+		+	ish	=	replenish

FIGURE 4–2
Wall charts of words with shared rimes help readers understand that when words have a common rime, they also have some of the same sounds.

What Analogy Strategy Users Know about Phonological Awareness Users of the analogy strategy are aware of beginning sounds in words. They know that **fun** begins with "f" and **sun** begins with "s." They are also aware of rhyming sounds in words. Because of this knowledge, they can identify words that share rhyming sounds, such as **fun, run,** and **spun.** Likewise, the strategy users can give examples of words that begin with the same sounds, such as **fun, fat,** and **five.** They also can separate words into onsets and rimes. For example, they can separate **fun** into "f" and "un." Furthermore, the strategy users know how to blend beginning sounds (onsets) and the sounds of vowels and ending consonants (rimes) together to form recognizable words. They can, for instance, blend "f" and "un" together to pronounce "**fun.**"

What Analogy Strategy Users Know about Code Cues We know that beginning readers who are aware of rhyme in spoken language use the analogy strategy to identify unfamiliar words that share written rimes (Goswami & Mead, 1992). Hence, analogy strategy users recognize and remember onset letter-sound combinations and rime letter-sound combinations in the context of real words (Ehri & Robbins, 1992). For instance, learners recall that the **f** in **fun** represents "f" and that the **n** in **name** represents "n." Analogy strategy users treat rimes as complete units, not as individual letter-sound combinations. Consequently, when they see the words **fun** and **sun,** they know that the **un** represents "un" in each word. Likewise, they know that the **ift** in **sift** and **drift** represents "ift."

What Analogy Strategy Users Do with Their Knowledge   Suppose for the sake of illustration that Tamara, who is a first grader, does not automatically recognize the word **tent** in the sentence **Jane saw a large tent in the forest.** Suppose further that Tamara cannot figure out **tent** from picture cues, syntactic context cues, semantic context cues, or background knowledge. However, Tamara brings to reading the knowledge of onsets and rimes in words she knows how to read. Here is how Tamara uses the analogy strategy:

1. Tamara notices a familiar onset and a familiar rime in **tent.** She recalls that the **t** in **tell** represents "t," and that the **ent** in **went** represents "ent."
2. Tamara exchanges the "w" in **"went"** for the "t" in **"tell,"** which leaves "t" + "ent."
3. She then blends "t" + "ent" to pronounce "tent."
4. Last, Tamara checks to make sure that "tent" is a good fit for the sentence. She asks herself: Does **tent** sound and look right? Does this seem like language? Does **tent** make sense in the passage? Do I know what the author means? If the answers to these questions are yes, Tamara stops decoding and continues reading. If the answers are no, Tamara tries once again to figure out **tent.**

Tamara would not have been successful if she had not been able to exchange the onset in one word (the "w" in **"went"**) for the onset in another word (the "t" in **"tell"**). Also known as initial consonant substitution, this ability is so important for strategic code use that all learners who successfully use word identification strategies know how to replace one onset with another.

EXCHANGING ONSETS

If you see that . . .

learners know the sounds represented by the **ent** in **went** and the **t** in **tell** but cannot use this knowledge to pronounce "tent," then it is quite probable that learners cannot exchange onsets.

The thing to do . . .

is to give learners opportunities to develop this ability by using the activities called Building Words with Onset-Rime Tiles and Mystery Words on Mini-Chalkboards (described in this chapter) and Fish for Onsets (described in Appendix A).

THE CROSS-CHECKING STRATEGY

In the example in the previous section, the last thing Tamara did was to verify that **tent** made sense in the sentence. When readers make sure that the words they identify fit the reading context, this is called **cross-checking**. Cross-checking is a strategy all by itself and the last step in word identification. Good strategic code users always cross-check, regardless of whether they identify words with the analogy strategy or some other strategy.

Cross-checking ensures that word identification supports comprehension. When readers cross-check, they actively think about meaning. They take into account the overall sense of the surrounding phrases, sentences, and paragraphs, as well as sentence structure, code cues, and their own personal reasons for reading. Once satisfied that the newly identified word makes sense in the context, readers immediately focus their attention back on reading the text.

When readers cross-check, they get valuable feedback on the success of their own decoding efforts. Thus, one consequence of cross-checking is metacognitive, or conscious, awareness of the success of word identification. Readers know whether a decoded word is acceptable or unacceptable for the reading passage. An acceptable outcome is a real, meaningful word that is sensible in the context; an unacceptable outcome is either a nonsense word or a word that does not fit the context.

Readers who cross-check put only as much mental energy into decoding as is necessary to identify a word as consistent with the author's message. Readers who cross-check know whether to stop word identification and proceed with reading the text or to give word identification another try. When a word makes sense, decoding stops and comprehension moves forward unimpeded by the confusion created by unknown words. On the other hand, if decoded words do not make sense, then cross-checking lets readers know that they have not constructed a meaningful message.

Readers who use the cross-checking strategy are guaranteed of a good fit between identified words and authors' messages. Readers who do not cross-check accept the results of decoding even if those results are nonsense. For these reasons, cross-checking is absolutely essential, and hence this strategy must be used every time readers use word identification strategies to figure out the identity of unfamiliar words.

IMPLICATIONS OF THE USE OF ANALOGIES FOR TEACHING

Making analogies from the known to the unknown is an important part of learning. Both preschoolers and school-age learners solve problems by applying what they know about familiar situations or conditions to unfamiliar ones (Brown, Kane, & Long, 1989). Teachers know this and are quick to help

FIGURE 4–3
Readers use the cross-checking strategy to monitor their own word identification so as to keep word identification and reading meaning based.

learners appreciate connections between the words that learners know how to read and the words that learners do not how to read. Whenever teachers point out shared onsets and rimes among known and unknown words, they are helping readers use the analogy strategy. For example, if readers do not automatically recognize **tent** and if picture and context cues are not strong enough to help the reader figure out this word, then teachers might say something like, "Look at the word **tent** in this sentence. Now, look at this word (pointing to **went** in another sentence). If this (pointing to **went**) represents **"went,"** what do you think this word (pointing to **tent**) might be?" Or teachers might point to **tent** and say, "Can you think of another word that you know that begins with a **t**? Can you think of another word that ends with **ent**? Now, how can you use this to help you figure out **tent**?"

Though readers could separate words into the beginning consonant-vowel combination (**te**) and the ending consonant(s) (**nt**), they prefer to divide syllables into onsets and rimes (Santa, 1976–1977; Wise, Olson, & Treiman, 1990). What's more, readers are much more likely to make analogies between words that share a rime, such as **tent** and **went**, than between words that share a beginning consonant-vowel combination, like the **te** in **tent** and the **te** in **test** (Goswami, 1990; Goswami & Bryant, 1992). In addition, the use of analogous onsets and rimes places fewer demands on phonological awareness and code knowledge than word identification with individual letter-sound combinations. The reason is that rimes are treated as intact units.

While analogy strategy users need to know that rimes like **"ent"** come at the end of **"bent,"** **"went,"** and **"tent,"** they do not have to be aware of the individual sounds in rimes. Remembering that **ent** represents **"ent"** is far less challenging than remembering that the **e** represents the sound of **"e,"** **n** the sound of **"n,"** and **t** the sound of **"t."** Thus, readers who remember the rimes in written words put less mental energy into code reading than do learners who remember individual letter-sound combinations.

Blending ability helps readers apply the analogy strategy (Uhry & Shepherd, 1993). And blending onsets and rimes is much easier than blending individual sounds. Readers who blend onsets and rimes into words have fewer individual sounds to manipulate and consequently fewer sounds to keep in memory than readers who blend individual sounds into words. This, in turn, reduces the probability of reversing sounds, deleting sounds, or adding sounds. From a practical point of view, readers who are less phonologically aware and who therefore might not be successful in sounding out and blending **tent** as "**t**" + "**e**" + "**n**" + "**t**" may be able to decode **tent** when it is divided into "**t**" + "**ent**" (Ehri & Robbins, 1992).

Since identifying words with the analogy strategy makes fewer demands on readers' phonological awareness, it is a more accessible strategy for learners who are less phonologically aware. For this reason, the analogy strategy is a good place to begin with readers who have difficulty decoding words letter-sound by letter-sound.

Why Onsets and Rimes?

Onsets and rimes are reasonably dependable maps to sound; as a result, readers can place a certain amount of confidence in them. Onsets are consonants and consonants are far more reliable representations of sound than are vowels. Readers who see the onset **s** in **sack** and the onset **br** in **brake** have solid clues to pronunciation. This is not the case with vowels. Vowels represent more than one sound, as with the **a** in **sack**, **brake**, **saw**, and **car**. But, when syllables are divided into onsets and rimes, the trick vowels are not quite so troublesome. The reason is that vowels are learned as part of a chunk of letters and sounds. For this reason, readers who learn rimes do not have to understand why the **a** in **sack** is pronounced one way and the **a** in **brake** another way. Instead, learners remember that the **ack** in **sack** represents "**ack**" and the **ake** in **brake** represents "**ake**." No further analysis is called for.

Second, remembering rimes sidesteps the need for readers to learn exceptions to the alphabetic code. For example, the sound represented by the **o** in **told** should be the same as the **o** in **clock**, since both vowels are followed by two consonants. This is not so, of course. Learners would be confused if they tried to read **told** as though the **o** represented the sound in **clock**. However, the sound represented by the **o** in **told** is not at all troublesome when remembered as part of the rime **old**. Learners who know how to read the rime in **told** have an alphabetic code cue to the identification of any word that shares this rime; for example, **gold**, **behold**, **scold**, and **enfold**. The net effect is that even vowels that can stand for a variety of sounds are easily remembered and decoded when learned as part of frequently recurring rimes.

Which Onsets and Rimes Are Important?

For readers using word identification strategies, any onset is worth exploring. This is so because a combination of onsets and the reading context gives learners powerful cues to the identification of unfamiliar words. In many cases, considering the onset along with syntactic context cues and semantic context cues gives readers enough information to identify unfamiliar words. In other cases, this combination of information substantially narrows the field of plausible words. Additionally, calling attention to onsets, in combination with the reading context, keeps word identification meaning based.

Whereas any onset is worth learning, some rimes are more important than others. Worthwhile rimes are those that recur regularly in words. The idea is to learn those rimes that are used to build many different words, not rimes that are part of a mere handful of words. By focusing on frequently occurring rimes, readers have the information they need to decode a great many different words. As a consequence, teachers should provide readers with plenty of opportunities to apply the analogy strategy. The more often the analogy strategy is used, the more powerful a tool it becomes. Look for frequently occurring rimes in the literature learners enjoy, as well as in Appendix C. Look, too, in *The Random House Rhyming Dictionary* (Stein, 1990) and *Webster's Compact Rhyming Dictionary* (1987) for lists of literally thousands of words that share patterns of ending letters and sounds. All things considered, the analogy strategy is well within the capabilities of most beginning readers, as well as a beneficial way to add words to the reading vocabularies of older readers.

ACTIVITIES TO INCREASE THE STRATEGIC USE OF ONSETS AND RIMES

To explore onsets and rimes with learners, discuss the onsets and rimes in words from familiar stories and poems; point out shared onsets and rimes; compare and contrast words; make lists of words that share onsets or rimes and put the lists up in your classroom. As readers use the analogy strategy, give them opportunities to explain their reasoning. Ask questions like those in Chapter 1, which help readers reflect on their own use of word identification strategies:

1. Does what you just read sound like a real word?
2. Does what you just read sound like language?
3. Does the word make sense in the passage?
4. How did you figure out that word?
5. What other kinds of words can be figured out just the way that you figured out this one?
6. When would you use this same way to figure out another word?
7. What did you learn today that will help you be a better reader?

Also ask questions that specifically help readers develop sensitivity to analogous onsets and rimes. For example, you might ask, "What word do you already know how to read that can help you figure out this new one?" Or you might ask, "Can you think of a word you know that begins with the same letter(s)? Can you think of a word you know that ends with the same letters?" Encourage learners to find helpful words on wall charts, pocket charts, and bulletin boards, as well as in storybooks and poems.

The five activities described in this section are a basic framework to help learners explore many onsets and rimes. It is up to you to decide which onsets and which rimes to examine with learners. Onsets are everywhere, so they are relatively easy to select. As for rimes, my suggestion is that you first look for frequently occurring rimes in the everyday reading materials learners enjoy. And, of course, look in Appendix C and in rhyming dictionaries like those mentioned earlier. Not only do activities like those described here give readers opportunities to think analytically about onsets and rimes, they are also flexible enough to be integrated into all kinds of listening, reading, and writing experiences in your classroom.

✸ Building Words with Onset-Rime Tiles

In this activity, learners build words by lining up small tiles that have onsets or rimes written on them. Learners should know the meaning of the words they build. And the words used for building should be printed on the pages of the storybooks shared in your classroom, written on the wall charts displayed in your classroom, and used by learners in the messages they write.

FIGURE 4–4
Putting words with the same rime in a pocket chart helps readers discover the letter patterns in words that look and sound alike.

Two versions of this activity are described here: one to build words by exchanging onsets; the other to build words with different onsets and different rimes. Building Words with Onset-Rime Tiles is appropriate for learners of any age who need experience strategically using onsets and rimes to identify unfamiliar words.

Things You'll Need: One set of onset-rime cards that combine to build often-seen and often-used words; as many sets of onset-rime tiles as there are cooperative groups or individual learners in your class; a pocket chart; words to build that are part of the spoken and written language in your classroom—words found on bulletin boards, wall charts, and signs, and in the stories children have written and in big books, storybooks, and poems. (See Appendix B for how to make onset-rime cards and tiles.)

Exploration: For the version Exchange Onsets, put a rime card (perhaps **at**) in a pocket chart and discuss the sounds that the rime represents (**"at"**). Next, put an onset card in front of the rime (a **b** for instance). Explain that when an onset (**b**) is added to a rime (**at**), the letters stand for **"bat."** Now, take away the onset (**b**) and replace it with a different onset (**f** perhaps). Show learners that when one onset (**f**) replaces another onset (**b**), a whole new word is built (**"fat"**). Do this several times, exchanging onsets to build different words.

For the version Build with Different Onsets and Different Rimes, put an onset and a rime card side by side in a pocket chart. Build one word, pointing out the onset and the rime (**bat**, perhaps). Use a different onset and the same rime to build another word (**fat**, for instance). Now, there are two words in the pocket chart—**bat** and **fat**. Build several words with the same rime and leave each in the pocket chart. Then introduce another onset-rime combination (perhaps **m** and **an**). Build different words with the new rime (**fan, can,** and **pan,** perhaps). Line up words with the same rimes in columns and support learners as they make inferences about the sounds that analogous onsets and rimes represent in words.

Guided Practice: For the Exchange Onsets version, give learners several tiles with the same rime (**ip** for instance) and several tiles with different onsets (such as **l, d,** and **s**). Ask learners to put the rime tile (**ip**) in the center of their work space and then say something like, "Look for a tile that makes the sound you hear at the beginning of **sat** and **silk**." Once learners identify the tile with **s**, say, "Put the **s** in front of the **ip** tile. What word have you built?" Now, tell learners to take the **s** away and exchange it for the **l** tile. "What is the new word?" Repeat several times, always watching to see that learners make the correct exchanges.

For the Building with Different Onsets and Different Rimes version, pass out several onset tiles, such as **b, f, w, t,** and several tiles for each of two different rimes, **ent** and **ish** for example. Challenge learners to build as many words as they can think of that are spelled with the onsets and rimes space. Ask learners to count the number of words they build, to write down the

FIGURE 4–5
The use of a pocket chart to build words helps learners gain insight into the sounds that analogous onsets and rimes represent in words.

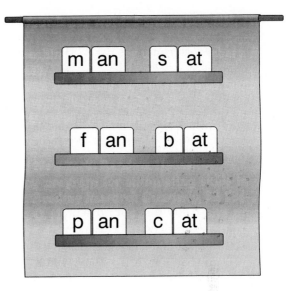

words, and to share words with others. Make a bar graph showing the number of words built out of different onsets and rimes; discuss quantity; relate ideas to math concepts.

Transfer: Challenge learners to read everything on the walls, windows, and doors of your room—wall charts, posters, bulletin boards, stories learners have read, stories learners have written on their own, stories learners have dictated. Learners can read individually or together in pairs. Make sure learners point to each word as it is read. (For helpful ideas, look in Appendix B.) Ask learners to write down words that are spelled with a particular onset or rime. Then, when everyone has read everything in the room and made lists of words that are spelled with the same onset or a rime, have learners compare lists, talk about words, find words in the room, and read sentences in which words are written.

✳ Pair-a-Rime

Here learners create fanciful word pairs that share a rime, from intriguing words in the classroom, in books, and in poems. In so doing, learners have opportunities to consider how some words that are spelled similarly also sound similar. This activity is effective for second graders and up.

Things You'll Need: Paper, pencils, crayons.

Exploration: Ask learners to find interesting words in the classroom, in familiar books, and favorite poems. Then write words on the chalkboard and invite learners to make up fanciful pairs of words that share a rime, such as

brown crown and **red Fred**. Write examples on a wall chart; discuss ways in which words that share a rime sound alike and look alike. (Sometimes two-word rimes are called Hinky Pinks [Gunning, 1992].)

Guided Practice: Challenge learners to create and illustrate imaginative, and perhaps unconventional, word pairs. Interesting characters, places, and things that learners find in familiar books are especially good to use as one of the words in a rhyming pair. Figure 4–6 shows rime pairs and pictures created by a multiage group of second and third graders. Put pictures on the bulletin board, thus setting the stage for the transfer activity that follows.

Transfer: Invite learners to work collaboratively to write definitions for the word pairs created. For example, learners might define a **soggy doggy** as "**a drippy dog**" or "**a wet pet**." Ask learners to write definitions on tagboard strips. Then (1) fasten word pairs and pictures on a bulletin board, (2) prop definitions written by different cooperative groups on the chalk tray, and (3) invite learners to match word pairs with definitions. This is lots of fun and

FIGURE 4–6
Learners think about rime and about word meaning when they create and illustrate pairs of words that share the same rime.

happy
pappy

FIGURE 4–6, *continued*

71

offers many opportunities for learners to talk about rimes, words, and definitions. Combinations of word pairs, pictures, and creative definitions make a great bulletin board.

❋ Writing Tongue Twisters

Learners' natural attraction to alliteration makes creating tongue twisters fun, a great way to explore onsets, and an imaginative way to transfer learning. Use this activity with first, second, and third graders; give more support to younger learners, less support for older learners.

Note: Not all tongue twisters repeat the same onsets. When you select tongue twisters, look for those that have a great many words with the same beginning sound.

Things You'll Need: Tongue twisters remembered from childhood or a good book with lots of twisters, such as *World's Toughest Tongue Twisters* (Rosenbloom, 1986) and Charles Keller's *Tongue Twisters* (1989).

Exploration: Ask learners to listen as you say a twister or two. Ask learners to say the tongue twister in chorus with you. Challenge them to say the twister on their own; ask them to identify the repeated sound. Call attention to alliteration by asking learners to discover the quality that makes twisters unique.

Guided Practice: Share books that highlight alliteration, such as the sophisticated and zany ABC book *Aster Aardvark's Alphabet Adventure* (Kellogg, 1992) or the captivating book *Animalia* (Base, 1987). To explore alliteration further, write a tongue twister on the chalkboard and ask learners to read it with you in chorus. Ask a volunteer to underline all the instances of the same onset; count how many times words begin with the same letter and the same sound. Point to each word as it is read. Invite the whole group to write a tongue twister together.

Transfer: The playful, engaging, and alliterative language in books such as *Aster Aardvark's Alphabet Adventure* and *Animalia* invites learners to create their own alliterative messages. First and second grade learners enjoy making up twisters as a group activity and then dictating as you write on chart paper. Third grade learners like to work cooperatively to write their own tongue twisters. Share the alliterative tongue twisters learners write (as shown in Figure 4–7); read twisters aloud in chorus; put them on wall charts; ask learners to tape-record tongue twisters and make tapes available for everyone's listening pleasure! Or follow the example of authors like Kellogg and Base. Fasten together learners' alliterative sentences and illustrations to make a book of playful, alliterative language that is created by the readers and writers in your classroom.

FIGURE 4–7
Writing and illustrating tongue
twisters gives learners
opportunities to identify the
onsets in words and to
creatively use this knowledge.

✳ Mystery Words on Mini-Chalkboards

In this activity, learners use onset and rime clues to figure out mystery words, which are then written on mini-chalkboards. Everyone in the group responds, which gives you valuable insight into how learners use code knowledge. Mystery Words is suitable for first, second, and third graders. Relate Mystery Words to social studies, science, health, and mathematics vocabularies by using words from these content areas.

Things You'll Need: As many mini-chalkboards as there are learners in your classroom. (See Appendix B for a helpful hint.)

Exploration: Explain that learners are to use clues to figure out mystery words that the learners have read in a familiar storybook or poem, to write words on mini-chalkboards, and then hold boards in the air. Then write two clue words on a large chalkboard in your room (**rice** and **bug**, perhaps), tell the learners the book or poem that contains the mystery word, and say, "The mystery word starts with the sound heard at the beginning of **rice** and rhymes with **bug.** What is the mystery word?" When learners discover the mystery word, **rug,** write it on the large chalkboard. Explain how and why clues are used. Encourage learners to share how they discover mystery words from clues.

Guided Practice: Give each learner a mini-chalkboard, a piece of chalk, and a cloth to use as an eraser. Use the same procedure just described, only now ask learners to write the mystery word on their mini-chalkboard and hold up chalkboards when finished. Another version is to ask learners to think of the mystery word and then to write two or three words that have the same letter pattern—**hug, rug, dug.**

Transfer: Select familiar words from the stories and poems learners share in your classroom or from science, social studies, math, and health subjects. Write a riddle and a clue on the chalkboard. Explain that learners are to use the rime in the clue word to help them solve the riddle. For example, if learners are familiar with the poem "What Is Gold" from *Hailstones and Halibut Bones* (O'Neill & Wallner, 1961), you might write riddles for the words **fish, wish,** and **dish** (which are part of the poem):

> *I live in water.*
> *I have fins and gills.*
> *What am I?*
> *Clue: wish*

Challenge learners to think of a word that ends like **wish,** begins with a different sound, and fits the sentence. Erase the **w** from **wish;** write **f** in its place. Now, write another riddle on the chalkboard, only this time use **fish** as the clue word. Continue using clue words from the poem. Last, reread the poem "What Is Gold" (O'Neill & Wallner, 1961), looking and listening for these and other words that share spoken and written rimes.

✸ Predicting and Writing Rhyme

In this activity, learners predict words that share rimes in familiar poems, and, as a transfer activity, add new and creative endings to poems. Learners of every age, from the youngest to the oldest, can predict words that share rimes (the rhyme) and add new endings to rhyming poems, provided that poems have been shared in class.

Things You'll Need: Familiar poems like traditional nursery rhymes, long-time favorites such as *Oh, A-Hunting We Will Go* (Langstaff, 1989), humorous poems such as those found in Sendak's *Chicken Soup with Rice* (1962), thoughtful and fanciful poems such as the ones in Silverstein's *Where the Sidewalk Ends* (1974), or poetry that tells a story such as *Everett Anderson's 1, 2, 3* (Clifton, 1977).

Exploration: Share poetry. Read poems; write them on wall charts. Have learners read and reread them in chorus. Make a list of words that share rimes.

Guided Practice: Select a familiar poem and put it on a wall chart in your classroom. Find words that share rimes. Now use a sticky piece of paper to cover up a word that shares a rime with another word. For example, if the word **train** appears on one line and then the word **rain** appears in the next line or two, cover up **rain**. Ask learners to read the poem aloud, and when learners come to the covered-up word, ask learners to predict the word under the paper. Once learners make their prediction, take off the sticky paper to reveal the written word. Discuss spoken rhyme and written rime; point out words on wall charts and bulletin boards; have learners find rimes in books and poems.

Transfer: Challenge learners to write their own versions of a familiar, favorite poem by adding a new ending.

For first and second graders, begin by writing a new ending as a whole-group activity. As the group writes, point out how to preserve the poet's sense of rhyme and rhythm. When the new ending is written, read the poem in chorus with the class, sweeping your hand under the words as they are read aloud. When learners understand what they are to do, invite younger ones to create their own personal endings for the same poem that the group wrote an ending for. The endings in Figure 4–7 were written by first graders after their teacher shared the big book *Oh, A-Hunting We Will Go* (Langstaff, 1989). When finished, ask younger children to illustrate their work. Then ask younger children to read their poems with new endings and to share their illustrations.

Older learners (third graders and up) enjoy writing new endings (either individually or in groups) for poems that are their own personal favorites. For example, poems such as "The Toucan" (in *Where the Sidewalk Ends,* Silverstein, 1974) is particularly suited for older learners. Not only does "The Toucan" have an easy-to-follow rhyme and rhythm, but Silverstein literally invites learners to add to this poem. Also have them make an illustration of their ending.

Once learners have written endings for their personal favorites, ask them to trade their poems with a classmate. To do this, learners give a classmate the original poem and the new ending they have written. (Tell learners to hold onto the illustration they made for the ending, for the illustration will be needed later.) Now, challenge classmates to read the original poem, to read their classmate's new version, and to illustrate the new ending. This way each new ending has two artistic interpretations: one made by the author of the new ending and one by a classmate. Now have learners compare artistic interpretations, discuss the feelings poems convey, and contrast points of view as expressed in words and in pictures.

FIGURE 4–8
Writing new endings for familiar poems helps readers gain insight into words that share letter and sound patterns.

FIGURE 4–8, *continued*

RIMES AND INSIGHT INTO THE ALPHABETIC CODE

As you plan reading and writing experiences that capitalize on rime, it is important to make sure that learners have lots of opportunities to develop code knowledge of many different rimes in words. This is vital because the number of words learners can identify with the analogy strategy is limited by the onsets and rimes learners can remember in words.

Code knowledge of rimes is useful only so long as learners have words in their reading vocabularies that are spelled with the letters that represent the rimes. For example, if learners do not have a word spelled with **ent** in their reading vocabulary, such as **went**, then the analogy strategy is useless for identifying **tent**. It can be used only when a word spelled with **ent** is in their reading vocabulary. As a consequence, learners need a reasonably large pool of words in memory from which to make comparisons.

With a decent size pool of remembered words, learners have a firm basis for making analogies between familiar and unfamiliar words. The more words with varied rimes learners have in their reading vocabularies, the more useful the analogy strategy.

When you explore rimes with learners, it is important to know that beginning readers who rely mainly on rimes to make analogies are actually not as expert at word identification as beginning readers who pay attention to individual letter-sound combinations (Bruck & Treiman, 1992). As already explained, learners who use the analogy strategy do not have to look inside rimes to figure out the sounds letters represent (learners do not have to know the sound the **a** represents in **at** and **ack**, for instance). And so they know less about how the alphabetic code works at a level that is smaller than beginning onsets and ending rimes (that is, at the level of letter-sound relationships). Therefore, learners who rely on analogy are limited in their ability to use the alphabetic code, since they may not be able to make sense of unknown words that do not have overlapping onsets and rimes.

Finally, though the analogy strategy is a helpful and productive tool for learners to use to identify unfamiliar words, it is not entirely suited to unlocking the complete range of words in our alphabetic writing system. Our alphabet is basically a written map for the sounds in words, not the rimes in words. Anyone who reads and writes a language written in an alphabet must understand how letters represent sounds in words. Readers who know this use the letter-sound strategy to identify words. Actually, learners develop the analogy strategy and the letter-sound strategy about the same time. So, my recommendation is that you use the activities in this chapter to increase learners' strategic use of onsets and rimes, and the activities in Chapter 5 to increase their strategic use of letter-sound combinations. After all, word identification is more than one strategy. It is a whole collection of different strategies; the more strategies learners have at their fingertips, the better.

REFERENCES

Baron, J. (1979). Orthographic and word-specific mechanisms in children's reading of words. *Child Development, 50,* 60–72.

Base, G. (1987). *Animalia.* New York: Henry N. Abrams.

Bowey, J. A. (1990). Orthographic onsets and rimes as functional units of reading. *Memory and Cognition, 18,* 419–427.

Brown, A. L., Kane, M. J., & Long, C. (1989). Analogical transfer in young children: Analogies as tools for communication and exposition. *Applied Cognitive Psychology, 3,* 275–293.

Bruck, M., & Treiman, R. (1992). Learning to pronounce words: The limitations of analogies. *Reading Research Quarterly, 4,* 374–388.

Clifton, L. (1977). *Everett Anderson's 1, 2, 3.* New York: Henry Holt & Company.

Ehri, L. C., & Robbins, C. (1992). Beginners need some decoding skill to read words by analogy. *Reading Research Quarterly, 27,* 12–27.

Fowler, C. A., Treiman, R., & Gross, J. (1993). The structure of English syllables and polysyllables. *Journal of Memory and Language, 32,* 115–140.

Goswami, U. (1986). Children's use of analogy in learning to read: A developmental study. *Journal of Child Psychology and Psychiatry, 31,* 301–311.

Goswami, U. (1990). A special link between rhyming skill and the use of orthographic analogies by beginning readers. *Journal of Experimental Child Psychology, 49,* 323–340.

Goswami, U., & Bryant, P. (1992). Rhyme, analogy, and children's reading. In P. B. Gough, L. C. Ehri, & R. Treiman (Eds.), *Reading acquisition* (pp. 49–64). Hillsdale, NJ: Lawrence Erlbaum Associates.

Goswami, U., & Mead, F. (1992). Onset and rime awareness and analogies in reading. *Reading Research Quarterly, 27,* 153–162.

Graves, M. F., Watts, S., & Graves, B. (1994). *Essentials of classroom teaching: Elementary reading methods.* Boston: Allyn & Bacon.

Gunning, T. G. (1992). *Creating reading instruction for all children.* Boston: Allyn & Bacon.

Keller, C. (1989). *Tongue twisters.* New York: Simon & Schuster.

Kellogg, S. (1992). *Aster Aardvark's alphabet adventure.* New York: William Morrow.

Langstaff, J. (1989). *Oh, a-hunting we will go.* Boston: Houghton Mifflin.

O'Neill, M., & Wallner, J. (1961). *Hailstones and halibut bones.* New York: Doubleday Books for Young Readers.

Rosenbloom, J. (1986). *World's toughest tongue twisters.* New York: Sterling Publishing.

Santa, C. M. (1976–1977). Spelling patterns and the development of flexible word strategies. *Reading Research Quarterly, 12,* 125–144.

Sendak, M. (1962). *Chicken soup with rice.* New York: Scholastic.

Silverstein, S. (1974). *Where the sidewalk ends.* New York: Harper Collins.

Stein, J. (1990). *The Random House rhyming dictionary.* New York: Random House.

Treiman, R. (1992). The role of intrasyllabic units in learning to read and spell. In P. B. Gough, L. C. Ehri, & R. Treiman (Eds.), *Reading acquisition* (pp. 65-106). Hillsdale, NJ: Lawrence Erlbaum Associates.

Uhry, J. K., & Shepherd, M. J. (1993). Segmentation/spelling instruction as part of a first-grade reading program: Effects on several measures of reading. *Reading Research Quarterly, 28,* 218–233.

Webster's compact rhyming dictionary (1987). Springfield, MA: Merriam-Webster.

Wise, B. W., Olson, R. K., & Treiman, R. (1990). Subsyllablic units in computerized reading instruction: Onset-rime vs. post vowel segmentation. *Journal of Experimental Child Psychology, 49,* 1–19.

THE LETTER-SOUND STRATEGY

Identifying Words by Their Letters and Sounds

This chapter explains the letter-sound strategy. Here you will discover how learners use the letter-sound strategy, why the manner in which letters are sequenced from left-to-right is important for word identification, why grouping letters into neighborhoods is important, and ways to support learners as they use this strategy as a pathway to word identification.

<h1 style="text-align:center">K E Y   I D E A S</h1>

---

* Letters that routinely appear right next to one another in words and that signal pronunciation make up a neighborhood. Our alphabetic writing system has many different letter neighborhoods.
* Learners who use the letter-sound strategy associate sounds with letters in neighborhoods and blend sounds together to pronounce words that make sense in reading contexts.
* Letter neighborhoods can be grouped into three groups: those that are less challenging, more challenging, and most challenging to learn.

Unlike the turtles in Wen Ting's drawing (Figure 5–1), the alphabet is not a jumble of topsy turvy letter-sound combinations. Readers do not tumble aimlessly about as they learn about our alphabetic writing system, nor do they stand on their heads when they use letter-sound combinations to unlock the pronunciation of unfamiliar words. For readers who have never before come across the words **topsy, turvy,** and **turtles** in print, the letter-sound strategy is a quick and sure route to pronunciation. Readers who use the letter-sound strategy take advantage of the most basic units of our alphabetic code—the letters of the alphabet and the sounds they represent in words.

LETTERS AND THEIR NEIGHBORS

The twenty-six letters in our alphabet are a hardworking bunch. The same small group of twenty-six is systematically arranged, rearranged, and

FIGURE 5–1
Unlike the jumbled turtles in Wen Ting's drawing, the letter-sound combinations of the alphabetic writing system have enough predictable structure to be a useful pathway to word identification.

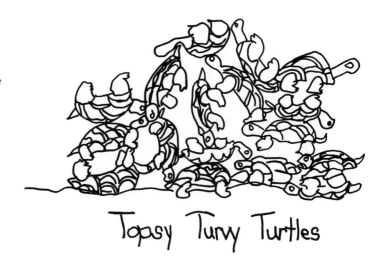

sequenced to build literally tens of thousands of words. With all this arranging and sequencing, it is inevitable that certain letters routinely appear right next to one another in spelling. This creates a type of spelling context—a neighborhood—in which certain letters are frequently and predictably the neighbors of other letters. With many fewer letters (only twenty-six) than sounds (as many as forty-three or so), English spelling contains a host of letter neighborhoods that signal pronunciations.

Letter neighborhoods are pronounceable letter sequences that represent one or more sounds in words, such as the **s** in <u>s</u>at, the **sh** in <u>shaft</u>, the **ine** in <u>line</u>, and the **ince** in <u>since</u>. Because there is almost always more than one way to group the letters in unfamiliar words, learners who are trying to identify words must consider which letter sequences form pronounceable neighborhoods and which do not. To do this, learners consider the letters in unfamiliar words from left to right. The reason to do this is that the way letters are sequenced from left to right affects the sounds letters represent in words.

For example, the letter **a** represents one pronunciation when it is followed by a consonant and an **e** in the word **bl<u>ade</u>** (the vowel-consonant-e neighborhood, or **VCe** for short), another pronunciation when followed by one or more consonants in **c<u>at</u>** and **sh<u>aft</u>** (a vowel-consonant neighborhood, described as **VC/VCC**), yet another pronunciation when preceded by the letter **o** in **c<u>oa</u>t** and **t<u>oa</u>st** (a vowel-vowel neighborhood, expressed as **VV**), and still another pronunciation when followed by an **r** in **c<u>ar</u>t** and **f<u>arm</u>** (an **r-controlled** neighborhood, or **Vr** for short). Some of the letter neighborhoods are summarized in Table 5–1. Look in Appendix D for detailed explanations and lists of words that include neighborhoods.

Readers may use their knowledge of letter neighborhoods to gain insight into the sounds that many different letters represent in words. For example, readers may generalize their knowledge of the sound that the vowel in the **VC/VCC** neighborhood represents to help them identify words such as **sh<u>aft</u>** (VCC), **j<u>ob</u>** (VC), and **l<u>eft</u>** (VCC). Though the underlined letters in these three words are different, the letters form a **VC/VCC** neighborhood, and it is the neighborhood that signals the sounds letters are likely to represent.

As learners gain reading experience, they become sensitive to letter neighborhoods that recur in many different words. Sensitivity increases as readers move up in the elementary grades (Juel, 1983) and is significantly related to reading ability (Massaro & Hestand, 1983). And so, the more opportunities learners have to strategically use letter neighborhoods as they read and write, the more learners will know about the manner in which the letters in neighborhoods represent sound.

Strict and Lenient Neighborhoods

Just as strict zoning codes limit the types of buildings developers are permitted to construct in certain areas of your community, so too do strict letter neighborhoods limit the sounds learners need to associate with letters in

TABLE 5–1
Summary of Letter Neighborhoods[1]

Consonant Neighborhoods	Examples
Single Consonant Usually represents the sounds associated with the underlined letters in the examples	boat, cat or city, dot, fish, game or gem, hat, jet, kite, lamp, monkey, nut, pan, queen, rain, seal, toad, valentine, wag, fox, yell, zoo
Twin (Double) Consonant Generally represents the same sound as the single consonant	mm in hammer, b in rabbit
Consonant Blend Sounds that are blended together when pronounced	black, clam, flag, glad, place, sleep, brave, crab, drag, fry, grape, prize, train, scale, skate, small, snack, space, stone, swim, twig, scrap, splash, sprain, squirrel, strap, chrome, school, three
Consonant Digraph Two or more letters that represent a sound that is different from the sounds letters represent individually	chair, phone, shade, thank, then, wheat, catch
Qu Represents "**kw**" as an onset and in the middle of some words, and "**k**" when it is a final sound	queen, frequent, antique
S as a Next-Door Neighbor As an onset, **s** represents "**s**." In the middle or at the end of words, **s** represents either "**s**" or "**z**."	Onset "**s**" in sack and save Middle "**s**" in person and tassel Middle "**z**" in resent and closet End "**s**" in toss and bus End "**z**" in close and dresses
C or g plus a, o, and u **Ca**, **co**, and **cu** usually represent "**k**." **Ga**, **go**, and **gu** usually represent "**g**."	"**k**" in camel, color, and Cuba "**g**" in game, got, and gum
C or g plus e, i, and y **Ce**, **ci**, and **cy** generally represent "**s**." **Ge**, **gi**, and **gy** generally represent "**j**" as in **jelly**.	"**s**" in cedar, city, cypress "**j**" in gem, gist, energy

[1]Look at Appendix D for more detailed explanations and examples.

words. Learners can place a lot of confidence in strict letter neighborhoods because these neighborhoods offer few, if any, choices as to the sounds represented. For instance, the **sh** forms a consonant digraph neighborhood that is completely restricted. The letter combination **sh** is pronounced as **"sh"** in words like **shelf, trash, shepherd, admonish,** and **eggshell;** there are no other possibilities from which to choose. Under ideal conditions, every neighborhood would be completely restricted, and therefore learners could depend on neighborhoods 100 percent of the time.

TABLE 5–1, *continued*

Vowel Neighborhoods	Examples
VC/VCC²	
Vowels generally represent the short sound when the following next-door neighbor is a consonant.	VC: m<u>an</u>, p<u>eg</u>, m<u>ix</u>, j<u>ob</u>, g<u>um</u>, vin<u>yl</u>
A consonant neighborhood before the vowel forms a CVC (**cat**), CCVC (**brat**), CVCC (**back**), or CCVCC (**black**) sequence and does not affect the sound that the vowel in the VC/VCC neighborhood represents.	VCC: l<u>ast</u>, b<u>ent</u>, l<u>ift</u>, r<u>ock</u>, d<u>ust</u>, m<u>yth</u>
VCe	
A vowel with a consonant and a final **e** as next-door neighbors usually represents a long sound and the **e** is silent. A consonant neighborhood before the vowel forms a CVCe (**save**) or CCVCe (**slave**) sequence, and does not affect the sound that the vowel in the VCe neighborhood represents.	s<u>ave</u>, th<u>eme</u>, d<u>ime</u>, b<u>one</u>, c<u>ube</u>, t<u>ype</u>
VCCe	
A vowel with two consonants and a final **e** as next-door neighbors usually represents the short sound and the **e** is silent. A consonant neighborhood before the vowel forms a CVCCe (**dance**) or a CCVCCe (**prance**) sequence, and does not affect the sound that the vowel in the VCCe neighborhood represents.	d<u>ance</u>, b<u>adge</u>, ch<u>ance</u>, inv<u>olve</u>, br<u>onze</u>, d<u>ense</u>, h<u>inge</u>, imp<u>ulse</u>, s<u>ince</u>, w<u>edge</u>, f<u>udge</u>
V V	
In the combinations of **ai**, **oa**, **ay**, **ee**, **ey**, and **ea**, the first vowel generally represents a long sound and the second is silent.	ch<u>ai</u>n, fl<u>oa</u>t, cl<u>ay</u>, b<u>ee</u>f, hon<u>ey</u>, b<u>ea</u>ch

²V = vowel, C = consonant

However, zoning codes, like letter neighborhoods, are not always restrictive. When your city council or county commissioners pass lenient zoning codes, developers are free to build anything they desire. As a consequence, you cannot predict from one building to the next whether you will find a home, store, factory, hospital, or school. The same is true for letter neighborhoods. Lenient neighborhoods put fewer restrictions on pronunciation than do strict neighborhoods. Because of this, learners have more than one pronunciation from which to choose.

For example, **oo** is a moderately lenient neighborhood in that learners have two sounds to choose from—the sound heard in **moon** or the sound heard in **book**. The **ough** neighborhood is quite lenient, for learners who come across this neighborhood have four different pronunciations to con-

TABLE 5–1, *continued*

Vowel Neighborhoods	Examples
Double oo Usually represents sounds that are heard in **cool** or **cook**	f<u>oo</u>d, m<u>oo</u>n, sh<u>oo</u>k, st<u>oo</u>d
Vowel Diphthongs **Ow** and **ou** often represent the sounds heard in **cow** and **out**, while **oi** and **oy** represent the sounds heard in **oil** and **boy**.	br<u>ow</u>n, d<u>ow</u>n, cl<u>ou</u>d, l<u>ou</u>d c<u>oi</u>n, s<u>oi</u>l, dec<u>oy</u>, t<u>oy</u>
Vr **R** affects pronunciation so that vowels cannot be classified as short or long.	<u>ar</u>m, f<u>er</u>n, sh<u>ir</u>t, c<u>or</u>n, b<u>ur</u>n
CV/CCV The vowel may represent the long sound.	CV: l<u>a</u>ter, b<u>e</u>long, p<u>i</u>lot, ban<u>jo</u>, b<u>u</u>gle CCV: cr<u>a</u>zy, pr<u>e</u>dict, ch<u>i</u>na, pr<u>o</u>gram, br<u>u</u>tal
Y When **y** is the only vowel in a final syllable, it generally represents the long **e** sound.	Final syllable: cand<u>y</u>, tin<u>y</u>, bab<u>y</u>, lad<u>y</u>
When **y** is the only vowel in a word, it generally represents the long **i** sound.	Only vowel: sk<u>y</u>, fl<u>y</u>, m<u>y</u>, tr<u>y</u>
Au and Aw Usually represent the sound in **fault** and **straw**.	h<u>au</u>l, exh<u>au</u>st, l<u>aw</u>n, j<u>aw</u>
Ew and Ue Usually represent the sound in **blew** and **blue**.	ch<u>ew</u>, gr<u>ew</u>, tr<u>ue</u>, val<u>ue</u>

sider: The **ough** might sound as it does in **bough**, or **ough** might correspond to the sounds heard in **cough, though,** and **enough.** Toss in the letter **t** at the end—thus creating **ought**—and **though** becomes **thought**!

Strict letter neighborhoods are easier to learn and easier to use than lenient neighborhoods. This is so because strict neighborhoods limit the pronunciations that learners need to remember and apply when identifying words. When learners come across strict neighborhoods in spelling, they do not have to think about several possible pronunciations. This makes decoding faster, more effective, and less attention consuming.

THE TROUBLE WITH RULES

If our writing system were a parcel of land, it could be rezoned. Lenient neighborhoods could be made to be more restrictive and hence more predictable maps for sound. Since it has not proven to be feasible to rezone our writing system, researchers have put tremendous energy into finding out which letter sequences in spelling are dependable maps for pronunciation and which are not. In their quest, researchers have investigated forty-five different phonics rules that are supposed to describe the laws governing letter-sound relationships (Bailey, 1967; Clymer, 1963; Emans, 1967).

Take the rule that says, "A vowel in the middle of a one-syllable word represents the short sound." In theory, this rule is supposed to explain the **VC/VCC** neighborhood. In practice, it makes make our alphabetic writing system seem more complicated than it is. Researchers have found this rule to be relatively unreliable. In a sample of primary grade reading material, Clymer (1963) and Emans (1967) found the middle vowel rule applied 62 and 73 percent of the time, respectively. Bailey (1967) considered material read by first through sixth graders and found that this rule was useful 71 percent of the time.

This rule distorts our perception of the alphabetic writing code because it overlooks the fact that some vowels in the middle of one-syllable words do not reside in a **VC/VCC** neighborhood. The words **hew** (Emans, 1967) and **her** (Bailey, 1967) were cited as exceptions to the middle vowel rule. Though **hew** and **her** are exceptions to the phonics rule, these words are not exceptions to our alphabetic writing code. These words contain two different letter neighborhoods that signal two different pronunciations: The sound represented by the **e** in **hew** is quite consistent, for the **e** resides in the **ew** neighborhood which is found in words like **jewel, chew,** and **threw** (as explained in Appendix D). The **e** in **her** is perfectly regular, too, for the **e** in these words resides in an **r-controlled** neighborhood (**Vr**), and so the sound it represents is characteristic of this neighborhood (as described in Appendix D).

Aside from making the code more complicated to learn, there is another drawback to memorizing rules: Just because learners recite rules does not mean that learners know when and how to apply rules. In fact, some learners are quite skilled at reciting rules yet do not have the foggiest notion of how to strategically use the rules they put so much effort into memorizing. The reason rules are not applied is that learners do not connect rules with the way letters are sequenced in words. Learners parrot rules—they recite the wording of rules but do not analyze the sequence of letters in written words and do not relate rules to words they read and write.

Rules encourage learners to think of letter-sound combinations as isolated bits of the code because the explanations they learn are often isolated from the words learners read and write everyday. When rule-based code knowledge is not connected to real words, learners may not create the images of pronounceable letter sequences in words, which is the foundation of knowledge of the letter neighborhood code and the bedrock of strategic code use.

Rather than focus on the rules themselves, a more beneficial approach is to sensitize learners to the way neighborhoods affect pronunciation and to ground neighborhoods in the spelling of words learners encounter in their reading and writing. A letter neighborhood orientation requires that learners pay attention to the way letters are sequenced in words, not to phonics "rules." By analyzing specific letter neighborhoods in words, learners discover logical, sequential, and predictable neighborhoods within the context of words they read and write everyday. As a result, learners not only acquire knowledge of how letter sequences form neighborhoods, but develop mental images of how neighborhoods look in real words and create mental pictures of words in which neighborhoods appear.

UNLOCKING PRONUNCIATION WITH THE LETTER-SOUND STRATEGY

Learners who use the letter-sound strategy have the full strength and power of the alphabet at their fingertips. Thanks to their constant self-monitoring with the cross-checking strategy, the words that they identify and pronounce are both understandable and contextually sensible. Users of the letter-sound strategy invest a sizeable amount of mental attention in word identification. But, like so many things in life, the extra time and energy invested in something worthwhile is more than offset by the rewards.

The advantage of the letter-sound strategy is that it can be used to identify any word that sounds the way it is spelled. The reward for readers who use this strategy is that they identify a large number of written words with a relatively small amount of code knowledge. This, in turn, helps learners build their reading vocabularies. The letter-sound strategy also helps learners become independent readers because it gives them a way to identify a great many unfamiliar words on their own without skipping words or asking someone else for help. And, of course, as a pathway to the identification of a good number of unfamiliar words, the letter-sound strategy supports the comprehension of increasingly more challenging text.

What Letter-Sound Strategy Users Know about Phonological Awareness   Users of the letter-sound strategy know (1) how to separate spoken words into individual sounds and (2) how to blend individual sounds together to form spoken words. They take it for granted that blended sounds form sensible words. Accordingly, learners are perpetually on the lookout for meaning as they blend, are quick to discover when a group of blended sounds is gibberish, and do not tolerate the creation of meaningless mumbo jumbo. The more learners use the letter-sound strategy, the greater their insight into phonological awareness and the more they learn about our alphabetic code. Consequently, as the learners in your classroom use the letter-sound strategy over and over again, they become better and better at separating and blending sounds, and their code knowledge of letter neighborhoods increases, too.

What Letter-Sound Strategy Users Know about Code Cues   Learners who use the letter-sound strategy know how the letters in neighborhoods signal pronunciation. In addition, given the complexity of our English alphabetic code, these learners realize that there is no guarantee that the first try at word identification will always result in a meaningful word. If it so happens that their first try falls short, they draw upon their considerable storehouse of code knowledge (and well-developed phonological awareness) to fix mistakes and correct misidentifications.

What Letter-Sound Strategy Users Do with Their Knowledge Suppose that Leslie comes across the word **shaft** in the sentence **A shaft of moonlight fell across the rabbit's cage and spilled onto the floor below,** which is in Deborah and James Howe's tale of a vampire rabbit named *Bunnicula* (1979, p. 20). Leslie uses the alphabetic code just exactly the way it is intended, as a sound-based representation of speech. In so doing, she reaps the full benefit of reading a language written in an alphabet, and here is how she does it:

1. Leslie groups the letters in **shaft** into pronounceable neighborhoods. In so doing, she recognizes that **s** and **h** (**sh**) belong in one neighborhood (the consonant digraph neighborhood) and then realizes that the letters **a + f + t** reside in another neighborhood (the **VC/VCC** neighborhood).
2. Leslie then associates **sh** with "sh" and **a, f, t** with the sounds "a" + "f" + "t."
3. Now she blends "sh" + "a" + "f" + "t" to pronounce "shaft."
4. Last, Leslie cross-checks to make sure that "shaft" fits the reading context. She asks herself: Does **shaft** sound and look right? Does this seem like language? Does **shaft** make sense in the passage? Do I know what the author means? If **shaft** makes sense, Leslie stops decoding and turns her full attention to *Bunnicula,* finishing the page and reading the rest of the chapter. If the answers are no, she returns to decoding.

Leslie's phonological awareness and code knowledge are well developed. But learners need not be experts at separating and blending to begin using the letter-sound strategy. All learners need is just enough phonological awareness to separate and blend the sounds in short words. Likewise, learners need enough code knowledge to associate sounds with the letters in neighborhoods in short, uncomplicated words.

Sounding out a short word like **big**, which has only three sounds and predictable associations between sounds and the letters in neighborhoods, is far less taxing than sounding out a long word like **ostrich**, which has six sounds and many more letters in neighborhoods. For this reason, it is quite possible, and indeed highly likely, that some learners you teach who have no difficulty whatsoever sounding out a word like **big** will have difficulty using the letter-sound strategy to identify longer words like **ostrich**.

In the example with Leslie, **shaft** is among the words she recognizes in conversations. So, as soon as Leslie pronounces "shaft," she knows what it means. When Leslie connects the written word (**shaft**) with the meaning of a familiar spoken word ("**shaft**"), Leslie adds a new word to her reading vocabulary. But what would happen if **shaft** was not among the words Leslie recognizes in everyday conversations? The type of word identification strategy Leslie used (as well as all other strategies explained earlier) works when, and only when, readers connect the meaning of printed words with the meaning of spoken words (as discussed in Chapter 1).

Expert users of the letter-sound strategy may identify the letter neighborhoods in words on their own without the guidance and support of their teachers. Inexperienced users of this strategy benefit from their teachers' help. Teachers can support learners (1) by helping them find words in reading and writing that have the same letter neighborhoods, (2) by encouraging them to look for neighborhoods in the words they do not automatically recognize, (3) by talking with them about the neighborhoods they find in words, and (4) by modeling the use of the letter-sound strategy. To identify the letter neighborhoods in a word, I suggest that readers do the following:

1. Look at all the letters in the word, and think about their left-to-right sequence.

   For example, on seeing the word **crimson** for the first time, look at the whole word; consider all the letters from left to right.

2. Look at the first letter(s). Ask, "Is it a consonant(s)? If so, to what letter neighborhood does it belong? What sound(s) does it represent?" If the first letter is a vowel, go to the next step.

   In the example of **crimson**, **cr** is a consonant blend neighborhood that represents the sounds of "**cr**."

3. Look at the first vowel letter(s)in the word. Ask, "In what neighborhood does the vowel letter(s) reside? What sound(s) does it represent? Is there a consonant(s) following the vowel in the neighborhood? If there is a consonant, what sound(s) does it represent?"

   The first vowel in **crimson** resides in a **VC/VCC** neighborhood (**im**). This vowel represents the short **i** sound (as heard in "**him**"), and the consonant represents the sound of **m** that is heard in "**mitt**."

4. "Are there other letters in the word?" If so, repeat steps 2 and 3 to identify the letters in neighborhoods and the sounds that the letters represent.

   In this example, the single consonant letter **s** represents "**s**." It is followed by the **VC/VCC** neighborhood of **on**. The letter **o** and its neighbor, the letter **n**, represent the short **o** heard in "**olive**" and the sound of **n** heard in "**nap**."

5. Does the word have a special ending, such as **-ing**, **-ed**, **-s/-es**, or **-ly**. If so, "What sound(s) does the ending represent?"

In this example, step 2 requires that users of the letter-sound strategy decide whether the first vowel in **crimson** resides in the **CV/CVV** neighborhood, **cri**, or in the **VC/VCC** neighborhood, **im**. Identification of **cri** as a **CV/CVV** neighborhood in **crimson** would leave the **mson** letter sequence to be analyzed. The sequence of **ms** in **mson** is confusing. Though **ms** occurs in words like **hamster** and **damsel,** and is present when there is a suffix attached to words such as **palms** and **aims, ms** is not a frequently used letter sequence, and does not occur at the beginning of English syllables. (**"Mson"** does not form a legal sequence in English pronunciation.) On the other hand, the identification of the **VC/VCC** neighborhood **im** leaves the sequence **son** to be analyzed. This is consistent with English letter sequence and with English pronunciation.

So the correct identification of letter neighborhoods is **cr** (consonant blend), **im** (**VC/VCC**), **s** (single consonant), and **on** (**VC/VCC**). Users of the letter-sound strategy know that a consonant neighborhood at the beginning of the **VC/VCC** neighborhood does not affect the sound that the vowel represents. For example, the sound that the vowel represents in the word **it** is short, which is typical for vowels in a **VC/VCC neighborhood.** Even with the addition of a single consonant neighborhood, **l,** to form a **CVC** sequence, **lit,** or a consonant blend neighborhood, **sl,** to form a **CCVC** sequence, **slit,** the letter **i** still represents the short vowel sound. Thus, the **cr** before the **im,** and the **s** before the **on** do not change the short sound that the vowels in the **VC/VCC** neighborhood represent in **crimson.** As this example illustrates, the identification of letter neighborhoods hinges on the consideration of all the letter in words, and on attention to the left-to-right sequence of letters.

There are six guidelines that readers may use to assist them when they decide whether the letter sequence in a word constitutes the **CV/CCV** or the **VC/VCC** neighborhoods. First, if readers see two consonants between two vowels in a long word (as in **rabbit** and **crimson**), the first consonant most often goes with the preceding vowel, thus forming the **VC/VCC** neighborhood (**rab-bit** and **crim-son**) and a resulting short vowel sound. Second, advise readers that if there is only one consonant between two vowels in a long word (as in **silent** and **feline**), many times the first vowel is part of a **CV/CVV** neighborhood and is often long. Third, the consonant blend neighborhood frequently stays intact, as in **secret** (**se-cret**) and **membrane** (**mem-brane**). Fourth, the consonant digraph neighborhood usually stays intact in words, as in **bishop** (**bish-op**), **author** (**au-thor**), and **fathom** (**fath-om**). Fifth, when words end in a **Cle** (such as the **ble** in **stable, cle** in **cycle, dle** in **cradle, gle** in **bugle, kle** in **wrinkle, ple** in **dimple, tle** in **title,** and **zle** in **puzzle**), the **Cle** is usually a neighborhood. Sixth and last, remind readers that prefixes and suffixes are usually intact units in words, such as **prepaid** (**pre-paid**), and **slowly** (**slow-ly**).

The **VC/VCC** neighborhoods in **crimson** (**im** and **on**) include consonant and vowel letters. Readers must therefore know the sound that the vowel letters represent, as well as the sound that the consonants represent. By and large, consonant neighborhoods are relatively dependable maps for sound. For example, the consonant digraph neighborhood **sh** represents the same sound in **she** (a **CV/CVV** neighborhood) as it does in **fresh** (a **VC/VCC** neighborhood). This consistency is observed for the **st** blend neighborhood in **sta-dium** (**CV/CVV**) and in **blast** (**VC/VCC**), and for the **m** in **me** (**CV/CVV**) and in **time** (**CVe**). As a consequence of the general dependability of consonant neighborhoods, the learners in your classroom may not be troubled by them when they are within vowel neighborhoods, provided that learners recognize consonant neighborhoods, and know the sounds they represent.

When readers use the letter-sound strategy to pronounce words, they blend together the sounds that the letters in a neighborhood represent. In so doing, readers may pronounce the syllables in words. Syllables consist of one or more sounds, and each has a vowel sound, as explained in Chapter 4. Syllables may be whole spoken words (as the one-syllable word **ban**) or parts of spoken words (as the two-syllable word **banjo,** which is divided into **ban-jo**). Syllables are units of pronunciation and hence do not have an absolute parallel in written language. For this reason, users of the letter-sound strategy may not know where one syllable in a word stops and another syllable in a word begins until they know how to pronounce the written word (Ives, Bursuk, & Ives, 1979).

The syllables in written words may be obvious to expert readers because they know how to pronounce the words that authors write. For example, readers who know the pronunciation of **sinus** may use this knowledge to divide **sinus** into two syllables—**si-nus**. On the other hand, users of the letter-sound strategy who do not know how to pronounce this word cannot be absolutely certain which sequence of letters represents syllables—**si-nus** or **sin-us**—until they successfully pronounce **sinus**. The identification of letter neighborhoods and the association of sounds with the letters in neighborhoods provide readers the information they need to pronounce words. The pronunciation of words may in turn give readers insight into the way that words are divided into syllables.

The more learners read and write, the more likely they are to see the same letters sequenced in words. Reading and writing the same sequences of letters in words over and over again gives learners opportunities to form images of these sequences in their minds. Learners may then fuse the frequently occurring letter sequences together and treat them as intact chunks. This results in pronunciation without analyzing the individual letter-sound associations in neighborhoods. Chunks may be frequently occurring rimes, such as the **ot** in **lot,** meaningful letter groups, such as the **multi** (meaning "many") in **multiply,** or meaningless sequences larger than rimes, such as the **tion** in **nation**. The use of chunks is a more streamlined word identification strategy than the association of sounds with the letters in neighborhoods, and is explored in the next chapter.

When the words that authors write are not in readers' speaking or listening vocabularies, sounding out helps with pronunciation, but not with meaning. Under this condition, word identification does not meet its goal because meaning eludes readers. For this reason, when you explore the letter-sound strategy (and previously described strategies) with learners, make sure that the unfamiliar words learners meet in books are already in the learners' speaking or listening vocabularies. If you suspect that words are not in learners' speaking or listening vocabularies, then it is important to build enough background knowledge to add words to their speaking or listening vocabularies.

Alternatively, under some conditions, the reading context gives strong clues to word meaning. In this situation, it is important to support learners as they combine context clues with the pronunciation that they derived from the letter-sound strategy (and other strategies). Generally speaking, learners develop the ability to combine context clues—to determine word meaning—with the letter-sound strategy—to arrive at pronunciation—after they have had a good bit of experience reading. Look for this ability to begin to mature as learners move into the fourth grade and beyond.

Correcting Misidentifications

Users of the letter-sound strategy are experts at correcting their own misidentifications. If the sounds Leslie blends together do not make a sensible word, cross-checking brings the misidentification to light. Should this be the case, there are three ways Leslie might make a correction:

1. Reblend the same sounds, perhaps gliding sounds together more smoothly or changing the order of sounds and then cross-check for meaning.
2. Associate different sounds with the same letters in neighborhoods and then reblend sounds to form a new word that is cross-checked for meaning.
3. Redo the entire process—regrouping letters into pronounceable letter neighborhoods, associating sounds with the letters in neighborhoods, blending, and cross-checking all over again.

The learners whom you teach are bound to prefer easier, less attention-demanding ways to correct misidentifications over energy-draining alternatives. So you will notice that successful word identifiers often try reblending as their first attempt to correct mistakes. Then, if reblending does not work, they may try different letter-sound combinations. Only when all else fails do learners typically redo the entire process of reidentifying letter neighborhoods.

Users of the letter-sound strategy expect the words they decode to be real words and to make sense in the reading context. The motivation to connect meaning with written language is so strong that even when learners are asked to read nonsense words they change the pronunciation of nonwords into real words (Laxon, Smith, & Masterson, 1995).

Not all misidentifications interfere with comprehension, so not all misidentifications need correction. Learners have greater tolerance for misidentifications when they read a novel for pleasure than when they read a content subject textbook to learn new information. In this example, Leslie is reading *Bunnicula* for pleasure, so she is less concerned with absolute accuracy than if she were reviewing a chapter in her science book to complete an assignment. As a consequence, the misidentifications Leslie chooses to ignore as she reads *Bunnicula* for pleasure may well be, and in some cases absolutely ought to be, corrected if she were reading for technical information in content subjects.

The Role of Minor Mistakes   Learners take minor mistakes in stride. Minor mistakes do not derail decoding because strategy users actively look for sensible connections between the words they recognize in everyday language and the words authors write in books, poems, plays, and articles. Accordingly, as learners cross-check, they find words in their speaking or listening vocabularies that sound similar to minor mispronunciations. When this happens, learners associate minor mispronunciations with real words that make sense in the reading context. Once plausible words are identified, learners automatically adjust pronunciations so that the sounds in the word they decode match words in their speaking or listening vocabularies. The net effect is that slight letter-sound association mistakes and blending miscalculations do not require extra special effort to repair.

IMPLICATIONS FOR TEACHING

Awareness of letters in a single consonant neighborhood emerges early, as we see in the note Roger taped to the gerbil cage in his first grade classroom (Figure 5–2). Roger wrote this note to tell his classmates about the feisty habits of the resident pet, Biscuit. Roger's warning reads: "Biscuit Bites. Don't bother Biscuit because he bites." Roger uses invented spelling when he writes. That is, he spells words the way he hears them. He begins words with single consonants and ends words with consonant letters, too. Roger even includes consonants in the middle of words, as in Biscuit (spelled **Bekst**) and bother (spelled **brtr**). And, when we look closely at Roger's note, we can infer that he is beginning to discover the manner in which vowels represent sounds.

FIGURE 5–2
The invented spelling in Roger's note shows that he thinks carefully about the relationship between the letters in written words and the sounds in spoken words.

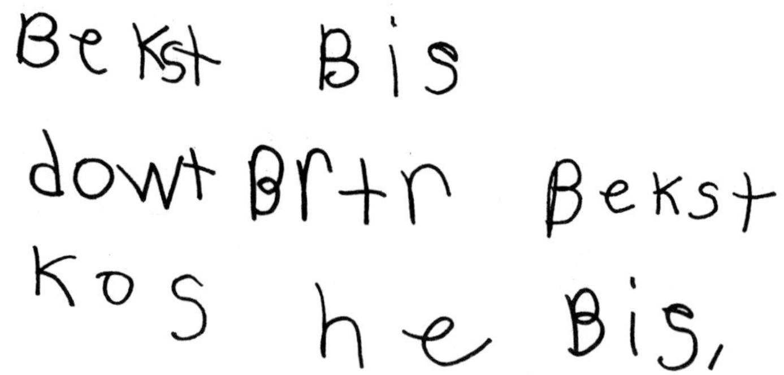

INVENTED SPELLING

If you see that . . .

kindergartners and first graders spell words the way they sound (such as **bekst** for **Biscuit**), you can infer that these learners are thinking carefully about the way our writing system represents sound.

The thing to do . . .

is to give learners lots of opportunities to read, write, and explore the code. When you do this, you will notice that learners move through various stages as they learn to spell (Gentry, 1987).

As strategy users add words to their reading vocabularies and learn more and more about letter neighborhoods, they use invented spelling in fewer and fewer words. Eventually, words are spelled conventionally. Look for this transition from the end of the first grade and into second grade, depending on the individual learner's phonological awareness and code knowledge.

Though Roger seems to know that vowels are important, he is far from understanding vowel letter neighborhoods. This is quite natural because vowels reside in many different neighborhoods and hence offer many choices for pronunciation. It certainly stands to reason, then, that learners need time and reading experience to develop sensitivity to vowel letter neighborhoods and to use this knowledge to learn words (Fowler, Shankweiler, & Liberman, 1979; Zinna, Liberman, & Shankweiler, 1986). Of the forty-five phonics rules researchers use to explain letter-sound correspondences, fully two thirds pertain to vowels (Bailey, 1967; Clymer, 1963; Emans, 1967). Perhaps this explains the reason learners misidentify the sounds represented by vowels far more frequently than the sounds represented by consonants.

Though it takes more reading and writing experiences to develop knowledge of vowel letter neighborhoods than the single consonant neighborhood, one sequence for learning letter neighborhoods is not necessarily superior to another. In fact, there is no prescribed order in which neighborhoods should be explored, no learning hierarchy, no sequence chiseled in stone. You and the learners whom you teach are free to explore letter neighborhoods in any order whatsoever.

While learning sequences in whole language and literature-based classrooms emerge from learners' experiences in reading and writing, you will find prescribed teaching-learning sequences in basal programs, in workbooks, and sometimes in textbooks on the teaching of reading. If you have the freedom to devise your own sequence, my advice is to first consider the words learners read and write everyday. The neighborhoods that occur frequently in these words are the neighborhoods to be learned first. All things being equal, I find it useful to group letter neighborhoods into those that are less challenging, more challenging, and most challenging for the learners whom I teach.

Less Challenging Neighborhoods

The single consonant neighborhood at the beginning of words (the onset) is, in my view, the easiest for strategy users to learn and use. Single consonant onsets are especially obvious and can be readily combined with syntactic context cues and semantic context cues, which keeps word identification and meaning driven from the start. It is not surprising, then, that many learners first pay attention to the single consonants at the beginning of words. Then, as learners gain more experience reading and writing, they notice this neighborhood at the end of words. Hence, the single consonant neighborhood at the end of words is also relatively easy.

The learners whom I teach find the **VC/VCC** neighborhood (explained in Appendix D) to be the least challenging of the neighborhoods that include a vowel letter. The vowels in this neighborhood usually represent the short sound, as in **at**. Should a consonant neighborhood come before the **VC/VCC** neighborhood in words such as in **cat** or **chat**, the **VC/VCC** neighborhood still represents a short vowel sound in these words.

I find that this vowel neighborhood is most easily explored after strategy users have learned to recognize rimes like those in **cat** and **tent**. This puts learners in a position to use their knowledge of rimes to develop code knowledge of the **VC/VCC** neighborhood. Once learners know a few rimes, I encourage learners to look inside the rimes they know to discover how the **VC/VCC** neighborhood represents sound. Looking inside rimes requires that learners focus on the individual letters in the **VC/VCC** neighborhood, think analytically about the **VC/VCC** sequence, and use this code knowledge to pronounce many different combinations of vowels and their next-door consonant neighbors.

Letters that form a consonant blend neighborhood (as the **cl** in **clam** or the **st** in **step**) are also in the easier-to-learn category for the learners whom I teach. When letters reside in a consonant blend neighborhood, they represent the same sounds as they do in the single consonant neighborhood; the only difference is that the blended neighbors are pronounced by blending sounds together rather than saying sounds separately. The consonant blend neighborhood is a strict neighborhood; as a result, readers have very little new information to develop in order to effectively use their code knowledge.

Since two-letter blends are less challenging than three-letter blends, I focus first on blends in a neighborhood made of two letters (**st**) and then move to blends in a neighborhood made of three letters (**str**). I leave any blend neighborhood that includes a digraph (as the **ch** portion of **chr** in **chrome**) until after strategy users have developed knowledge of how letters in a digraph neighborhood represent sound.

More Challenging Neighborhoods

As for more challenging neighborhoods, I find that the consonant digraph neighborhood, such as the **ph** in **phase** and the **th** in **this**, is harder to learn than the single consonant neighborhood or the consonant blend neighborhood. The digraph neighborhood creates whole new, multiletter symbols for sounds. Hence, the learners I teach cannot generalize, or transfer, the code knowledge they already have to the consonant digraph neighborhood. With the exception of **sh**, letter combinations that form the consonant digraph neighborhood are moderately lenient in that strategy users have at least two options for pronunciation (see Appendix D for an explanation).

With regard to the vowel neighborhoods set out in Appendix D, five fall into the more challenging category for the learners whom I teach:

1. Vowel-consonant-e (**VCe**) neighborhood, as in **save** and **life**. Readers know that a consonant neighborhood at the beginning of the **VCe** neighborhood in words forms a **CVCe** (**name**) or **CCVCe** (**blame**) sequence and the beginning consonant neighborhood does not affect the sound that the vowel in the **VCe** neighborhood represents.

    Though the final **e** is a good reminder of the presence of this neighborhood, some learners overlook it, hence treating letters as if they reside in a **VC/VCC** neighborhood instead of a **VCe** neighborhood. Additionally, there are some obvious exceptions to the **VCe** neighborhood (see Appendix D for an explanation).

2. Consonant-vowel (**CV/CCV**) neighborhood, as in **me** and **spider**. This neighborhood frequently comes at the beginning of words, which makes it more obvious than neighborhoods that come in the middle of words. What's more, a beginning **CV/CCV** neighborhood gives readers lots of excellent information to combine with context cues. Still, this neighborhood has some exceptions (particularly in unaccented syllables) and hence takes more experiences with print than neighborhoods in the less challenging category (see Appendix D).

3. Vowel-vowel (**VV**) neighborhood, which is formed when the following two vowels are next-door neighbors: **ai** (**sail**), **ea** (**cream**), **ee** (**seed**), **oa** (**goat**), **ay** (**lay**), and **ey** (**honey**). For the most part, **ai** (**sail**), **ea** (**cream**), and **oa** (**boat**) require that learners pay attention to the middle of words. The vowel combinations **ey** (**honey**) and **ay** (**play**) frequently require that learners pay attention to the ending letters in words. The pattern **ee** can occur at the end of words (**see**) and in the middle of words (**seed**).

4. Double **oo** neighborhood as in **book** and **cool**. The neighborhood **oo** does not represent a long sound as do other **VV** neighborhoods and, in fact, can stand for two sounds, as heard in **school** and **cook**. Generally, this neighborhood pops up early when learners read the word **school**, which creates many opportunities to call attention to it. Look in Appendix D for examples of words with the **oo** neighborhood and a

way to help strategy users manage the two options for its pronunciation.

5. **Diphthong** neighborhood, which is formed when **ow, ou, oi,** and **oy** are next-door neighbors. The neighborhood **ow** represents the sounds heard in **c<u>ow</u>; ou** the sounds heard in **<u>ou</u>t; oi** the sounds heard in **<u>oi</u>l; oy** the sounds heard in **b<u>oy</u>.** Since the sounds represented by the diphthong neighborhood are different from the sounds that letters represent in other neighborhoods, strategy users must learn something totally new about the code. And, added to this, **ow** sometimes represents the long "o" sound, as heard in **cr<u>ow</u>.** For these reasons, letters in the diphthong neighborhood take more attention and more experiences with print than letters in less challenging neighborhoods.

Most Challenging Neighborhoods

As for the most challenging neighborhoods, I find that the neighborhood made up of **c** or **g** plus a vowel, as in **<u>cir</u>cus** and **<u>ge</u>m,** is quite challenging for the learners whom I teach. This is also true for the **ew** and **ue** neighborhoods in **ch<u>ew</u>** and **bl<u>ue</u>,** as well as the **aw** and **au** neighborhoods in **s<u>aw</u>** and **s<u>au</u>cer.** Likewise, the **r-controlled (Vr)** neighborhood, as in **<u>car</u>** and **<u>cur</u>l,** can be quite puzzling to strategy users, perhaps because at first glance the **Vr** neighborhood resembles the **VC/VCC** neighborhood.

I also find that it takes the learners whom I teach a while to develop knowledge of the vowel-consonant-consonant-e (**VCCe**) neighborhood, as in **<u>ten</u>se** and **ch<u>an</u>ce.** Perhaps this is so because the **VCCe** neighborhood resembles the **VCe** neighborhood and is large, consisting of four or more letters.

The **CLe** neighborhood is also quite challenging for the learners whom I teach. This neighborhood consists of sequences like the **ble** in **marble** and the **ple** in **staple,** and typically comes at the end of words. The final **e** is the result of the evolution of English spelling, and so the sounds that **CLe** represents are not completely apparent from the letter sequence. For example, the **ble** is pronounced as "bul" in **marble** and the **ple** is pronounced as "pul" in **staple** (see Appendix D). This is different from the sounds represented by the **bl** consonant blend neighborhood in **black,** and the **pl** consonant blend neighborhood in **place.**

In the final analysis, all of the most challenging neighborhoods typically require that learners have much more practice reading all sorts of books, poems, articles, and stories, and many more opportunities to write all sorts of stories, poems, and messages. So, if the learners whom you teach take longer to figure out how to strategically use neighborhoods with **c** or **g** plus vowel, and the **ew, ue, aw, au** neighborhoods, **CLe** and **Vr** neighborhoods, this is perfectly natural.

LOOKING INSIDE WORDS

If you see that . . .

strategy users *only* identify sounds represented by consonant letter neighborhoods at the beginning and the end of words, in all likelihood they are overlooking the middle letters. Since vowel letter neighborhoods often occur in the middle of words, this is an important oversight. Since vowel letter neighborhoods are generally trickier than consonant neighborhoods and since words cannot be pronounced without a vowel, readers absolutely must pay attention to the vowels in the middle of words.

The thing to do . . .

is to focus learners' attention on the middle vowel and its immediate neighbors. When learners come across an unfamiliar word in a sentence, ask them to think of a word that begins and ends with the sounds represented by letters in neighborhoods at the beginning and end of the word, has a sound like that represented by the middle letter neighborhood, and makes sense in the sentence. Additionally, use activities that call for building words with letter tiles and solving word puzzles, both described later in this chapter.

Neighborhoods That Require Little Exploration

I find that some neighborhoods require only a minimum of learners' attention, or no special attention at all, depending on learners' ability to absorb, infer, and internalize code knowledge. By and large, the learners whom I teach have little or no trouble with the consonant twin neighborhood, such as the double **ll** in **pull** or the double **bb** in **bubble**. So I do not focus much, if any, special attention on this neighborhood. As for **gh**, I do not single out this combination as residents of particular neighborhoods; instead, I present these letters as parts of rimes whenever possible. And, so long as **qu** is considered as an intact neighborhood, the learners whom I teach have not had difficulty with the **qu** in **queen** and **quack**. For one thing, with the exception of a few words (**quick** and **quite**, for example), learners do not come across many words that include this neighborhood in spelling. Second, **qu** is a predictable neighborhood that nearly always represents the sounds heard in **queen**, so learners can count on it most of the time.

ACTIVITIES TO INCREASE THE STRATEGIC USE OF LETTER NEIGHBORHOODS

The five activities that follow are blueprints for instruction and learning of letter neighborhoods. These activities do not zero in on specific letter neighborhoods; it is up to you to decide which letter neighborhoods to explore and when to do so. The activities encourage learners to think analytically about letter neighborhoods and to strategically apply this information. If plain old-fashioned practice is called for, look in Appendix A.

✳ Building Words with Letter Tiles

This activity is like the word building activity in Chapter 4, only here learners use tiles with letters written on them instead of tiles with onsets and rimes. Not only is word building appropriate for learners of any age, but this type of activity has definitely withstood the test of time, for it has been around for decades in one form or another (Cunningham & Cunningham, 1992; Gunning, 1992; Reed & Klopp, 1957). This activity is appropriate for learners in any grade, so share it with those learners who need to gain greater insight into the letter neighborhoods in words.

Things You'll Need: Letter cards; a pocket chart; as many sets of letter tiles as there are individual learners or learning partners in your classroom (see Appendix B); words from familiar books, favorite poems and plays, and learners' own writing; old magazines, newspapers, and advertising flyers for making scrapbooks.

FIGURE 5–3
Letter tiles are easy to make, inexpensive, and give learners opportunities to think about the way that the letters in a word's spelling form neighborhoods that represent pronunciation.

Exploration: Begin by exploring the words learners hear and see around them every day. Point out words on the wall charts and bulletin boards in your classroom. Write words on the chalkboard that include the same neighborhood, the **VC/VCC** neighborhood, for example. Discuss this letter neighborhood, and the sounds that the letters in this neighborhood represent in words. Do the same for a second neighborhood, the **VCe** neighborhood for instance. Then challenge learners to find other words that include the same neighborhoods (the **VC/VCC** and **VCe** neighborhoods) on the wall charts and bulletin boards in your classroom, in books and poems, and in the stories learners write. Write the words learners find on the chalkboard. Now explain that learners are going to build words that have the same neighborhoods as the familiar words on the chalkboard.

Model word building by putting letter cards one after the other in a pocket chart. Discuss why certain letters form neighborhoods and why the letters in neighborhoods represent the sounds that they do.

For example, you might put cards with the letters **p, f, i, n,** and **e** written on them in the top row of a pocket chart. Then pronounce the word "**pin.**" Pronounce "**pin**" a second time, "rubber banding" it so that learners have an opportunity to hear each of the sounds. Ask learners to think of letters on the top row of the pocket chart that represent the sounds they hear in "**pin.**" Show learners how to line up the **p,** the **i,** and the **n** one after the other to build the word **pin.** Leave the word in its pocket, and put new letter cards for **p, i,** and **n** on the top row of the pocket chart, thereby reproducing the original five letters. Now build the word **pine.** Follow this procedure to demonstrate how to build **fin** and **fine.** Invite learners to come up to the pocket chart and participate in word building. Talk about words, letter neighborhoods, and the sounds the neighborhoods represent. When learners understand how to build many different words from the same set of letters, it is time for guided practice.

Guided Practice: Pass out four or more tiles to individual learners or learning partners, and ask learners to build a word. For example, if learners have letter tiles with **s, t, p, o, a, r** on them, learners might build the word **stop.** Talk about the letter neighborhoods in the word learners have built and ask learners to change that word, **stop** for instance, into another word, **star** perhaps. Continue building, asking learners to change one word into another— **star** to **part; part** to **tar; tar** to **top; top** to **port; port** to **sport,** for example. (Look in Appendix A for What's in a Name? which is a fine complement to this activity, not to mention a favorite of the learners whom I teach.)

Transfer: Have the learners make scrapbooks. Have the learners work in small groups to cut out words from magazines that share the same letter neighbmrhood and paste these words onto large pieces of paper. Learners then write sentences on the pages, using as many of the words on each page as possible in sentences. (Younger learners may dictate to you, to a parent volunteer, or to some other accomplished reader.) Last, fasten pages together

FIGURE 5–4
Learners gain insight into the letter neighborhoods in words when they use neighborhoods to build words.

to make a scrapbook. Make the scrapbook available for everyone to read and enjoy; send it home overnight with learners to share with their families; share it with other classrooms in your school.

✳ Venn Diagrams

Venn diagrams are overlapping circles in which shared characteristics are inside the overlapping portion and unique characteristics are inside each separate circle (Figure 5–5). Making diagrams calls for discussion, analytical thinking, and group interaction. So, move the furniture, clear work spaces,

FIGURE 5–5
Venn diagrams give learners opportunities to explore letter neighborhoods that represent more than one sound in words.

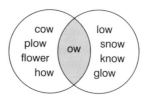

and give learners who are third graders and older plenty of support as they delve into letter neighborhoods.

Things You'll Need: One piece of chart paper for each cooperative group in your class; markers; poems or books written in verse that have a good selection of words that include the letter neighborhoods learners are to explore.

Exploration: Read books written in verse or poems that have a good selection of words that include the same letter neighborhood. Talk about the images that the books and poems create in readers' and listeners' minds. Then point out that some of the words authors use have the same letter neighborhoods.

Draw two overlapping circles on the board. Write a neighborhood that represents more than one sound (**ow**, for instance) in the overlapping portion. Write a word that represents one pronunciation (**snow**, perhaps) in one circle; a word that represents another pronunciation (**cow**, for example) in the other circle. Challenge learners to think of words in which **ow** represents the sounds heard in **snow** and in **cow**. Support learners as they draw conclusions about the way that **ow** signals pronunciation.

Guided Practice: Invite learners to work collaboratively and cooperatively to make their own Venn diagrams (Figure 5–6). Challenge learners to find words written on the wall charts and bulletin boards in your classroom that include the letter neighborhood featured in the Venn diagram they are working on. Invite them to find words with the letter neighborhood in poems and in books written in verse. For example, words with the **ow** neighborhood are sprinkled throughout many of the short poems in *Hailstones and Halibut Bones* (O'Neill, 1961), so this would be a book that learners might read in their search for words.

When they have finished, invite groups to share their diagrams with the entire class, to explain letter neighborhoods, to talk about the words they found, and to discuss spelling. Display diagrams in your classroom and encourage learners to use diagrams as resources.

Transfer: Have learners complete modified cloze sentences. When learners read modified cloze sentences, they think about syntactic context cues, semantic context cues, and code cues in order to figure out the identity of words. To construct modified cloze sentences, delete portions of words so as to focus learners' attention on certain letter neighborhoods. For example, a sentence from *Tuck Everlasting* (Babbitt, 1975) would look like

> Though it was very l_ now, almost midnight, the wind_s glowed golden; the family h_ gone to bed. (p. 59)

In this example, learners are challenged to use their knowledge of the **VCe** (**l<u>a</u>te**), **ow** (**wind<u>ow</u>s**), and **VC/VCC** (**h<u>a</u>d**) neighborhoods along with information gleaned from the sentence context. I suggest that you begin by focusing attention on one letter neighborhood at a time, choosing a neighborhood

FIGURE 5–6
When learners make Venn diagrams, they discuss the letter neighborhoods and explore the ways that neighborhoods represent sounds in words.

from which learners would benefit by using in context. Then, when learners have developed greater knowledge of letter neighborhoods, focus attention on more than one letter neighborhood at a time. As for cloze sentences, use ones from familiar books and poems or from the stories learners write. This way learners bring plenty of prior knowledge and reading experiences to this activity.

✳ Word Puzzles

This activity challenges learners who are second graders and older to solve puzzles that include a clue word (like **steam**) and a set of instructions (**- ea + or =**) that transform the clue into a solution word (**storm**), as shown in Figure 5–7. Puzzle solvers delete letter neighborhoods, add neighborhoods, and cross-check to verify solutions by finding words in content subject textbooks, storybooks, or poems. (Solution words in Figure 5–7 are from the zany rhyming book *Father Fox's Pennyrhymes* [Watson, 1971].)

Things You'll Need: A good imagination to create puzzles; colored chalk; words from familiar reading material; multiple copies of content subject textbooks, storybooks, novels, or poems.

Exploration: Read and share a variety of stories and poems, or look inside the content area textbooks that learners are reading in your classroom. Discuss the letter neighborhoods in words, focusing attention on one or two neighborhoods that recur frequently in words and that learners could use to identify words with the letter-sound strategy.

Write three or four puzzles on the chalkboard. Use colored chalk to highlight the transformations learners are to perform. To demonstrate how to solve the puzzle **steam - ea + or = _** , first read the clue word. Then show learners how to take away the **ea** (**VV**) letter neighborhood and add the **or** (**Vr**) neighborhood to form **storm**.

Guided Practice: The examples in Figure 5–7 challenge learners to use the **Vr** letter neighborhood to solve puzzles. I have found that puzzles are most effective when learners begin solving them by changing only one kind of letter neighborhood to find solutions. I also suggest beginning with less challenging letter neighborhoods, such as onsets, the **VC/VCC** vowel neighborhood, or consonant blends. As learners' code knowledge and phonological awareness increases, make puzzles with the more challenging and the most challenging neighborhoods. From a familiar book, poem, or textbook, select words that include the important letter neighborhood(s) that have been discussed previously. Then make puzzles in which the solution words are words from the familiar text. And as learners become better at solving puzzles, I suggest that a variety of letter neighborhoods be used in the same puzzle. Write several puzzles on sheets of paper and ask learners to work either individually or with a partner to find solutions. Encourage puzzle solvers to explain in their own words how and why transformed words create solution words. Challenge learners to reread the book, poem, or selection in the content area textbook, to think about the author's message, to consider the words in the message, and to find the solution words in the text.

coin	–	oi	+	or	=	____	steam	–	ea	+	or	=	____
sheet	–	ee	+	ir	=	____	house	–	ou	+	or	=	____
coat	–	oa	+	ar	=	____	dealing	–	ea	+	ar	=	____

FIGURE 5–7
Finding solutions to word puzzles calls for thinking analytically about the sounds that the letters in neighborhoods represent in words.

Transfer: Invite learners to work collaboratively and cooperatively to create their own puzzles for words, finding words in a variety of books—content subject textbooks, storybooks, novels, and poems. As groups of learners make puzzles, ask them to (1) underline the words in puzzles that are from books and (2) write the page numbers where words appear. When the puzzles are complete, groups trade puzzles, as well as the books that contain solution words. Groups then solve one another's puzzles and verify their solutions by finding the underlined words in books.

✳ Letter Neighborhood Togetherness Charts

In this activity, learners in the second grade and up make large charts that show how three- or four-letter neighborhoods represent the same sounds. For instance, a chart that depicts letter neighborhoods that represent the long **o** sound might be divided in four equal sections. One section might have a picture of a stove with the word **stove** written under the picture; another section might have a picture of a boat and the word **boat;** a third section might have a picture of a snowman with the word **snowman;** and a fourth section might have a picture of a gold bar with the word **gold.** Learners look at the picture and the word in each section of the Letter Neighborhood Togetherness Chart, think about the letter neighborhood that represents the long **o** sound, and add words to each section that uses the same letter neighborhood to represent the sound of long **o.** In this example, learners might work together to write words such as **pole, hope, bone,** and **alone** in the section in which the word **stove** depicts the **CVe** neighborhood. Learners might then write words such as **coat, toad, float,** and **soap** in the section that depicts the **VV** neighborhood of **oa** in **boat,** and so on.

Charts are terrific to hang on the walls of your classroom and a great source for lively discussions about how and why our alphabetic code represents sounds in many different, but predictable, ways.

Things You'll Need: As many large sheets of chart paper as there are cooperative groups in your classroom; colored markers; a cardboard box, two dowels, a knife, and tape to make a movie projector (see Appendix B, Homemade Movie Projectors).

Exploration: Challenge learners to think of words that have a certain sound, the long **o** sound for instance. Invite learners to think of words from memory and to look for words on the wall charts in your classroom, and in dictionaries, storybooks, and textbooks. Write words on the chalkboard. Make a long list; cover the entire board with words! Stop when the chalkboard is covered. Explain that there are several ways that the letter sequences in words represent the sound. In the example of long **o,** you might focus on the **VV** neighborhood of **oa,** the **VCe** neighborhood (as in **home**), the **ow** neighborhood (as in **low**), and the **old** rime (as in **fold**).

Ask learners to look for the words on the chalkboard list that use a particular neighborhood to represent the sound, such as words in which the **oa** represents the long **o** sound. Use a piece of colored chalk to draw a lacy cloud around each word. (Draw clouds around all the words on the list in which **oa** represents long **o**, such as **coat, boat,** and **foam.**) Then ask learners to find all the words in which a different neighborhood represents the same sound, such as the **VCe** neighborhood that represents the long **o** sound. Use a different color of chalk to make lacy clouds around the words that include this neighborhood. Continue until all the words with the letter neighborhoods have been found. (Depending on the letter neighborhoods that are explored in this activity, some of the words on the chalkboard may not be spelled with one of the neighborhoods, such as the word **toe** or the word **locate.** Discuss the idea that the same sound can be represented by more letter sequences than the ones learners have focused their attention on.) Then explain that learners are to make a Letter Neighborhood Togetherness Chart of words in which the same sound (in this case long **o**) is represented by different letter neighborhoods (in this example, **oa [VV], VCe, ow,** and **old**).

Divide a piece of chart paper into equal parts; write a word and draw a picture in each section, as shown in Figure 5–8. Write words in the correct sections of the chart. Support learners as they draw the conclusion that some words share sounds, but not letter neighborhoods. Now, ask learners to think of words that have the same sounds as the words on the chart. Discuss the idea that different letter neighborhoods can represent the same sounds.

Guided Practice: Challenge learners to work cooperatively and collaboratively to make Letter Neighborhood Togetherness Charts. For the first chart-making experience, I find that expanding the chart made by the whole class works best. Later, challenge groups to devise charts for many different neighborhoods. Remind learners to look for words on wall charts and in dictionaries, storybooks, and textbooks. Share finished charts with the class; ask learners to compare and contrast words and to explain how different letter neighborhoods signal pronunciation.

Transfer: Invite learners to write and produce movies. To begin, ask groups to write a short story and to divide the story into brief episodes. Then give groups opportunities to revise and edit their stories. Next, ask groups to partition a long piece of butcher paper into movie frames by drawing horizontal lines at equal distances. In every frame, learners write text and draw a picture for one episode in the story. (Leave one or two blank frames at each end of the butcher paper.) Fasten the butcher paper to dowels and insert it in a homemade movie projector (explained in Appendix B).

Now it's movie time. Put the spotlight on each group as they simultaneously turn the dowels to display one illustration after the other and read the accompanying text. After the presentations, invite the learners to talk about the movies, about meaning, about interesting words, and about some of the letter neighborhoods in the words in the movie scripts.

FIGURE 5–8
Making letter neighborhood charts creates opportunities for learners to compare and contrast different letter neighborhoods that represent the same sounds in words.

✴ Word Group Discovery

The Word Group Discovery activity provides opportunities for first grade learners and up to discover the syntactic, semantic, and code properties that glue categories of words together. This activity is appropriate for any letter neighborhood and is similar to many of the sorting activities that are so effective (Henderson, 1990; Miller & McKenna, 1989; Powell & Hornsby, 1993) and is most successful when strategy users work with a learning partner or in cooperative groups.

Things You'll Need: As many sets of small word cards as there are cooperative groups in your class; a few large word cards with tape on the back; lunch-size paper sacks; storybooks; poems; science, social studies, language, and mathematics textbooks; gallon-size plastic bags that lock at the top, a hole punch, and ribbon to make books.

Exploration: Select interesting words from familiar storybooks and poems and content area books. Write these words on cards. Tape several large word cards randomly to the chalkboard (perhaps cards with **snake, grain, snail,** and **grape** on them) and challenge learners to think of ways words are alike. Learners might, for example, point out that some words belong together in the same groups because they share the same letter neighborhoods (such as **CVe** or **gr**), that some are nouns and others verbs, that some are things to eat, to wear, animals, and so forth. Rearrange word cards to show different groups. Talk about how and why words are grouped and regrouped in many different ways.

Guided Practice: Give each cooperative group of learners several small sacks and one container with an assortment of small word cards inside. (Old margarine containers make good holders for small word cards.) Ask learners to put words that belong to the same group in the same paper sack. The words learners sort should be words that learners know how to read. For first and second graders, write the names of word groups on sacks so that learners know before hand the groups to which words belong, as in Figure 5–9. Challenge older learners to devise their own word groups and to write word group names on sacks. When finished, learners empty each sack, cross-check to make sure all the words inside are group members, and then write each word on the side of the sack in which it belongs. Ask learners to read the words when they take the word cards out of the sacks. Last, bring the whole class together: Invite the learners to compare and contrast word groups and talk about how and why the same words are grouped in different ways.

Transfer: Have the learners make bag books, which are lots of fun, lend themselves to group interaction, and are great to share. Explain that learners are to write a story and to put the pages inside sealable plastic bags which are then fastened together to make a book. (See Appendix B.) When stories are complete, share them with the class; read them aloud. Invite the learners to talk about sequence in stories, about words, about meaning, and about letter neighborhoods.

FIGURE 5–9
Sorting helps learners discover letter neighborhoods that occur in many different words.

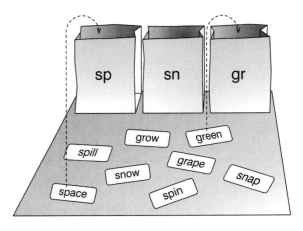

FIGURE 5–10
Writing gives learners
opportunities to use their
knowledge of letter
neighborhoods to
communicate through written
language.

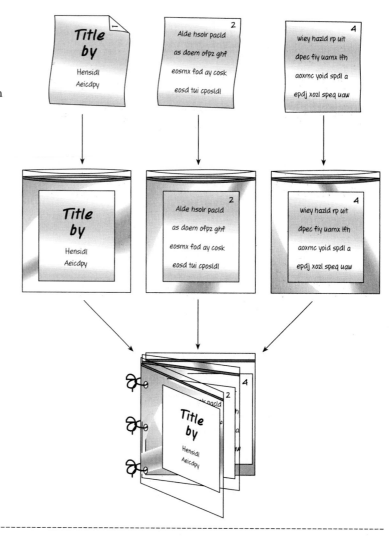

FINAL OBSERVATIONS

In the final analysis, though the letter-sound word identification strategy is
an especially useful tool, it is also especially challenging because of its heavy
demands on phonological awareness and code knowledge. Learning to use
the letter-sound strategy is well worth the effort, however, for this strategy
taps into the basic feature of alphabetic writing—the sounds represented by
letters in neighborhoods. And, in addition, the letter-sound strategy paves the
way for the chunk strategy, which is the streamlined strategy considered in
the next chapter.

REFERENCES

Babbitt, N. (1975). *Tuck everlasting.* New York: Bantam Skylark Books.

Bailey, M. H. (1967). The utility of phonic generalizations in grades one through six. *The Reading Teacher, 20,* 413–418.

Clymer, T. (1963). The utility of phonic generalizations in the primary grades. *The Reading Teacher, 16,* 252–258.

Cunningham, P. M., & Cunningham, J. W. (1992). Making words: Enhancing the invented spelling-decoding connection. *The Reading Teacher, 46,* 106–115.

Emans, R. (1967). The usefulness of phonic generalizations above the primary grades. *The Reading Teacher, 20,* 419–425.

Fowler, C. A., Shankweiler, D., & Liberman, I. Y. (1979). Apprehending spelling patterns for vowels: A developmental study. *Language and Speech, 22,* 243–252.

Gentry, J. R. (1987). *Spel . . . is a four-letter word.* New York: Scholastic.

Gunning, T. G. (1992). *Creating reading instruction for all children.* Boston: Allyn & Bacon.

Henderson, E. H. (1990). *Teaching spelling* (2nd ed.). Boston: Houghton Mifflin.

Howe, D., & Howe, J. (1979). *Bunnicula.* New York: Avon Books.

Ives, J. P, Bursuk, L. Z., & Ives, S. A. (1979). *Word identification techniques.* Chicago, IL: Rand McNally.

Juel, C. (1983). The development and use of mediated word identification. *Reading Research Quarterly, 18,* 306–327.

Laxon, V. A., Smith, B., & Masterson, J. (1995). Children's nonword reading: Pseudohomophones, neighborhood size, and priming effects. Reading Research Quarterly, 30, 126–144.

Massaro, D. W., & Hestand, J. (1983). Developmental relations between reading ability and knowledge of orthographic structure. *Contemporary Educational Psychology, 8,* 174–180.

Miller, J. W., & McKenna, M. (1989). *Teaching reading in the elementary classroom.* Scottsdale, AZ: Gorsuch Scarisbrick, Publishers.

O'Neill, M. (1961). *Hailstones and halibut bones.* New York: Doubleday.

Powell, D., & Hornsby, D. (1993). *Learning phonics and spelling in a whole language classroom.* New York: Scholastic Professional Books.

Reed, L. C., & Klopp, D. S. (1957). *Phonics for thought.* New York: Comet Press Books.

Watson, C. (1971). *Father Fox's pennyrhymes.* New York: Harper & Row.

Zinna, D. R., Liberman, I. Y., & Shankweiler, D. (1986). Children's sensitivity to factors influencing vowel reading. *Reading Research Quarterly, 21,* 465–479.

C H A P T E R

THE CHUNK STRATEGY

Using Groups of Letters
to Identify Words

This chapter describes the chunk strategy. As you read this chapter, you will find out about the different types of chunks inside words, how learners use chunks to identify unfamiliar words, and ways to support learners as they streamline word identification with the use of the chunk strategy.

KEY IDEAS

----

* ✳ Chunks are groups of letters in words that learners recognize and automatically know how to pronounce.
* ✳ Meaningful chunks contribute to the pronunciation and to the definition of words, for example, the Latin root **port** meaning "carry"; nonmeaningful chunks contribute to pronunciation only.
* ✳ Learners who use the chunk strategy streamline word identification by pronouncing and blending groups of letters as intact chunks.

Look at Figure 6–1. At a mere glance, you know how to pronounce **astroport**, recognize that it probably is an interstellar station for the space traveling public, know that it is a noun, and, if asked, could use **astroport** in a sentence. All this is quite interesting, since **astroport** is not a real word, at least not yet.

The way to unlock the word's pronunciation and at the same time to get insight into its meaning is to divide **astroport** into two large chunks—**astro** and **port.** Each chunk is spelled the way it sounds and contributes to the word's definition, provided you know that **ast(er)** means "star" and **port** means "to carry." With this knowledge, you have the information you need to infer that an **astroport** is a site to which space travelers are transported, just as an airport is a site to which airline passengers are transported.

FIGURE 6–1
Meaningful chunks give insight into pronunciation and word meaning. The student who drew this picture used knowledge of **astro** and **port** to show what they might mean if put together.

After reading and writing the same letter groups time and time again, learners perceive groups of letters as large, intact units (Stuart & Coltheart, 1988). In so doing, learners chunk, or join together, groups of letters in their minds. The use of chunks significantly reduces the energy readers put into word identification and, when readers know the meaning of chunks, provides them with insight into the definition of words.

Learners who use the chunk strategy do not recall analogous onsets and rimes in known words to identify unfamiliar words as do users of the analogy strategy, nor do they sound out and blend the letters that reside in neighborhoods as do users of the letter-sound strategy. Instead, users of the chunk strategy recognize and pronounce entire groups of letters in words. The chunk strategy is the most streamlined way to identify unfamiliar words. Accomplished strategy users realize this and hence use the chunk strategy whenever they have the opportunity. The use of chunks is not unique to reading, for you chunk all sorts of information. You use chunks all the time and you do this for good reason.

WHY CHUNKS?

You form chunks whenever you bundle several small bits of information together into one unit. For example, when you combine the letters **p + r + e** in **prepaid** into one whole unit, **pre**, you create a chunk in your mind. The reason you use chunks is to prevent a bottleneck in short-term memory. Short-term memory holds all the information about whatever you happen to be paying attention to at the moment. All information goes through short-term memory on its way to long-term memory. Long-term memory, in turn, is the storehouse for all the information, words, ideas, and memories you accumulate throughout your life. So you want to get as much information as possible out of short-term memory and into long-term memory.

While there is a great deal of space to store information in long-term memory, the storage space in short-term memory is extremely limited. In fact, only five to seven thought units are held in short-term memory at one time (Miller, 1956), and this information lasts only a few seconds before it is either forgotten or moved into long-term memory. A bottleneck occurs when there are so many thought units in short-term memory that some are forgotten before information can be sent to long-term memory. A thought unit can be small (one letter, such as **p**) or large (a group of letters, as **pre**).

When you combine small bits of information (a single letter) together into a large chunk (a group of letters), you put more information into one thought unit. This makes it easier to keep more information in short-term memory because overcrowding is prevented. It also makes it possible to get more information into long-term memory because a number of small bits of information are grouped together in each thought unit.

Take something as ordinary as your social security number, which has nine digits. You use your social security number from time to time, so remembering the nine digits makes life less stressful. Rather than remembering the nine digits as separate thought units, you can choose to make it easy on yourself by combining digits into large chunks. So, instead of remembering nine things (3 + 2 + 1 + 6 + 5 + 8 + 7 + 9 + 0), you might choose to combine information into three chunks (321 + 65 + 8790). This makes recalling and repeating you social security number simpler.

The same principle holds for the nine letters in **astroport**. Learners who use chunks reduce information to just two thought units—**astro** and **port**. With only two thought units in short-term memory, learners are less likely to forget information. And what's more, there is room left over to make a little sense of **astroport** before it goes to long-term memory. Added to this, the use of chunks reduces the number of spoken language segments that must be blended. Blending a few large chunks—"astro" + "port"—makes it less likely that individual sounds will be forgotten or reversed.

Given the advantages of chunks, it is not at all surprising that as readers increase the number of chunks they recognize, their efficiency in word identification improves (Invernizzi, 1992). All in all, readers who use chunks put less mental attention and less mental energy into word identification than is the case with other forms of decoding. This means that readers using chunks return to textual reading more quickly and hence the disruption to comprehension created by unfamiliar words is decreased.

USING THE CHUNK STRATEGY TO IDENTIFY UNFAMILIAR WORDS

Learners who use chunks are not neophytes just cutting their teeth on our alphabetic writing system. Users of the chunk strategy bring to word identification considerable experience with the alphabetic code and with reading and with writing. In their search for familiar chunks in unfamiliar words, users of the chunk strategy consider the complete spelling of words and then target chunks selectively. Learners who do this have very good phonological awareness and in-depth code knowledge. And as learners gain greater experience communicating in written language as readers and writers, the number of chunks they can recognize in words increases, too.

What Users of the Chunk Strategy Know about Phonological Awareness   Users of the chunk strategy know that spoken words consist of all sorts of different-size groups, or chunks, of sounds, some small and some large. Added to this, they know that these sound sequences are part of a variety of words, as the **"ter"** in **"butter,"** **"terrific,"** and **"later."** Users of the chunk strategy also understand that some groups of sounds can be associated with a pronunciation but not with a meaning (the **"ter"** in **"after"**), and others can be associated with a meaning as well as pronunciation (the **"astro"** in **"astro-port"**). And, of course, users of the strategy can separate the spoken words they hear in everyday conversations into individual sounds and chunks, and they can blend individual sounds and chunks together to form recognizable words.

What Chunk Strategists Know about Code Cues   Users of the chunk strategy recognize and use many sizes and types of chunks, some meaningful (as the **astro** in **astroport** or the **pre** in **prepaid**) and some nonmeaningful (as the **ter** in **after** or the **tion** in **nation**). Chunks are like large envelopes that contain all the information needed to identify and pronounce whole groups of letters in words. Unlike users of the letter-sound strategy, who associate sounds with the individual letters that reside in neighborhoods, chunk strategists instantly know how to pronounce the chunks they recognize in words. When Leslie (Chapter 5) used the letter-sound strategy to unlock the pronunciation of **shaft**, she recognized the **VC/VCC** neighborhood in which **a**, **f**, and **t** reside, and then used this knowledge to determine the sounds that each letter represented—"a," "f," and "t." Had Leslie recognized **aft** as an intact chunk, she would have instantly known that **aft** represented "aft." When learners use chunks, it takes them less mental attention to identify words and, by extension, requires less time away from understanding authors' messages.

What Users of the Chunk Strategy Do with Their Knowledge   The chunk strategy hinges on learners' abilities to recognize and use the chunks in words, as you will see when Brian comes across the word **antiseptic** in this sentence from his science book (Hackett, Moyer, & Adams, 1989): "Perhaps you recall getting a cut on your knee. Someone may have disinfected the cut with an **antiseptic**" (page 27).

Brian's science class has already discussed antiseptics and their function, so this word is in his speaking and listening vocabularies. Added to this, Brian knows that **anti** contributes to the meaning of many different words. He knows that **anti** means "against" when it is in common words like **antismoking, antitheft,** and **antiaircraft**. And he knows the meaning of the word **antibody** because this term was explored in a preceding section of the science book.

All things considered, Brian brings a good deal of knowledge to word identification: He knows (1) what the word **antiseptic** means, (2) how **anti** contributes to a word's definition, (3) how letters form neighborhoods in words, and (4) how to recognize many different types of chunks in the words he reads. Here is how Brian goes about using the chunk strategy:

1. Brian identifies **anti, sep,** and **tic** as chunks. In so doing, he instantly recalls pronunciation, which results in "anti" + "sep" + "tic."
2. Next, Brian blends "anti" + "sep" + "tic" into "antiseptic."

3. Last, Brian cross-checks to make sure than he can pronounce and understand the word in the context in which it is used in his science book. He asks himself: Does **antiseptic** sound and look right? Does this seem like language? Does **antiseptic** make sense in the passage? Do I know what the author means? If **antiseptic** makes sense, Brian stops decoding and continues reading the passage. If the answers are no, he returns to decoding.

Brian could have divided **antiseptic** into chunks in more than one way. In the way he separated them, the first group of letters is a meaningful chunk that is two syllables long (**anti**) and the last two chunks correspond to individual syllables (**sep** and **tic**). But there are other chunks Brian might have chosen. Though the **septic** in **antiseptic** is a meaningful chunk, it is not in Brian's speaking or listening vocabulary. Had he known the meaning of **septic**, Brian might have divided **antiseptic** into two meaningful chunks—**anti + septic**. Or he could have divided **antiseptic** into **an + ti + sep + tic** or into **an + ti + septic**. Though the specific chunks used by individual strategy users vary depending on the code knowledge they bring to word identification, all users of the chunk strategy are sensitive to which letter groups are chunks and which are not.

Take the letter group **ing**, which is part of a great many words. Users of the chunk strategy know that **ing** represents meaning and sound in **playing** and a nonmeaningful rime chunk in **swing**. They also know that **ing** is not a chunk in the word **derringer.**

Learners recognize chunks by taking into account the position of the chunks relative to the surrounding letter neighborhoods. This explains why Brian did not identify the **ise** as a chunk in **antiseptic**. While the letter sequence **ise** is pronounceable if removed from the word **ant-ise-ptic**, and a viable chunk in a word such as **precise**, it is not consistent with the letter neighborhoods in the word. And so chunk strategy users like Brian use their knowledge of the letter neighborhoods to determine the groups of letters in unfamiliar words that are most likely to be chunks. This type of in-depth code knowledge is not an overnight phenomenon. Rather, it develops gradually over time as readers strategically use the alphabetic code to read and write.

Correcting Misidentifications

Users of the chunk strategy are not always successful on the first try. If the first try does not work, learners can do the following:

1. Rechunk (divide words into different chunks and then reblend).
2. Fall back on the letter-sound or analogy strategy.
3. Look up words in the dictionary.
4. Ask expert readers for help.

Learners use these options wisely so as to identify words that make sense in the sentences they read. In order to rechunk or fall back on the letter-sound or analogy strategies, learners must bring a great deal of code knowledge and a great deal of phonological awareness to reading. With its dependence on in-depth code knowledge, the chunks strategy does not come into its own until after learners have had experience using the analogy and letter-sound strategies.

The Roots of the Chunk Strategy

The chunk strategy is rooted in both the analogy strategy and the letter-sound strategy. In fact, there is reason to believe that the very origin of the chunk strategy lies in the use of rimes and letter neighborhoods to identify words (Ehri, 1991). When analogy strategy users employ the rimes in familiar words to identify unfamiliar words, they learn how to capitalize on large, regular letter groups in spelling. This helps learners develop a mind-set to look for and to use "rime" chunks. So, the use of analogous rimes presents early opportunities for learners to strategically use chunks and, in this sense, constitutes a step toward the more sophisticated chunk strategy.

When learners use the letter-sound strategy, they think analytically about the letter neighborhoods in words. In so doing, they have opportunities to form hypotheses about the presence of recurring letter groups within and across neighborhoods. As a consequence of reading and writing the same letter groups, learners eventually fuse letters together to recognize common chunks (Stuart & Coltheart, 1988). Learners then refine their knowledge of chunks through even more reading and writing experiences and, as reading maturity increases, so too does the ability to take advantage of chunks (Santa, 1976–1977).

Once the chunk strategy develops, it co-exists with the analogy and letter-sound strategies. As is to be expected with such a streamlined route to word identification, there are some interesting implications for teachers, which you will learn about in the next section.

IMPLICATIONS FOR TEACHING

Users of the chunk strategy recognize many different-size chunks and many different types of chunks (Gibson & Guinet, 1971; Invernizzi, 1992; Santa, 1976-1977). Chunks are either (1) **nonmeaningful** groups of letters that contribute to pronunciation only or (2) **meaningful** groups of letters that contribute to pronunciation and to the definition of words.

Nonmeaningful Chunks

Many of the syllables in words, such as the **sep** in **antiseptic** or the **der** in **spider,** are nonmeaningful chunks inasmuch as they signal pronunciation, yet give no clue as to a word's definition. Accurately speaking, the frequently occurring rimes in Appendix C are also nonmeaningful chunks, as the **at** in

cat and **democrat** or the **end** in **send** and **blend.** Rimes are detected and used for word identification and for spelling far earlier than more complicated letter sequences like **astro** and **port** (Invernizzi, 1992). Look in Chapter 4 for teaching activities for chunks that are rimes.

Meaningful Chunks

Meaningful chunks provide insight into the definition of words, which explains why they have been found to be so important for word recognition (Nagy, Anderson, Schommer, Scott, & Stallman, 1989). Insight into meaning is particularly important for older readers, say fourth graders and above, who meet a good many new and challenging words in content subject textbooks and leisure reading materials. However, the large number of completely new words—words unknown by ear and by eye—is somewhat counterbalanced by the insight into word meaning that meaningful chunks provide.

Once learners combine the strategic use of meaningful chunks with syntactic context cues and semantic context cues, growth in reading vocabulary serves to extend and expand the number of words in learners' speaking and listening vocabularies. Now, at last, learning by eye surpasses learning by ear. Whereas young learners depend on their speaking vocabularies to develop their reading vocabularies, older learners (those in the fourth grade and above) use reading as the basis for developing their speaking and listening vocabularies. One way older readers do this is to strategically use the meaningful chunks in words to gain insight into both pronunciation and definition. Five types of meaningful chunks are described in the next sections:

1. Prefixes, which are attached to the beginning of words
2. Suffixes, which are attached to the end of words
3. Greek and Latin roots, which are chunks borrowed from these two languages
4. Compound words, which are two words glued together to form a third word
5. Contractions, which are speaking and writing shortcuts

Prefixes and Suffixes Prefixes are separate syllables attached to the beginning of words and hence are usually quite easy to recognize. Prefixes either change the meaning of the base word completely, as in **non + fatal = nonfatal** (which results in an opposite), or make meaning more specific, as in **pre + pay = prepay** (which means to pay "before"). In Appendix E, you will find a list of prefixes and their meanings.

Suffixes, on the other hand, are the chunks that are attached to the end of words. These chunks are recognized by learners (Gibson & Guinet, 1971). Some suffixes change grammatical function. For example, the addition of **ly** to **bright** changes an adjective (**the bright sun**) to an adverb (**the sun shone brightly**). Other suffixes clarify meaning or add information. In addition, frequently used suffixes may add information or clarify meaning, as in **cat + s = cats** (s marks the plural); **cup + ful = cupful; friend + ship = friendship; sea + ward = seaward.** Appendix F lists suffixes that are frequently used in English and hence are useful chunks for readers to know.

The strategic use of prefixes and suffixes is important because the number of words with prefixes and suffixes that learners encounter doubles from fourth to fifth grade, and doubles again by the seventh grade (White, Power, & White, 1989). It is estimated that fifth graders may meet an average of about 1,325 words a year that include the prefixes **in-, im-, ir-,** and **il-** (meaning "not"), and **un-, re-,** and **dis-.** Seventh graders may well decode 3,000 words each year, and perhaps as many as 9,000 words, with these prefixes as well as a variety of suffixes. As learners move into higher and higher grades, their knowledge of suffixes increases (Nagy, Diakidoy, & Anderson, 1993). So, it is not surprising that fourth, sixth, and eighth graders use their code knowledge of suffixes to read new words in context and that sixth and eighth graders are better at this than fourth graders (Wysocki & Jenkins, 1987).

Though older readers meet a great many prefixes and suffixes, words with prefixes or suffixes do not make up the major portion of text in the storybooks younger children read (Ives, Bursuk, & Ives, 1979). Nevertheless, it is wise to begin to explore meaningful chunks early, and suffixes are a better investment in learning than are prefixes (Durkin, 1993). This is so because authors who write for young readers frequently use words that end with **-s**

FIGURE 6–2
Reading, writing, and spelling give learners opportunities to gain insight into the prefixes and suffixes that are meaningful chunks attached to many different words.

(es), **-ing**, and **-ed,** which makes these suffixes extremely important (Temple-ton, 1991). These three suffixes make up to 65 percent of the suffixes that learners in grades 3 through 9 are likely to read (White, Sowell, & Yanagi-hara, 1989). The majority of readers become aware of **-s(es), -ing,** and **-ed** by the end of the first grade, and **-er, -est,** and **-ly** by the end of the second grade.

By the third grade, learners have had enough reading and writing experi-ence to begin to explore suffixes like **-able** and **-ous** (Henderson, 1990). Gen-erally speaking, those suffixes that have a significant effect on word mean-ing—the **-less** in **faithless**—present greater learning challenges than more frequent endings that are part of the grammatical structure of English (the plural **-s** attached to **cats** or the past tense **-ed** in **played**). For this reason, endings like the **-or** in **actor** and the **-logy** in **biology** are more easily learned when readers are in the fourth grade and up.

By and large, readers learn the meaning of prefixes after they have learned easy-to-recognize suffixes. Prior to second grade, learners are likely to recognize and use the prefix **un-,** but not necessarily other prefixes. In gen-eral, third grade is the time when learners add important prefixes to their repertoire of code knowledge, such as **super- (superman), dis- (disagree), re-(redo),** and **pre- (pretest).**

Though there are a good many prefixes, White, Sowell, and Yanagihara (1989) found that a mere smattering, four to be exact, account for 58 percent of the words with affixes (prefixes and/or suffixes) that learners in grades 3 through 9 are likely to read. **Un-, re-, in-** (meaning "not"), and **dis-** are the four that occur most frequently. **Un-** accounts for the lion's share: A full 26 percent of words with affixes were found to begin with **un-.** While **un-, re-, in-,** and **dis-** are certainly useful, older learners benefit from knowledge of more difficult prefixes because these prefixes offer considerable insight into word meaning (Harris & Sipay, 1990).

My advice is to begin by exploring prefixes and suffixes that occur fre-quently or that have only a moderate effect on the meaning of words in books and poems that learners read, such as **-(es), -ing, -ed, un-, re-, in-,** and **dis-.** Then, as learners' code knowledge expands, introduce prefixes and suffixes that occur less frequently or that have a significant affect on meaning. As learners gain knowledge of prefixes and suffixes, they also gain the ability to dramatically expand their reading vocabularies, which in turn makes it feasi-ble to read increasingly more complex and conceptually demanding text.

Greek and Latin Roots   Greek and Latin roots are meaningful chunks that have been borrowed from these two languages to create English words. When the scholars, philosophers, and authors of the Renaissance became interested in writing in their own language, English, they borrowed liberally from ancient Greek and Latin (Ayers, 1980). Just as the great thinkers and writers of the Renaissance used Greek and Latin words to coin lots of new words, so too do we continue this tradition today. When we ventured into space in the middle of this century, a new word was needed for space explorers. Rather than devising a whole new word from scratch, the term **astronaut** was coined by combining the Greek root **aster,** meaning "star," with **naut,** meaning "sailor." Considering the Greek origin, modern day **astronauts** are **star sailors**, a term that suggests all sorts of engaging images.

Words that share the same Greek or Latin roots, such as **infirm, firmament,** and **confirm**, form meaning families (Henderson, 1990; Templeton, 1991). By organizing words into meaningful families, strategy users not only have opportunities to figure out meaning, but a platform for using analogy to figure out the meaning of unfamiliar words with the same root. For example, **aqua** (a Latin root) means "water," and therefore words with this root also have something to do with water, as in **aquarium, aquatic, aqueduct,** and **aquaplane**. Likewise, **poly** (a Greek root) means "many"; thus, **polynomial, polygon, polysyllabic,** and **polygamy** all pertain to conditions in which there are many different facets, sides, conditions, or individuals.

Content subjects in the upper grades are peppered with words built from Greek and Latin roots—**carnivorous, democracy, multiple, polygon, document, epidermis, corpuscle,** and **dogmatic,** to mention but a few. Learners who use their knowledge of one word that contains a Greek or Latin root (**astronomer**) to infer the meaning of another word that has the same root (**astroport**) have a valuable route to word identification and vocabulary building. From a practical standpoint, you can expect learners who recognize and appreciate the chunks made up of Greek and Latin roots to learn a great many technical terms with relative ease and to do so with less guidance from you than their classmates who do not understand the contribution Greek and Latin roots make to English words.

Though Greek and Latin roots are powerful tools for word identification, learners are not likely to figure out the meaning of roots from normal reading experiences. In part, this is because roots are semihidden in words and in part because each word that includes a root has a slightly different meaning (**aquarium** and **aquaplane** both pertain to water but the meaning of individual words is quite different). Consequently, to develop the ability to strategically use Greek and Latin roots, learners need explicit explanations of them, modeling of how to use them to unlock word meaning, as well as many opportunities to read and write words with them.

In Appendix G, you will find lists of common Greek and Latin roots, their meanings, and examples of words that contain roots. As with all appendixes in this book, there are many items from which to choose, so select those roots you believe will be beneficial for the learners whom you teach. Use Greek and Latin roots in meaningful reading contexts, relate the roots to learners' everyday life experiences, discuss and explore roots, and support learners as they use roots to expand and refine their reading, writing, speaking, and listening vocabularies.

Compound Words Compound words are formed when two words—for example, **finger** and **print**—are glued together to create a third word—in this

FIGURE 6–3
Learners develop the ability to recognize the Greek and Latin roots in content area words when they read, write, find words in textbooks that have such roots, and watch their teachers model how to use the meaning of roots to gain insight into the definition of words.

case, **fingerprint.** Compounds differ depending on how far afield meaning wanders from the definitions of the individual words that are put together (Miller & McKenna, 1989). In the case of **fingerprint,** the general definition of each word is unchanged. A second sort of compound is made of words whose meanings are somewhat different than that of the combined form, such as **basketball, driveway, skyscraper,** and **spotlight.** In a third category of compounds, the meaning of the compound has practically nothing to do with the meaning of the individual words. Examples include **butterfly, fireworks, dragonfly, hardware, turtleneck,** and **peppermint.** Knowing the words that make up this sort of compound provides precious little insight into the meaning of the compounds themselves.

The strategy users whom I teach find compound words to be the easiest meaningful chunks to learn. Perhaps this is because compounds are made of two whole words and hence are not overly challenging to identify. And when the words that make up compounds are already in learners' reading vocabularies, pronunciation is merely a question of saying the words together. As for the meaning of compounds, I find that learners are intrigued by the changes in meaning that occur when words are glued together. First graders enjoy finding words that are glued together in compounds. Older learners, on the other hand, have had so many rich experiences with print that the compounds they see in everyday reading usually pose no challenge whatsoever.

Contractions   Contractions are formed when one or more letters (and sounds) are deleted from words. Missing letters are replaced in writing by an apostrophe, which is a visual clue telling learners that a word is abbreviated, as in **hasn't, he's, she'll,** and **let's.** Words mean exactly the same thing whether they are written as a contraction or individually. First graders meet contractions in everyday reading material, so it is important that these readers learn to recognize the contractions they see in storybooks.

I suggest that you explore contractions as a whole-group activity with the use of a set of magnetic letters that includes a magnetic apostrophe. Invite learners to use magnetic letters to change words like **she** and **will** into **she'll,** as well as to reverse the process by changing contractions (**she'll**) into two words (**she** and **will**). Another way to explore contractions is to write two sentences on the chalkboard. In the first sentence, underline two words that can be combined to form an contraction. In the second sentence, leave a blank where the contraction should be. For example, you might write the following:

1. The dog <u>did not</u> find the bone.
2. The dog _ find the bone.

Learners read the first sentence, form a contraction from the two underlined words (**did** and **not**), and write the contraction (**didn't**) in the blank in the second sentence. Everyone then reads both sentences together in chorus while you sweep your hand under the words as they are read. When you do this, be sure to use sentences from storybooks the students have read so as to make sure that written language is familiar and a part of learners' background knowledge.

Learning about Chunks

The chunks learners routinely recognize are significantly affected by learners' level of reading maturity (Gibson & Guinet, 1971; Invernizzi, 1992; Santa, 1977–1977). Generally speaking, the less frequently chunks are used and the more technical the information chunks convey (as with Greek and Latin roots), the later chunks are learned. For instance, rimes are learned before Greek and Latin roots. Readers begin to learn compound words and contractions as early as first grade. Easy-to-recognize suffixes are learned before prefixes. What's more, some prefixes and suffixes are learned early, others later.

The chunks that are worthwhile exploring are those that are important parts of the words learners read and write. The more strategy users know about meaningful chunks, the more opportunities they have to use chunks to streamline word identification. However, it takes direct instruction for learners to develop code knowledge of some of the meaningful chunks in words. It is important, therefore, that you give strategy users many opportunities to learn about meaningful chunks through explicit instruction and to strategically use chunks while reading and writing.

ACTIVITIES TO INCREASE THE STRATEGIC USE OF MEANINGFUL CHUNKS IN WORDS

Asking learners to memorize the lists of chunks like those in Appendixes E, F, and G is pointless. Learners are unlikely to use the chunks on lists they have memorized to identify unfamiliar words in textbooks, novels, newspapers, and magazines. This is just as true for prefixes and suffixes (Lapp & Flood, 1992), as it is for Greek and Latin roots, compounds, and contractions. All this means that you make a significant contribution to learning when you support learners as they identify and use meaningful chunks in the words they read and write (Wysocki & Jenkins, 1989). Use the five activities that follow to give learners opportunities to recognize chunks, remember chunks, and strategically use chunks as part of ongoing classroom learning. Use those activities you believe will be most beneficial and adapt activities to suit your own special classroom environment.

✳ Coin-a-Word

New words are added to our language all the time and here is a chance for the learners in your classroom to have a hand in the process. The goal of the activity is to increase learners' insight into, and their creative use of, meaningful Greek and Latin roots, prefixes, and suffixes. To accomplish this, learners coin their own words, which means that they must have some familiarity with meaningful chunks before they embark on this activity. Coin-a-Word is especially suited to social studies and science, and best used with learners who are in the fifth grade and up. (**Astroport**, the word at the beginning of this chapter, is an invention of a fifth grader.)

Things You'll Need: Wall charts of the prefixes, suffixes, and Greek roots and Latin roots that strategy users encounter in their content area textbooks and in books written by their favorite authors; a wall chart of common nouns; a good imagination!

Exploration: On the chalkboard, write words that include meaningful chunks. Invite learners to find words with the meaningful prefixes, suffixes, and Greek and Latin roots in their science, mathematics, and social studies texts, and to find words on the wall charts in your classroom. For example, the words **antibody** and **antiseptic** may be selected from the science book; the words **antismoking** and **antiaircraft** from a wall chart. Talk about the meaning of prefixes, suffixes, and Greek and Latin roots in the words on the chalkboard. Then make a list on the chalkboard of the prefixes, suffixes, and Greek roots and Latin roots that are included in the words that learners have just discussed.

Show learners how to combine these meaningful chunks to create new words. Invite learners to coin words as a group; talk about meaningful chunks; discuss word meaning; use coined words in sentences. (Look in Appendix A for an activity called Creative Compounds, which is similar to this one and suitable for first through third graders.)

Guided Practice: Challenge learners to work individually or in groups to combine chunks to form totally new words, to write a definition of each new word, and to illustrate each coined word. Put the coined words and illustrations on bulletin boards, along the chalk tray, or anywhere else where they can be plainly seen so that learners can use them in the transfer activity that follows.

Transfer: Invite cooperative groups of three or four learners to make crossword puzzles with the words they find in content area textbooks and with the words they have coined. Each crossword puzzle should include (1) a brief definition of each word and (2) either the page where the word is written in a content area textbook **or** a note that the word is an invention on display in the classroom. Last, invite groups to trade puzzles and to solve the puzzles their classmates have created.

✳ Explosion

Best suited for sixth graders and above, the activity Explosion uses chunks from words in the content area subjects that are part of the middle school curriculum. This activity ties in nicely with materials learners are studying in English, social studies, and health, and can be used over and over with different words throughout the school year.

Things You'll Need: Tagboard sentence strips cut into halves; markers; masking tape; dictionaries; scissors; colored construction paper; glue; tape.

Exploration: Select a content area word that learners have read in a textbook and that has an easy-to-spot root, plus a prefix or a suffix (or both). Write the word on the chalkboard, discuss word meaning, and point out meaningful chunks. Read the sentence(s) in the textbook that include the word. Talk about the word's meaning in the sentence(s). Underline each chunk in the word. Then explain that the word is made up of several different chunks (prefixes, suffixes, or Greek and Latin roots) and that the chunks contribute to the word's definition. Invite learners to use their background knowledge, the dictionary, or explanations in the textbook to help them understand the meaning of each chunk. Explore the idea that each of the chunks may be a part of many different words.

Now divide the word into meaningful chunks and write the chunks about twelve to fifteen inches apart. Ask learners to think of words that include one of the chunks. Write the words under the chunks, thereby forming lists of words that include the same chunks.

Guided Practice: Divide a different word from a content area subject into meaningful chunks, and write each chunk on a separate piece of tagboard. Tape tagboard strips fairly far apart on the chalkboard. Follow the procedure previously described, but do not ask learners to think of examples of words that include the chunks and do not make lists of words. These are activities that the learners will carry out in groups. Pass out dictionaries, content area textbooks, blank tagboard strips, markers, and tape to groups of learners. Assign, or invite groups to choose, one meaningful chunk from the tagboard pieces taped to the chalkboard. Invite each group to find words in dictionaries and context area textbooks that include the meaningful chunk that the group is responsible for. Groups are to write each word with a chunk on a blank tagboard strip (as shown in the photograph of sixth graders in Figure 6–4) and then tape the tagboard strip under the designated chunk on the chalkboard. Conclude by inviting volunteers from each group to discuss word meaning, talk about meaningful chunks, and explain how the chunks contribute to the definition of the words on the tagboard strips.

Transfer: Have learners use their knowledge of chunks to write character descriptions. Discuss characters in the books learners are currently reading.

FIGURE 6–4
Learners gain insight into word meaning when they work cooperatively to explore meaningful prefixes, suffixes, and Greek and Latin roots in words from content area subjects.

Ask learners to draw a picture of a well-known character on one piece of paper. On a second piece of paper, ask each learner to write (1) words that describe the character and (2) sentences that describe the character. Tape the pictures to the chalkboard. Read the learners' character descriptions one by one, but do not tell which character is being described. Challenge learners to identify the character and then tape the description next to the illustration. Once all characters are identified, remove the character descriptions from the bulletin board. Pass these out, and ask learners to underline words that include prefixes, suffixes, Greek roots, Latin roots, compound words, and contractions. Last, ask a few learners to make lists of descriptive words that include meaningful chunks. Leave the lists in your classroom for future reference.

✳ Word Webs

Word Webs have been used successfully for some time (Gunning, 1992; Templeton, 1991; Tompkins & Yaden, 1986) and are an engaging way to support learners as they think strategically about meaningful chunks. In my experience, the most intriguing webs are those that begin with a single prefix or root and then spin off into many different mini-webs, as shown in Figure 6–5. This is a challenging activity best suited for learners who are sixth graders or older, and most successful when learners work cooperatively in groups.

Things You'll Need: Dictionaries; paper and pencils; one large piece of chart paper for each cooperative group; colored construction paper, colorful markers, scissors, glue, and a large piece of tagboard for each cooperative group to make games.

Exploration: Select a meaningful chunk from a word in a novel, play, or textbook that learners are currently reading. On the chalkboard, write a sentence from a familiar book that includes a word with the meaningful chunk. Underline the word. Talk about the word's meaning in the sentences, and about the way that the meaningful chunk contributes to the word's definition. Then write the chunk in the center of the chalkboard and draw a bubble around it. Write the word from the sentence to the upper right of the chunk; make sure that the chunk and the word are at least twelve inches apart. Draw a line from the chunk to the word. Put a bubble around the word.

Challenge learners to think of words that include the meaningful chunk. Then, for each word learners think of, draw a line (called a web strand) that extends from the center chunk. At the end of the web strand, write a word that includes the meaningful chunk and put a bubble around that word, too. Next, create mini-webs around each word by adding prefixes or suffixes, as shown in Figure 6–5. When finished, talk about the words and support learners as they draw the conclusion that words that share meaningful chunks belong in a word family and hence there is a common meaningful thread that ties the words together.

Guided Practice: Ask learners to work together collaboratively and cooperatively to create their own word webs, using words found in materials they study throughout the day, as well as ones they find in dictionaries, wall charts, signs, and posters. After webs are perfected to the satisfaction of group members, invite the groups to share their webs with the entire class, explaining the connections among words, telling why and how each word is a member of the meaning family.

Transfer: Have the learners make and share games with younger learners. Discuss various learning games children have played in school and at home. Talk about how games are constructed and played, the importance of clear directions, good examples, and meaningful activities. Explain the types of meaningful chunks learners in lower grades find in reading materials and write these chunks on the chalkboard (or put chunks on a handout). Challenge groups to work collaboratively and cooperatively to make an easy-to-play game that includes frequently used meaningful chunks and that can be shared with learners in a lower grade. Try games out in your classroom and then arrange to go to a classroom of younger learners to share the games. It takes more than one day to plan, create, and share games, so budget adequate time in your daily schedule. You and the learners in your classroom will not be disappointed.

FIGURE 6–5
Creating word webs helps learners draw the conclusion that there is a common thread of meaning among words that share the same meaningful chunk.

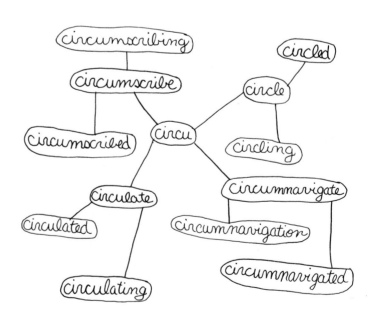

✳ Moving Words (Prefixes)

The goal of this activity is to increase learners' insight into the use of prefixes and to give them opportunities to think analytically about meaningful chunks. With its emphasis on easy prefixes and a lot of body movement, this activity is appropriate for second and third graders.

Things You'll Need: Large cards with prefixes written on them; word cards; masking tape; colored construction paper; markers; scissors.

Exploration: Select several words with prefixes from the books that learners read, and write sentences with them on the chalkboard. Underline the words that have prefixes attached to them, and talk about the affect that prefixes have on word meaning in the sentence. Then make two lists on the chalkboard: one of the prefixes and one of the words. Discuss the meaning of words and the meaning of prefixes. Ask learners which prefixes can be combined with which words. Make a wall chart for each prefix by writing the prefix at the top and words with the prefix underneath. Support learners as they draw the conclusion that some of the words, the word **paid** for example, may be combined with more than one prefix, **unpaid** and **repaid** for instance. Leave the lists in your classroom to serve as references for the guided practice and transfer activities that follow.

Guided Practice: Tape large cards with prefixes high enough on the wall so that prefixes can be seen from a good distance. Next, give each learner a word card. Ask learners to read the word and to look around for a prefix on the wall to which their word might be meaningfully attached. When found, learners stand underneath the prefix. Once everyone has found a prefix, ask each learner to read the word by itself and then to read the word a second time with the prefix attached.

Next, take the prefixes off the wall. Tape each prefix to the chalkboard and underneath each prefix tape the words to which the prefix might be attached. When finished, the chalkboard looks like a giant chart with columns of prefixes and words. Invite volunteers to read each prefix and then read each word, attaching the prefix to it. Now challenge learners to think carefully about the prefixes and words. Are there any mistakes? Does every combination make sense? If learners are unsure, ask them to check the dictionary. How about other combinations? Can some prefixes be attached to several different words? If so, which ones? Leave the chalkboard display up so that it can serve as a reference for the transfer activity that comes next.

Transfer: Have learners make a bar graph of prefixes in familiar books. Invite learners to find words with prefixes in the books they read every day. Have them look in content area textbooks, plays, short chapter books, the newspaper, magazines, and on signs and posters in the hallways of your school. Make a whole wall of words with the prefixes they find. Now count the number of times the same prefix occurs. Make a bar graph showing the

FIGURE 6–6
When learners combine words and prefixes they have opportunities to conceptualize prefixes as meaningful chunks attached to words.

frequency of occurrence and talk about how prefixes help authors share ideas with readers.

✳ Suffix Construction Project

This activity is a good way for learners in the fifth grade and up to review suffixes, not to mention a terrific vehicle to promote discussion, collaboration, and dictionary use.

Things You'll Need: Each cooperative group needs the following: a large piece of tagboard; a ruler; a dictionary; a pencil; a set of directions; a large piece of plain paper; colorful markers.

Exploration: After learners have had a great deal of experience reading and writing words with suffixes, write several suffixes on the chalkboard. Focus on only one suffix at a time, and ask learners to think of words to which the suffix may be attached. Make a list of words for each suffix. Talk about the meaning of the suffixes, and discuss their effect on the definition of words.

Then explain that groups are to make a chart that shows how prefixes and words are combined. Demonstrate by drawing a large rectangle on the chalkboard and then dividing it into four columns and four rows. Write a word beside each row and a different suffix at the top of each column. For each permissible combination of a word and a suffix, write the new word in the appropriate space in a row. Ask learners to double-check words in their dictionaries.

Guided Practice: Pass out a set of directions, a large piece of tagboard, a ruler, a colored marker, and dictionaries to each group of learners. Directions consist of two pages: One page is a list of twenty words and ten suffixes. The other page explains how to complete the construction project containing these steps:

1. Use a ruler to make a chart that has twenty-one rows and eleven columns.
2. Write ten suffixes at the top of the columns. Leave the first column blank.
3. Write twenty words in alphabetical order at the far left of rows. Begin in the second row.
4. Use the dictionary to check that each word and suffix combination makes a "real" word before writing it on the chart.
5. Color each empty space. These are ones for which you cannot combine the prefix and word to make a "real" word.
6. Sign the names of group members on the back of the chart when it is finished. Share charts with the class and discuss words.

Transfer: Challenge learners to create their own cartoons with the use of dramatic illustrations and dialogue balloons. Cartoon writing is a natural way to use suffixes and can be an individual or a small-group activity, whichever suits the organization in your classroom. Tell each writer (or group of collaborative writers) to divide a large piece of tagboard into boxes and then to use one box for each scene. Challenge writers to create fictional characters, to write dialogue using a smattering of suffixes, and to illustrate their work, as in

FIGURE 6–7
Learners treat suffixes as meaningful chunks when they attach them to words and then verify that the word and suffix combinations are meaningful.

the cartoon in Figure 6–8. Cartoons become a part of social studies learning when writers create fictional characters and events from social studies topics; the same is true of science, only in this case writers describe scientific events, real or imagined. Give learners opportunities to share cartoons with their classmates. Discuss the characters, events, and the dialogue. Challenge learners to identify words with suffixes. Explore why learners used the suffixes the way they did, and talk about how words with suffixes contribute to meaning.

FIGURE 6–8
Writing cartoons is a natural opportunity to use suffixes, and to explore the contribution that suffixes make to word and passage meaning.

FINAL OBSERVATIONS

In the normal course of learning to read, learners develop the ability to use a variety of word recognition strategies through in-depth literacy activities that are part of today's classrooms. The activities in this chapter are examples of ones to help learners use chunks to expand and refine their word identification abilities. Though most learners develop word recognition strategies as they advance in school, some learners have difficulty strategically using our alphabetic writing system. These learners are frustrated by the words they see on the pages of storybooks and novels and are unable to read magazine and newspaper articles at home. Learners are vexed by the ideas and concepts in content area textbooks because the technical vocabulary is out of reach. Learners who have had a great many reading and writing opportunities and who still cannot strategically use our alphabetic writing system need extra help to do so. This is the topic of the chapter that follows.

REFERENCES

Ayers, D. M. (1980). *English words from Greek and Latin elements.* Tucson, AZ: The University of Arizona Press.

Durkin, D. (1993). *Teaching them to read* (6th ed.). Boston: Allyn & Bacon.

Ehri, L. C. (1991). Development of the ability to read words. In R. Barr, M. L. Kamil, P. Mosenthal, & P. D. Pearson (Eds.), *Handbook of reading research* (Vol. II, pp. 383–417). New York: Longman.

Gibson, E. J., & Guinet, L. (1971). Perception of inflections in brief visual presentations of words. *Journal of Verbal Learning and Verbal Behavior, 10,* 182–189.

Gunning, T. G. (1992). *Creating reading instruction for all children.* Boston: Allyn & Bacon.

Hackett, J. K., Moyer, R. H., & Adams, D. K. (1989). *Merrill Science.* Englewood Cliffs, NJ: Merrill/Prentice Hall.

Harris, A. J., & Sipay, E. R. (1990). *How to increase reading ability* (9th ed.). New York: Longman.

Henderson, E. H. (1990). *Teaching spelling* (2nd ed.). Boston: Houghton Mifflin Company.

Invernizzi, M. A. (1992). The vowel and what follows: A phonological frame of orthographic analysis. In S. Templeton & D. R. Bear (Eds.), *Development of orthographic knowledge and the foundations of literacy* (pp. 105–136). Hillsdale, NJ: Lawrence Erlbaum Associates.

Ives, J. P., Bursuk, L. Z., & Ives, S. A. (1979). *Word identification techniques.* Chicago: Rand McNally.

Lapp, D., & Flood, J. (1992). *Teaching reading to every child* (3rd ed.). New York: Macmillan.

Miller, G. A. (1956). The magical number seven, plus or minus two: Some limits on our capacity for processing information. *Psychological Review, 63,* 81–97.

Miller, J. W., & McKenna, M. (1989). *Teaching reading in the elementary grades.* Scottsdale, AZ: Gorsuch Scarisbrick, Publishers.

Nagy, W. E., Anderson, R. C., Schommer, M., Scott, J. A., & Stallman, A. C. (1989). Morphological families and word recognition. *Reading Research Quarterly, 24,* 262–282.

Nagy, W. E., Diakidoy, I. N., & Anderson, R. C. (1993). The acquisition of morphology: Learning the contribution of suffixes to the meaning of derivatives. *Journal of Reading Behavior, 25,* 155–170.

Santa, C. M. (1976–1977). Spelling patterns and the development of flexible word recognition strategies. *Reading Research Quarterly, 12,* 125–144.

Stuart, M., & Coltheart, M. (1988). Does reading develop in a sequence of stages? *Cognition, 30,* 139–181.

Templeton, S. (1991). *Teaching the integrated language arts.* Boston: Houghton Mifflin Company.

Tompkins, G. E., & Yaden, D. B. (1986). *Answering questions about words.* Urbana, IL: National Council of Teachers of English.

White, T. G., Power, M. A., & White, S. (1989). Morphological analysis: Implications for teaching and understanding vocabulary growth. *Reading Research Quarterly, 24,* 283–304.

White, T. G., Sowell, J., & Yanagihara, A. (1989). Teaching elementary students to use word-part clues. *The Reading Teacher, 42,* 302-308.

Wysocki, K., & Jenkins, J. R. (1987). Deriving word meanings through morphological generalization. *Reading Research Quarterly, 22,* 66–81.

C H A P T E R

LEARNERS WHO NEED EXTRA HELP

This chapter explains why some learners need extra help and what you can do to help them. In this chapter, you will learn how to give extra help to learners who overrely on picture cues and incidental cues, do not effectively use the analogy and letter-sound strategies, or who speak languages other than English at home.

KEY IDEAS

- ＊ Some learners need extra help because they do not effectively use word identification strategies to identify the unfamiliar words they meet in text.
- ＊ Some learners whose families speak languages other than English need extra help because the language spoken at home is different from the language in which English-speaking authors write.
- ＊ When you give learners extra help, it is important to strike a balance between (1) the knowledge and abilities learners bring to reading and writing and (2) the challenges of reading interesting and age-appropriate literature and of writing for a variety of purposes.

Perhaps you are wondering why a chapter on learners who need extra help begins with a drawing of a seesaw (see Figure 7–1). As it turns out, a simple playground seesaw demonstrates a fundamental principle of physics that has a great deal of relevance to teaching and learning. Seesaws are simple levers. The purpose of levers is to make it easier to lift heavy loads, in this case the weight of playmates at either end of the seesaw. The seesaw board is the lever and the support on which the board is balanced is called the fulcrum.

The weight of the playmates in Rich's drawing (Figure 7–1) is about equal, so the effort needed to push each player into the air is exactly the same. Should a heavier playmate get on one end, the lighter playmate must push harder. And, if the heavier playmate weighs quite a bit more than the lighter playmate, the lighter playmate will not have the strength (or force) to lift the heavier one. The way to make the seesaw work is to balance the load at either end, to make the effort needed to lift each playmate equal to the weight of each child. Moving the fulcrum changes the balance point. With a new balance point, it takes less effort (force) to lift the heavier player (load).

Just as seesaw playmates differ in weight, so too do learners differ in the strategies they bring to reading. While some learners will develop a full comple-

FIGURE 7–1
A simple seesaw demonstrates a fundamental principle of physics that is relevant to supporting literacy in today's classrooms.

ment of word identification strategies through the normal reading and writing experiences in your classroom, other learners will need extra help. Learning experiences, just like seesaws, can be adjusted so that all learners are successful and so that all learners become expert users of word identification strategies.

Whereas the success of a seesaw hinges on finding the right balance point between the force and the load, the success of learning to strategically use our alphabetic writing system hinges on finding the right balance point between the force (learners' abilities) and the load (reading and writing activities). Sometimes classroom activities (the load) are too great for the knowledge and strategies learners bring to activities (the force). Under this condition, learners are in a similar position to that of a lightweight seesaw playmate who lacks the strength to lift a heavier playmate. When this happens, learners need extra help.

Learners who need extra help are successful when reading and writing activities (the load) are roughly balanced with learners' abilities to use strategies (the force). In practical terms, this means finding activities with which learners are successful and then using those activities to increase the learners' phonological awareness and code knowledge so that they can refine their existing strategies and develop new word identification strategies.

LEARNERS WHO OVERRELY ON PICTURE CUES AND INCIDENTAL CUES

Learners who overrely on picture cues and incidental cues take advantage of some, but not nearly enough, of the information available in written language. These learners do not strategically use onsets, rimes, letter neighborhoods, or chunks to identify the unfamiliar words authors write. Instead, learners overlook the actual words written on pages, focusing instead on pictures and, when pictures fall short, on colored ink, word shape, letter shape, and visual reminders like smudges and dog-eared pages.

Shandra

First-grader Shandra, whose story is shown in Figure 7–2, overrelies on pictures and incidental cues. From Shandra's writing, you might infer that she understands these principles: (1) that written language is made up of letters that are strung together from left to right and (2) that writing goes from top to bottom on the page. Shandra also seems to be developing awareness of punctuation and is working out exactly which written symbols—letters, numbers and shapes—make up words.

Even with these understandings, toward year's end, Shandra has fallen far behind her classmates. If you were to listen to Shandra read easy books with which she is familiar, you would hear something that sounds like fluent reading. Shandra's fluency is misleading, however. Shandra has memorized the text in familiar books. After reading the same short books time and time again, she knows the pictures and written sentences by heart. As a consequence, the fluent reading you hear is in actuality the result of Shandra reciting sentences much like preschoolers (Chapter 3) imitate the reading of adults by retelling stories from memory.

Though Shandra thinks about print, she does not pay attention to the rimes and letter neighborhoods in words. For this reason, Shandra recognizes a mere handful of words. What's more, the words she reads with ease in familiar stories are seldom recognized when she meets them in other reading materials. When the words that Shandra recognizes in often-read books are written in sentences on the chalkboard, in stories on wall charts, or in unfamiliar library books, Shandra behaves as though she had never seen these words before. For example, having read the word **down** without a moment's hesitation in a short, familiar storybook, Shandra read **down** as **"come"** in a storybook she had never seen before and pointed to **happy** when asked to find **down** in a sentence on a wall chart. Shandra needs to learn a good deal about written language, which brings us to the question of how to find the right balance point between the load and the force.

What Shandra Needs to Know and Be Able to Do   For starters, Shandra needs to become more print focused. She needs to know how the onsets, rimes, letter neighborhoods, and chunks in our alphabetic writing system represent pronunciation. She also needs to increase phonological awareness: Shandra

FIGURE 7–2
Learners who are glued to picture and incidental clues by the end of first grade may be trying to figure out exactly which written symbols—letters, numbers, or shapes—make up words.

needs to be able to identify the rhyme and individual sounds in words, and she needs to be able to blend individual sounds together. She also needs to learn to cross-check so as to keep word identification meaning centered.

Though the ultimate goal is for Shandra to develop the analogy, letter-sound, and chunk strategies, the most immediate aim is help her strategically use onsets and context cues together. Onsets are an excellent way to help learners like Shandra increase attention to print. This is so because onsets are quite predictable and, when used in conjunction with context cues, provide insight into a word's identity (as explained in Chapter 4). The rimes in words are the next thing to explore. As large bundles of sound, rimes require less phonological awareness than do letter neighborhoods (as mentioned in Chapter 2). Though Shandra needs to develop the letter-sound strategy, this strategy puts more demands on phonological awareness than does the analogy strategy. Hence, it is best to begin with analogous onsets and rimes, and then to move to letter neighborhoods. And, certainly Shandra needs to learn to cross-check, that is, to think about meaning and to use strategies to identify words that make sense in the messages authors write.

Learning Activities and Suggestions: Phonological Awareness Learners like Shandra who overrely on picture cues and incidental cues usually have low phonological awareness. These learners benefit from phonological awareness activities that target rhyme. Since spoken rhymes are easier to detect than individual sounds, the load is lighter when activities help learners develop sensitivity to rhyming sounds in words, heavier when activities focus on individual sounds. Activities such as Hands Up for Rhyme, Inventing Rhyme, and Picture-Rhyme Matching (Chapter 2) are beneficial. Rhyming Picture Book and Rhyming Lists in Appendix A are helpful because these two activities give learners opportunities to listen to spoken rhyme and to read written rime. I also suggest that you share books that have lots of rhyming words, such as those written by Dr. Seuss, make rhyming chants and poetry part of ongoing experiences, and provide lots of opportunities for learners to read and write every day.

Learning Activities and Suggestions: Code Cues Shandra and learners like her benefit from learning how to use onsets and the reading context to identify unfamiliar words. Because of the mutually supportive relationship between phonological awareness and code knowledge, you can expect the use of onsets and context cues to help learners like Shandra develop the ability to identify the beginning sounds (onsets) in words. To help learners use onsets and the reading context to figure out the identity of unfamiliar words, do the following: (1) show learners how to read to the end of the sentence and then (2) show them how to think of a word that makes sense and begins with the sound the first letter represents. Point out words in your classroom that begin with the same sounds and letters; make lists of words that begin with the sound; challenge learners to find examples of words in the storybooks they read. In this way, learners stay meaning focused and at the same time have opportunities to become aware of the beginning sounds in words.

Encourage learners like Shandra to pay more attention to print by asking learners to point to each word as it is read. Pointing to words as they are read reinforces the idea that specific written words represent specific spoken words. As a consequence of pointing to words, learners are encouraged to match the words they read with the words authors write. If you are not already sweeping your hand under words as you read them aloud, now is the time to begin to do so. Talk about print; point out individual words in big books, poems, and familiar storybooks. Make wall charts of often-used words, help learners like Shandra to write their names and the names of everyone in their family, and to collect words and put them on bulletin boards.

Invite learners to arrange words cards into sentences taken from familiar books. I use three different versions of this activity, depending on the abilities of the learners whom I teach:

1. The easiest version is to write a short, familiar sentence on a tagboard strip and to ask learners to arrange word cards so as to reconstruct the sentence. To do this, learners need only match the words on cards with the words on the tagboard sentence.
2. A more challenging version is to give learners word cards and then to say a sentence from a familiar storybook, and have learners arrange cards to form the sentence. Under this condition, learners must be able to read the words on cards, remember the sentence they hear you read, and then arrange words in the proper sequence.
3. The most challenging version is to ask learners to use word cards to make sentences that learners think of themselves. It is also challenging to change statements (The baby likes stuffed animals) into questions (Does the baby like stuffed animals?).

Additionally, invite learners to make their own personal dictionaries that include words they have seen in books and in the environment. Listed alphabetically, the words in personal dictionaries are perfect for calling attention to onsets and for increasing reading vocabulary. Dictionaries are references that are to be used regularly, so think of them as an ongoing part of learners' everyday reading and writing experiences, and include words from all the subject areas explored in your classroom.

Lessons that follow the plan given in the section "Teaching Code Cues in Context" in Chapter 3 are helpful because such lessons use familiar text to strengthen code knowledge and reinforce phonological awareness. Support cross-checking by asking learners if the words they read make sense and why (or why not) this is so. Additionally, choose easy books for daily reading and make sure that books repeat some of the same words several times. This gives learners plenty of opportunities to see words enough times to begin to learn them and to make inferences about code cues. Predictable books offer immediate success and for this reason probably will be one of the reading experiences learners enjoy.

LEARNERS WHO DO NOT EFFECTIVELY USE THE ANALOGY AND LETTER-SOUND STRATEGIES

Learners who do not effectively use the analogy and letter-sound strategies misidentify rimes, get bogged down in the middle of words, blend sounds into the wrong words, and associate the wrong sounds with the letters in neighborhoods. These difficulties impair word identification and, of course, interfere with comprehension. Because learners recognize only a few of the words authors write and because learners cannot effectively use the analogy and letter-sound strategies to identify unfamiliar words, learners pay little attention to written language and instead reconstruct the meaning of stories from their own background knowledge and picture cues.

Relying on background knowledge and picture cues works fine when stories are familiar. In fact, material that closely parallels learners' life experiences is understood remarkably well, given the fact that learners do not identify many of the words authors write. These are the learners about whom you hear teachers say, "He does not know many words in the story, but his comprehension is good." Or you hear, "Even though her reading vocabulary is weak, her comprehension is okay."

Bypassing a large number of words in favor of background knowledge and picture cues does not work at all well when reading materials do not closely parallel learners' own lives and fails altogether when learners read books and articles that introduce new ideas, concepts, and information. Comprehension suffers because learners do not have enough life experiences to fill in the gaps created by the many unfamiliar words and do not recognize enough words to reconstruct sensible messages based on what authors write. The difficulty is especially apparent when content subject textbooks introduce many new terms and concepts, when the topics of stories are outside learners' own personal experiences, and when books do not have a large number of highly descriptive illustrations.

To take a closer look at learners, consider the following descriptions of two learners who do not effectively use the analogy and letter-sound strategies. The first learner, Raymond, brings less code knowledge and phonological awareness to reading and writing than does the second learner, Mike. Raymond will benefit from extra help to develop the analogy strategy, Mike from extra help to develop the letter-sound strategy.

Raymond

By the end of the second grade, Raymond's reading progress has come to a near standstill. You can infer from his story (Figure 7–3) that Raymond uses some knowledge of onsets and ending letters when he writes and that he is working out how vowel letter neighborhoods represent sounds in words. He copies words from the print in his classroom, such as **was, Lisa,** and **bad,** and he conventionally spells a few high frequency words, such as **and** and **go.**

And, though letters and sounds are not always completely on target, many of the letters Raymond chooses are similar to the sounds represented in words.

Raymond's invented spelling includes words that generally begin with the right onsets, like the **b** for **but** (spelled **bot**), the **g** for **got** (spelled **gt**), and the **sh** for **she** (spelled **shi**). He thinks carefully about some of the sounds in words and then writes down letters he believes represent those sounds, as in **one**, spelled **won**. The way he pronounces the "ot" in "bot" is not far from the sounds heard in "**but.**" This is also true for the word **very**, spelled **vara**. Though Raymond strategically uses some code knowledge when he spells, he is a long way from spelling conventionally and a long way from reading the kinds of books his second-grade classmates enjoy. To develop the foundation upon which strategic code use rests, the load and the force must be brought into balance so as to nurture Raymond's growth and strategy development.

What Raymond Needs to Know and Be Able to Do   The most immediate aspects of phonological awareness that learners like Raymond need to develop are the abilities to do the following: (1) detect rhyming sounds and (2) blend beginning sounds and rhymes together to form words. Developing awareness of the individual sounds in words is also important, though this will occur after learners have begun to gain awareness of rhyming sounds.

If learners have difficulty with both the analogy and letter-sound strategies, as is the situation with Raymond, then analogous rimes are the place to begin teaching. Hence, the most immediate things that learners like Raymond need to know about the code are (1) how rimes represent sounds and (2) how to strategically use analogous rimes to identify unfamiliar words. As

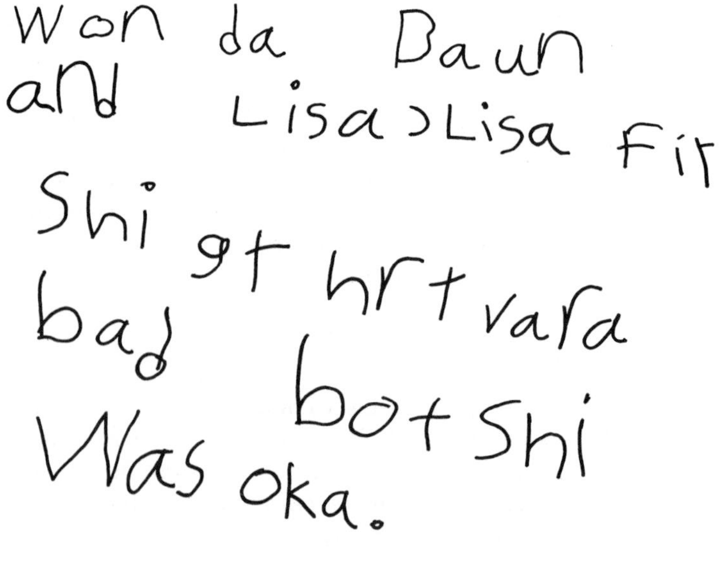

FIGURE 7–3
The writing of learners with underdeveloped phonological awareness and code knowledge may include words that are copied, high frequency words spelled conventionally, words spelled phonetically, and words in which the sounds do not match the letters.

learners begin to gain insight into the way that rimes signal pronunciation, then letter neighborhoods can be profitably explored. And, as learners understand how the letters in neighborhoods represent sounds, they have opportunities to strategically use this code knowledge.

Learning Activities and Suggestions: Phonological Awareness   It is highly probable that learners like Raymond will have difficulty detecting rhymes and individual sounds in spoken words. Should this be the case, my advice is to concentrate first on developing sensitivity to rhyming sounds and then to introduce activities that support awareness of individuals sounds. The reason to follow this sequence is that: (1) this is the normal development sequence in which phonological awareness progresses and (2) identifying rhyming sounds in words is much easier than identifying individual sounds in words.

Look in Chapter 2 for activities to develop the ability to detect rhyme. And when you share these activities with learners, be sure to include Arm Blending (which is also described in Chapter 2). Learners like Raymond find blending quite difficult, and Arm Blending is a highly successful technique. The description in Chapter 2 says to divide words into individual sounds, which places high demands on learners like Raymond who are uncertain of the rhymes in words. I suggest that you lighten the load by dividing words into beginning sounds (onsets) and rimes. Hence, the word **"bat"** would be separated into **"b"** and **"at,"** which is well within Raymond's capability. Modify the directions in Chapter 2 by placing your hand on your shoulder when you say **"b"** and then in the crook of your elbow when you say **"at."** Arm Blending is easy, gives learners a visual and kinesthetic platform from which to blend, and transfers to many different reading situations. This, in turn, increases the force learners like Raymond bring to reading, which means that learners are then capable of reading materials in which authors use more challenging words. Combine phonological awareness activities with reading and give learners plenty of opportunities to write.

Learning Activities and Suggestions: Code Cues   If learners like Raymond are to develop greater force, they must bring greater code knowledge to reading and they must use word identification strategies in support of comprehension. Since Raymond is not able to sound out words with the letter-sound strategy, the way to lighten the load is to concentrate first on developing the analogy strategy.

From his writing, you can infer that Raymond understands onsets, so rimes are a good focus for learning. Activities that highlight written rime are important because this knowledge paves the way for development of the analogy strategy. To help Raymond and learners like him expand their knowledge of rimes, invite learners to work collaboratively to make wall charts of words that share the same rimes. This activity is appropriate for many learners, so include learners who are glued to picture and incidental cues, as well as learners who strategically use large chunks. When the charts are complete, tape them to the chalkboard and challenge learners to explain reasons why words are included in lists and to think of other words that might be added. In so doing, learners have opportunities to think critically about spelling and everyone has a chance to participate.

The activities in Chapter 4 are helpful, especially Building Words with Onset-Rime Tiles. Include some activities from Appendix A that reinforce code knowledge, especially from the section Activities to Increase Onset-Rime Knowledge, such as Easy-to-Do Ideas, Giant Word Chains, Onset Houses, Rime Tic-Tac-Toe, Onset-Rime Tachistoscope, Muffin Tin Words, Egg Words, and Fish for Onsets. And be sure to give learners ample opportunities to find rimes in the words they read in storybooks and poems.

When learners have code knowledge of the frequently occurring rimes, challenge them to look inside rimes to discover the letters in neighborhoods. Focus first on the **VC/VCC** neighborhood. Many rimes represent this neighborhood, and therefore the **VC/VCC** neighborhood presents opportunities to build on the knowledge learners already have. Then support learners as they compare and contrast this neighborhood with the **VCe** neighborhood. An effective way to do this is to challenge the whole class to think of words that include a **VC/VCC** or a **VCe** neighborhood in their spelling. Compare and contrast the spelling of the words. Discuss the sounds that vowel letters represent in these two neighborhoods. Talk about how and why learners might use this information when they read. Then invite learners to work with a partner or in small groups to make charts of words that are spelled with a **VC/VCC** neighborhood and a **VCe** neighborhood, as shown in Figure 7–4. Ask learners who have less code knowledge to work with those who have more code knowledge. And encourage learners to find words that include the **VC/VCC** and **VCe** letter neighborhoods in their spelling on the bulletin boards, wall charts, and chalkboards in your classroom. Support learners as they work with one another to make charts; share finished charts with the

FIGURE 7–4
Making wall charts of words that are spelled with different neighborhoods gives learners opportunities to compare and contrast neighborhoods and to analyze the relationships among the letters in neighborhoods and the sounds in words.

whole class; display charts in your classroom; use them as references. Consult the neighborhoods in Chapter 5 that are less, more, and most challenging, and look in Appendix D for an explanation of letter neighborhoods.

The effect of beginning with large segments of spoken and written language (rimes) and then moving to smaller segments (the letters that reside in letter neighborhoods) is that activities progress from less demanding to more demanding. Hence, the load is first brought into line with learners' abilities and then gradually increases as learners become capable of handling more challenging word identification activities during reading.

Mike

Mike, whose story is shown in Figure 7–5, has developed some code knowledge of onsets, rimes, and letter neighborhoods. Even so, Mike has not developed enough code knowledge to support reading the normal fourth-grade reading materials in his classroom. Hence, the force that Mike brings to reading and writing is far less than the load imposed by everyday fourth-grade reading and writing activities.

When Mike writes, he conventionally spells highly frequent words, such as **it, all, you, bad, day,** and **have.** He also uses invented spelling, as we see in the word **weight,** written as **wate.** In so doing, Mike uses a **VCe** neighborhood (**ate**), which suggests that he has some code knowledge of this more challenging vowel letter neighborhood (Chapter 5). Mike still has a good deal to learn about the letter neighborhoods in words, for even with the support of story context, you cannot decode words such as **fuh** (intended to be the word **thing**), **ararer** (meant to be **another**), and **hate** (supposed to be **heavy**). Nevertheless, Mike's beginning sentence introduces readers to action and his thoughts flow logically. And, what's more, Mike is an enthusiastic learner when the load and the force are in balance.

What Mike Needs to Know and Be Able to Do   Mike needs to know more about the letter neighborhoods in words and needs to be able to strategically use this knowledge when he reads and writes. Additionally, Mike needs to increase phonological awareness of the individual sounds in words and needs to learn to blend sounds together without adding sounds, deleting sounds, or reversing sounds. Mike also needs to continue to be meaning focused, to use context cues along with code cues, and to cross-check for meaning.

Learning Activities and Suggestions: Phonological Awareness   Learners like Mike benefit from activities that increase their phonological awareness of the individual sounds in words and increase their ability to blend. The activities in Chapter 2 that call for tapping, counting, and listening for sounds are especially helpful. Arm Blending is always beneficial. Sliding Sounds Together is useful, too. Rather than always drawing a slide on the chalkboard (as described in Chapter 2), I suggest that you give learners sheets of paper

FIGURE 7–5
The reading and writing ability
of learners like Mike, who is
midway through the fourth
grade, will improve when they
increase sound awareness and
code knowledge.

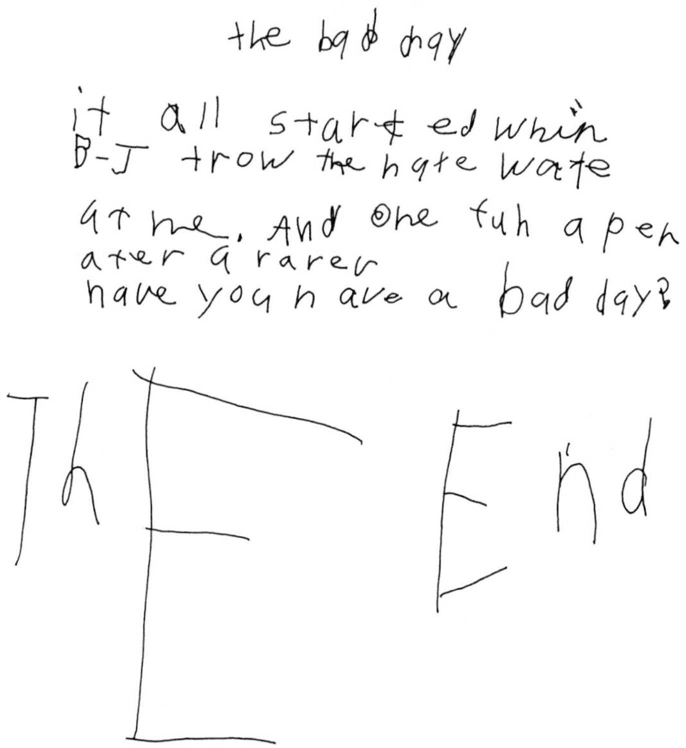

the bad day

it all start ed whin
B-J trow the hate wate
at me, And one tuh a pen
ater a rarer
have you have a bad day?

THE End

on which slides are duplicated. Ask learners to write the letters of words on the slide (beginning at the top and ending near the bottom), to say and blend the sounds represented by letters, and then to write the whole word at the bottom of the slide. Writing letters individually down the slide and writing the whole word at the bottom of the slide helps learners develop phonological awareness as well as code knowledge. The more learners like Mike know about phonological awareness, the better learners are able to strategically use code cues.

Learning Activities and Suggestions: Code Cues   If you have learners like Mike in your classroom, who need to increase their ability to use the letter-sound strategy, I recommend that you use the activity called Building Words with Letter Tiles (Chapter 5). Word building is exceptionally helpful, especially when learners consider the middle letters in words. Not only is word building an effective way to develop the insight readers need to unlock pronunciation, but this procedure shortens the time readers spend catching up with their classmates (Tunmer & Hoover, 1993).

The activity Word Puzzles (Chapter 5) combines phonological awareness with knowledge of letter neighborhoods and thus reinforces and extends the foundations upon which the letter-sound strategy rests. At first, have the learners solve puzzles as a large-group activity, and then, when learners are confident of their ability, invite them to solve puzzles cooperatively. Should learners need extra practice to learn the sounds that the letters in neighborhoods represent, look for activities in Appendix A like Letter Neighborhood Circle, Letter Neighborhood Bingo, and Letter Neighborhood Word Wheels.

I also recommend using mini-chalkboards to develop knowledge of code cues. Not only is spelling with mini-chalkboards a good way to extend learners' code knowledge, but it is a surefire way for you to find out who effectively uses letter neighborhood knowledge to spell and who does not. As the photograph in Figure 7–6 shows, learners do not always spell conventionally. Misspelled words are not penalized in any way, however. Learners simply erase misspellings and fix words with minimal disruption to learning. As learners spell, talk about letter neighborhoods, compare and contrast words, and discuss word meaning.

Learners like Mike also benefit from spelling words in salt (Appendix A). This activity is easy to use with a small group, shows words both in isolation and in a familiar sentence context, and allows learners to easily fix misspellings. Added to this, spelling in salt gives learners a sensory channel (touch) to help them learn words and to help them remember letter neighborhoods within the context of real words. Word Group Discovery (also described in Chapter 5) is an excellent whole-group activity that provides insight into ways words are grouped based on letter neighborhoods. Once learners gain a basic understanding of letter neighborhoods, encourage them to develop knowledge of the chunks in words. To do this, invite learners to make Venn Diagrams and Letter Neighborhood Togetherness Charts (described in Chapter 5).

All things taken together, learners benefit most when they have a great many experiences in reading and writing and many opportunities to use the analogy and letter-sound strategies. As learners use the analogy and letter-sound strategies, their phonological awareness increases. With greater phonological awareness and code knowledge, learners' ability to strategically

FIGURE 7–6

Writing words on mini-chalkboards is an effective way for learners to apply their knowledge of letter neighborhoods to spelling and to get immediate feedback on the words they spell.

use our alphabetic writing system also increases. Learners then are able to refine the analogy and letter-sound strategies, and to develop the ability to use chunks to help them identify words.

As a consequence, the force that learners like Raymond and Mike bring to reading is greater and, by extension, the load learners are capable of lifting is heavier. By carefully and systematically adjusting the balance, learners succeed, gain self-confidence, develop greater capacity to express themselves in writing, enjoy reading increasingly more difficult books, and eventually become independent readers.

LEARNERS WHO SPEAK LANGUAGES OTHER THAN ENGLISH AT HOME

Many learners whose families speak languages other than English benefit from extra help because the language spoken at home is different from the language in which English-speaking authors write. These learners bring to your classroom rich ethnic, cultural, and linguistic backgrounds. They also bring to reading a different complement of syntactic structures and vocabulary than do children whose families speak English. As a consequence, learners whose families speak languages other than English at home have three things to learn—a new spoken language, a new vocabulary, and a new written language, while native English speakers need only learn written English (Thonis, 1989). The challenge is even greater for older learners who must not only learn English but must also master the technical information taught in content subject classes (Freeman & Freeman, 1993).

Learners whose families speak languages other than English are most successful when they have opportunities to observe, infer, and grasp connections between spoken and written language (Verhoeven, 1990). Hence, one way to balance the load and the force is to explore speech and print together (Crawford, 1993). When learners understand how the English alphabet represents sounds, learners also have opportunities to become aware of syntactic structure (Dogger, 1981). Similarly, instruction in vocabulary not only increases learners' reading comprehension (Bartley, 1993), but also extends their use of spoken English, and this, in turn, enhances learners' abilities to form thoughts in English when they write.

Native language literacy is important for balancing the load and the force, too. Learners who are literate in their home languages find it easier to learn to read and write English than learners who are not literate in their native languages (Royer & Carlo, 1991). One reason for this is that learners who can read and write their home languages understand the purpose of reading and writing. Learners whose home languages are written in an alphabet may also bring to the English alphabetic code some, if not all, of the word identification strategies described in this book, albeit applied to word identification in their home languages.

FIGURE 7–7
Learners who speak a language other than English at home benefit from opportunities to talk about the messages they write, the stories they read, and the experiences they have in and out of schools.

Sometimes you will see the influence of their home languages as learners read and write, as shown in Juana's story (Figure 7–8). When Juana writes, she combines her knowledge of English with a rich knowledge of Spanish, her home language. Notice that Juana replaces **of** with **de,** the Spanish word that would ordinarily be used in this syntactic structure. Notice, too, that Juana writes **ticher** for **teacher.** The letter **i** in Spanish represents the sound heard in **routine**, not **line**, so Juana's spelling is consistent with her first language heritage. Juana is also aware of the way that the English alphabetic represents sound, as you can see in her spelling of **tois** for **toys.**

Chan, whose story is shown in Figure 7–9, has attended schools where English is spoken longer than Juana has. Hence, Chan brings greater knowledge of spoken and written English to reading and is therefore capable of lifting greater loads—he reads and understands more challenging materials than does Juana. Even so, Chan's home language, Vietnamese, sometimes crosses over into written and spoken English. For instance, when Chan writes, he does not always include all function words such as prepositions and conjunctions. And when Chan reads aloud, he pronounces **mother** as **"muder"** and leaves out most plurals, possessives, and many other word endings, thus reading **wanted** as **"want."** This is so even though Chan's story is a retelling of a familiar book, *The Great Kapok Tree* (Cherry, 1990), which his teacher has read several times in class, and that the class has discussed a good deal in relation to science.

The crossover, or transfer, of home languages to spoken and written English (substituting **de** for **of,** spelling **teacher** as **ticher,** omitting word endings and conjunctions, and using verbs inappropriately) suggests that learners are

FIGURE 7–8
The written messages of learners who speak languages other than English at home, such as Juana whose family speaks Spanish, may reflect a combination of learners' home language and English.

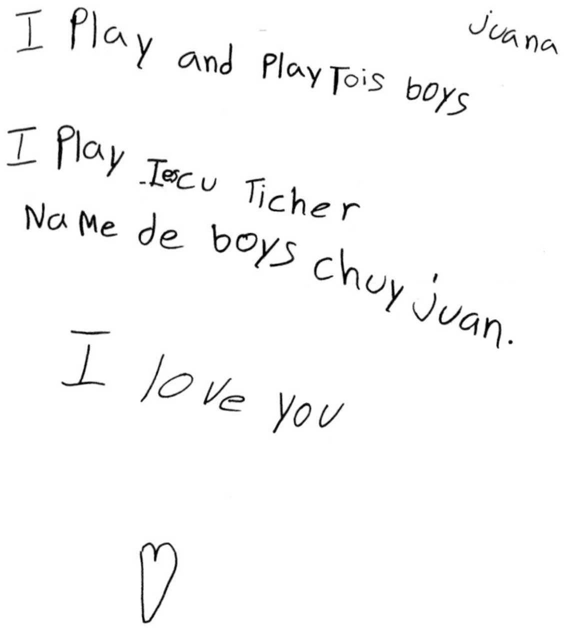

interacting with English text in meaningful ways. Transfer is, indeed, an important sign of progress toward English literacy. Though the home languages Juana and Chan speak result in different types of transfer, you can expect learners like these to learn to speak and read English equally well (Piper, 1993).

Both Juana and Chan are moving toward accomplished use of written English, each at a different point on a continuum. Given that learners bring a wealth of understandings and insights to written English, what types of materials are most likely to help balance the load and the force—to simultaneously support learners' strategic use of our alphabetic writing system and enhance comprehension? For one thing, you can support learners as they become literate in their home languages. For another thing, you can balance the load and the force so as to support the development of word identification strategies that are so important for literacy in written English. To this end, I suggest you consider achieving a point of balance with (1) the use of culturally familiar text, (2) use of predictable books, (3) promoting leisure reading, (4) reading aloud to learners, and (5) having learners write for a variety of purposes.

Use of Culturally Familiar Materials

The learners in your classroom who speak languages other than English at home will remember more information (Malik, 1990; Steffensen & Joag-dev, 1981) and make more elaborate connections when they read culturally famil-

The great kapot tree

The great kapot tree aise The raini forest.
The great kapot tree is larg.
The great kapot tree is where the animals live. The butterfly and The sasur live in The top loge. The monkey, the sloth live in The umbrella or canpy. The tree frog and the snak live in the understory. The Last is all the amimalscan live There.

Top

38 27

understory

umbrella

Last

FIGURE 7–9

The transfer of home languages to spoken and written English suggests that learners are interacting with English text in meaningful ways.

iar materials (Pritchard, 1990) than when they read materials that are far afield from their home cultures. Culturally unfamiliar materials require more background building and call for more explicit explanations than culturally familiar materials. Moreover, culturally unfamiliar text is not a good measure of reading ability and, in fact, is likely to underestimate learners' actual reading achievement (Garcia, 1991).

From a practical point of view, you will find that learners are better readers of the materials in your classroom—better at comprehending storybooks, novels, articles, and poems, and better at remembering information and concepts in content subject textbooks—when text is culturally relevant, worse readers when text is culturally unfamiliar. So, if you wish to get an informal assessment of learners' reading abilities, use materials that correspond to learners' background knowledge and experience, and avoid materials that are detached from learners' lives.

Establishing the right balance point depends to a considerable extent upon whether materials are culturally familiar to learners. This means that books, poems, articles, and plays that are culturally familiar to learners who speak English at home may not be suitable matches for learners whose families do not speak English at home. Furthermore, materials that are a good fit for Hispanic learners may not be such a good fit for Arabic, Asian, or Native American learners. This, of course, underscores the importance of being sensitive to learners' cultural heritage and personal life experiences.

The goal is to link learners' life experiences with classroom learning (Weaver, 1994). To do this, take frequent field trips; invite guest speakers whose home language is that spoken by the children whom you teach (in this case, Spanish for Juana and Vietnamese for Chan). Encourage learners to talk about their life experiences and incorporate those experiences into your everyday classroom routine. Cook learners' traditional foods; write signs in learners' home languages; make bulletin boards, wall charts, and labels in both English and the learners' home languages. Use pictures and real objects (an orange, a fork, a toy car) to support classroom discussions whenever possible. Read books and traditional tales that embrace learners' cultures; role-play, retell, and illustrate stories, folktales, and poems. Not only do such activities build a strong context for learning, but they provide ways to honor the cultures of learners as well.

Predictable Books

While there are many types of books and ways to share them, predictable books hold a special promise because they bring English syntax and English words within easy reach of young learners who are beginning to read a language different from the one spoken at home. Because the same English language patterns recur over and over again, predictable books encourage young, beginning readers to anticipate sentence structure. And, since the same words are read many times, learners have many chances to remember them, thereby building their reading vocabularies. The same characteristics that make predictable books useful for younger learners make these books beneficial for older learners who are novice readers of English (Arthur, 1991). So, do not hesitate to share predictable books with older learners who are crossing the threshold of English literacy, provided, of course, that books are culturally and developmentally appropriate.

Leisure Reading

There is nothing so powerful as enjoying a good book just for the pure fun of it. As learners read for pleasure, they use word identification strategies in context and have opportunities to develop a better understanding of English syntax. Intriguing storybooks, thrilling novels, touching poems, dramatic plays—all offer gateways to literacy. Take advantage, too, of the engaging magazines published for beginning and advanced readers: *Your Big Backyard* for young learners interested in the world of nature; *Odyssey* for third graders and up who are intrigued by space travel and the science of the universe; *Ranger Rick* for second graders through fourth graders who like to read articles about nature; *Disney Adventures* for readers interested in a pot-pourri of articles, ideas, and activities; and *Ladybug* (ages two through six), *Spider* (ages six through nine), and *Cricket* (ages nine through fourteen) for learners who are enchanted by stories, poems, and fantasy. This is just to mention a few. Look for books and magazines written in English and written in learners' home languages, as well. Set aside time each day for learners to read for pleasure and, while you make time for leisure reading, allow time for reading aloud to learners.

Reading Aloud to Learners

When you read storybooks, novels, plays, poems, and articles aloud, learners have opportunities to develop a sense of the structure of stories, to enjoy literature, and to have experiences with English print that may not be available in their homes. Look, too, for ways to combine read-aloud stories with writing activities. After books have been read aloud, discussed, and enjoyed, invite learners to write about a memorable event or a fascinating character. If you teach young learners, cut out the stories learners write, fasten the stories to construction paper, and staple construction paper sheets together to make a giant accordion book (Figure 7-10). Accordion books link reading and writing directly and are wonderful resources to share with younger learners. Older learners enjoy creating and publishing their own versions of favorite books

FIGURE 7–10
Writing retellings of familiar stories strengthens the connections among the reading, writing, speaking, and listening of learners who speak languages other than English at home.

and poems, not to mention rewriting the lyrics of songs, raps, and chants, which brings us to the use of writing to balance the load and the force.

Writing for a Variety of Purposes

Learners whose families speak languages other than English at home express their thoughts in writing long before they speak English proficiently (Hudelson, 1984). Writing helps learners reflect upon meaningful messages in print, creates opportunities to use English syntax and vocabulary in meaningful ways, and supports insight into our English alphabetic code. For these reasons, I suggest that you use the language experience approach with the less accomplished learners in your classroom and dialogue journals with the more accomplished learners whom you teach.

Language experience is an approach whereby the stories that learners read are stories written or dictated by them, are based on their life experiences, and reflect their spoken language. Language experience stories make a special contribution because the messages learners write are the materials read, which directly links the text with the learners' cultural background and daily experiences. Added to this, the words in language experience stories are a rich source of onsets, rimes, and letter neighborhoods to include in activities described in earlier chapters.

Dialogue journals, which are two-way communications between learners and their teachers, are particularly beneficial for learners who read and write English with enough independence to put their thoughts on paper. When learners like Chan write dialogue journals, they share their thoughts with their teachers. Their teachers, in turn, write reactions to learners' messages, including personal comments and descriptions of relevant life experiences. This gives learners opportunities to extend and refine their abilities to use the alphabet to write, as well as opportunities to learn how to form their thoughts in such a way as to communicate with English-speaking readers. Should you choose to use dialogue journals with the learners whom you teach, you can expect learners' confidence with written language to improve and their command of spoken English to increase, too (Nurss & Hough, 1992).

Language experience stories and dialogue journals are but two of the many ways to connect spoken and written English with learners' cultural heritage. Learners in the fourth grade and up enjoy writing cartoons (described in Chapter 7), especially when cartoons tap into learners' everyday life experiences. Adding new endings for familiar poems, writing stories, scripts for homemade movies, humorous jokes, riddles, and creating entertaining alliterative sentences also add a great deal to learners' overall understanding of spoken and written English.

Find lots of books, magazines, and newspapers written in learners' home languages and put them in your classroom library. Then create a classroom newspaper or magazine featuring articles written by learners. Articles can be

FIGURE 7–11
Writing creates opportunities for learners who speak languages other than English at home to gain insight into the English alphabetic code and to use English syntax and vocabulary to convey their ideas in written language.

in learners' home language and in English, too. This way everyone has an opportunity to share in literacy experiences. Locate pen pals who can write in learners' home languages. And locate, too, relatives of learners who will be learners' pen pals or who will visit your classroom to share their life experiences. Invite parents to volunteer in your classroom and celebrate holidays that are important to learners' families. This type of classroom activity is a rich source for writing collaboratively in large and small groups. Emphasize meaning as learners write, but also take the opportunity to discuss the onsets, rimes, letter neighborhoods, and chunks in learners' writing. In so doing, exploring the English alphabetic writing system will become an integral part of ongoing classroom activities in which learners read, write, speak, and listen to English.

FINAL OBSERVATIONS

All things considered, the greater the connection among everyday reading activities, writing, and strategic code use, the more opportunities learners have to transfer word identification to meaningful reading contexts. The challenge is to balance the load and the force so as to foster the development of word identification strategies, nurture literacy, and ensure that all learners become competent, meaning-driven strategy users. Balancing the load and the force creates a supportive learning environment; honors learners' individual differences, needs, and preferences; and provides the basis upon which learners successfully read a wide variety of storybooks, novels, poems, articles, plays, and content subject textbooks.

REFERENCES

Arthur, B. (1991). Working with new ESL students in a junior high school reading class. *The Journal of Reading, 34,* 628–631.

Bartley, N. (1993). Literature-based integrated language instruction and the language-deficient student. *Reading Research and Instruction, 32,* 31–37.

Cherry, L. (1990). *The great kapok tree.* New York: Harcourt Brace & Company.

Crawford, L. W. (1993). *Language and literacy learning in multicultural classrooms.* Boston: Allyn & Bacon.

Cricket. Mt. Morris, IL: The Cricket Magazine Group, Carus Publishing Company.

Disney adventures. Burbank, CA: Walt Disney Magazine Publishing Group.

Dogger, B. (1981). Language-based reading theories, English orthography, and ESL pedagogy. In C. W. Twyford, W. Diehl, & K. Feathers (Eds.), *Reading English as a second language: Moving from theory* (pp. 21–28). Monographs in Teaching and Learning, 4 (March).

Freeman, D. E., & Freeman, Y. S. (1993). Strategies for promoting the primary languages of all students. *The Reading Teacher, 46,* 552–558.

Garcia, G. E. (1991). Factors influencing the English reading test performance of Spanish-speaking Hispanic children. *Reading Research Quarterly, 26,* 371–392.

Hudelson, S. (1984). Kan yu ret an rayt en ingles: Children become literate in English as a second language. *TESOL Quarterly, 18,* 221–238.

Ladybug. Mt. Morris, IL: The Cricket Magazine Group, Carus Publishing Company.

Malik, A. A. (1990). A psycholinguistic analysis of the reading behavior of ESL-proficient readers using culturally familiar and unfamiliar expository text. *American Educational Research Journal, 27,* 205–223.

Nurss, J. R., & Hough, R. A. (1992). Reading and the ESL student. In S. J. Samuels & A. E. Farstrup (Eds.), *What research has to say about reading instruction* (2nd ed.) (pp. 277–313). Newark, DE: International Reading Association.

Odyssey. Peterborough, NH: Cobblestone Publishing.

Piper, T. (1993). *And then there were two: Children and second language learning.* Markman, Ontario: Pippin Publishing.

Pritchard, R. (1990). The effects of cultural schemata on reading processing strategies. *Reading Research Quarterly, 25,* 273–295.

Ranger Rick. Vienna, VA: National Wildlife Federation.

Royer, J. M., & Carlo, M. S. (1991). Transfer of comprehension skills from native to second language. *Journal of Reading, 34,* 450–455.

Spider. Mt. Morris, IL: The Cricket Magazine Group, Carus Publishing Company.

Steffensen, M. S., & Joag-dev, C. (1981). Cultural knowledge and reading: Interference of facilitation. In C. W. Twyford, W. Diehl, & K. Feathers

(Eds.), *Reading English as a second language: Moving from theory* (pp. 29–46). Monographs in Teaching and Learning, 4 (March).

Thonis, E. W. (1989). Language minority students and reading. *The Reading Instruction Journal, 32*, 58–62.

Tunmer, W. E., & Hoover, W. A. (1993). Phonological recoding skill and beginning reading. *Reading and Writing: An Interdisciplinary Journal, 5,* 161–179.

Verhoeven, L. T. (1990). Acquisition of reading in a second language. *Reading Research Quarterly, 15*, 90–114.

Weaver, C. (1994). *Reading process and practice: From socio-psycholinguistics to whole language* (2nd ed.). Portsmouth, NH: Heinemann.

LEARNING ACTIVITIES FOR PRACTICE AND REINFORCEMENT

If some of the learners whom you teach cannot explain in their own words how the English alphabetic writing system represents sound or take an inordinately long time to identify the unfamiliar words they meet in sentences, then the following practice and reinforcement activities will be beneficial. These activities are intended to be a part of, not separate from, the in-depth experiences with spoken and written language that are essential for becoming literate. As with all other learning activities in this book, select those that you think are most worthwhile for the learners whom you teach, modify them when necessary, and use the materials learners are reading and writing every day in activities.

ACTIVITIES TO INCREASE PHONOLOGICAL AWARENESS

The following practice and reinforcement activities give learners opportunities to develop greater insight into the word, rhyme, and sound segments of spoken language.

❋ Rhyming Picture Book

This picture book making activity gives kindergarten and first grade learners opportunities to gain insight into rhyme.

Things You'll Need: A large number of colorful pictures from magazines; scissors; glue; markers; very large sheets of paper or tagboard.

Exploration and Guided Practice: The Rhyming Picture Book can have as many or as few pages as meets the needs of the learners whom you teach.

Glue a picture to the top of each page, a **cat** perhaps. Then look at several other pictures, saying the word for each and asking learners if the word rhymes with the picture at the top of the page. Glue pictures that rhyme (in this example, whose names rhyme with **cat**) on the page and then write the words underneath the pictures. Ask learners to think of other rhyming words and, if you do not have pictures for words, invite learners to draw their own renditions. Write words under the pictures learners draw, too. Discuss the idea that some words that sound alike are also spelled alike. Fasten pages together to make a book. Display the Rhyming Picture Book in your classroom; share it with other classrooms; use it as a reference for writing poetry.

✳ Rhyming Lists

In this activity, kindergartners and beginning first graders create rhyming word lists from the words in favorite poems.

Things You'll Need: Paper; a marker; favorite poems.

Exploration and Guided Practice: Write a favorite poem of learners on a piece of chart paper. Read the poem in chorus with the learners and discuss rhyme. Invite learners to find all the rhyming words in the poem, writing words on the chalkboard. Next, challenge learners to think of other words that rhyme with one of the words in the poem. Make a list of the words. Do this for two or three rhymes. Then, for extra practice, invite learners to choose one rhyming list and to draw (or cut out) pictures of words on the list. When they have finished, you (or another accomplished reader) write the words under the pictures. Ask learners to tell you something about the pictures and then you can write the sentences on the page, too.

✳ Sandpaper Words

In this activity, learners trace words letter by letter and blend sounds as they do so. This gives learners opportunities to improve their insight into the sounds in words and to improve their ability to blend. Some knowledge of the sounds that letters represent is needed, which makes this activity suitable for mid-year first graders, as well as older learners.

Things You'll Need: As many words made of sandpaper letters as there are learners in a small group (look in Appendix B for instructions).

Exploration and Guided Practice: Demonstrate by moving your finger over each sandpaper letter in a word and blending sounds together as your finger goes from one letter to the next. Ask learners what word the sounds make. Show learners how the voice never stops but glides from sound to sound as the finger moves from letter to letter. Next, give learners sandpaper words to trace. Ask them to trace along with you, blending the sounds together as they do so. At first, your voice should lead learners' voices so that you blend sounds slightly ahead of learners. This way, your leading voice gives learners an expert model to follow as they blend. Later, when learners are more accomplished, align your voice with learners' voices. When learners are quite comfortable tracing and blending, ask them to trace and blend without your participation.

ACTIVITIES TO INCREASE ONSET-RIME KNOWLEDGE

These activities are intended for learners who are limited in their ability to use the analogy strategy because they lack code knowledge of onsets and rimes.

Easy-to-Do Activities

Here are four easy-to-do activities that you and the learners whom you teach will find enjoyable and worthwhile:

1. Invite learners to think of words that rhyme with food names, holidays, animals, community places, games, and toys. Then make lists of words that share a spoken rhyme and a written rime. Fasten lists to walls, bulletin boards, and doors. For example, learners might think of words that rhyme with **book**, such as **look, cook, hook, took, brook,** and **shook** or words that rhyme with school, such as **stool, cool, pool, fool, spool,** and **tool.**

2. Explore onsets with an old-fashioned celebration, an alliterative feast with all sorts of things that begin alike, such as popcorn, pizza, potatoes, pineapple, pretzels, and pie. Then write poems and stories about the experience, using lots of words that share onsets.

3. Create an alliterative shopping list of all sorts of things—real and imagined—that a store might sell. Make a game of it, saying "I went to the store and I found a bubble to buy." Then ask each learner to add something to the list that begins with the same letter and sound as **bubble— banana, basket, bread, book, balloon, bean.** Make a list on the chalkboard. Discuss onsets and invite learners to create their own imaginative shopping lists.

4. Invite learners to create their own personalized lists of words with shared onsets or rimes. They can put the lists in folders to be used as references for all sorts of reading and writing occasions.

✳ Giant Word Chains

In this activity, first grade learners make brightly colored paper chains with words that either have the same onset or have the same rime, depending on which aspect of print (onsets or rimes) you wish to emphasize. And, of course, such a large undertaking is a project that is best accomplished by groups of learners working together cooperatively.

Things You'll Need: Many colorful pieces of construction paper cut into strips about an inch wide; markers; tape or a stapler.

Exploration and Guided Practice: Explain that learners are to make a chain by writing words that begin alike (or words that end with the same letter pattern) on construction paper strips. Tape or staple the ends of strips into a circle, linking the circles with another to form a giant chain that makes an engaging display. Of course, the more words learners write, the longer the chain, so there is great incentive for them to think of a lot of words to make the chain as impressive as possible. Before you hang chains, make a wall chart list of words and count the number of words learners chained together. Drape chains over bulletin boards; hang them from one corner of the ceiling to the other; tape them to desks, windows, and walls.

✳ Onset Houses

This whole-group chalkboard activity is challenging and requires absolutely no materials and no preparation! Use this activity with first graders who are making average progress and with second graders who need extra practice with onsets.

Things You'll Need: No special materials are needed.

Exploration and Guided Practice: Write a word on the chalkboard, draw a rectangle around it, and say something like, "Today, we are going to build a house of bricks that have words inside them. This is the first brick and it has **big** written on it." Then draw another brick on the chalkboard. Explain that this empty brick needs a word inside, too. Ask, "Who can think of another word that begins like **big** and is spelled with a **b**?" The learner who thinks of a word, such as **baby**, comes to the chalkboard and writes the word inside the brick. Draw another brick, asking learners to think of a word that begins like **big** and **baby**. Continue building until the house is complete. Should learners have difficulty thinking of words, remind them to look at lists on wall charts and bulletin boards and to refer to any personal word lists they have made. For variety, put the bricks in different arrangements; for example, an igloo, a log cabin, a tepee, a fanciful castle, a strong fort.

✳ Rime Tic-Tac-Toe

This old standby is played much like the original version of game, except words sharing rimes are used instead of **X**s and **O**s. It is useful for learners who are in the second grade and up.

Things You'll Need: Laminated playing cards made of tagboard or heavy paper (explained in Appendix B; see "Rime Tic-Tac-Toe"); erasable marker.

Exploration and Guided Practice: Any learner who knows how to play Tic-Tac-Toe needs only cursory guidance to use this practice and reinforcement activity. Two learners play; each writes a word with the same rime as that at the top of the playing card (Figure A–1). The traditional rules hold—any three words joined in a horizontal, vertical, or diagonal direction win. Note: This activity can be modified so as to include words with prefixes and suffixes or to focus on words that include certain letter neighborhoods.

✳ Onset-Rime Tachistoscopes

A tachistoscope is a device through which a strip of tagboard is drawn to reveal one word at a time. Tachistoscopes challenge learners to read words made of different combinations of onsets and rimes, and they are suitable to learners of any age who need extra practice with onsets and rimes.

Things You'll Need: Several tachistoscopes, as shown in Figure A–2. While tachistoscopes can be purchased, they are extremely easy to make. (Look in Appendix B for directions telling how to make a tachistoscope.)

Exploration and Guided Practice: Show learners (1) how to thread the tagboard strip through the slits that form the window on the body of the tachistoscope and (2) how to line up onsets with rimes so as to form words. Tachistoscopes are used for individual practice, which means they fit nicely into learning centers.

FIGURE A–1
Tic-Tac-Toe challenges learners to think of words that have rimes, letter neighborhoods, or meaningful chunks.

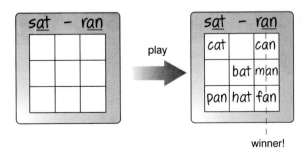

FIGURE A–2
Tachistoscopes give learners practice identifying words that are formed when different onsets are combined with the same rime.

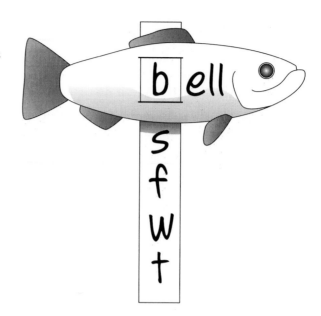

✳ Muffin Tin Words

This activity is for learners of any age who need more practice building words that are made of onsets and rimes. It is a particularly good activity for learning centers and yields a permanent record of the words learners build.

Things You'll Need:
A muffin tin (as described in Appendix B); onset-rime tiles; muffin word guides (also explained in Appendix B).

Exploration and Guided Practice: Explain that the muffin tin has small labels that tell which onset-rime tiles are inside each compartment. Give learners a muffin word guide, which has sample words with underlined onsets or rimes and several blank muffin circles underneath them (Figure A–3). Learners are to read the underlined words on the guide sheet and use onset-rime tiles to build other words that share the same onset or rime. As learners build words with onset-rime tiles, they write words in the blank "muffin" circles under each underlined word. Ask learners to count how many words they build. If learners build more words than fit in the blank muffins on the guide, ask them to write the extra words underneath the muffins. Have the learners add the words they build to their personal word lists.

FIGURE A–3
The muffin word guide that learners fill in when they combine onset tiles with rime tiles placed in a muffin tin is a permanent record of the words that learners build.

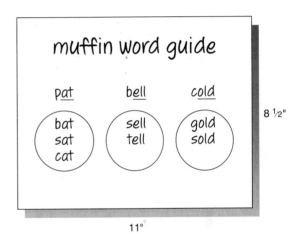

✳ Egg Words

This matching activity challenges learners to put together two halves of a colorful plastic egg—one half has an onset written on it and the other has a rime. The words formed by putting together egg halves should be ones that are often seen by learners in storybooks, poems, and articles. This activity is most suitable for first graders who have some experience reading. It is a good activity for centers and best done when learners work individually.

Things You'll Need: Many colorful plastic eggs; a permanent marker. (Instructions for making Egg Words are in Appendix B.)

Exploration and Guided Practice: To build egg words, learners put together two halves of colored plastic eggs that have a rime and an onset (Figure A–4). Put the eggs into a basket, separate them into halves, scramble the halves, and then challenge learners to put egg words together.

FIGURE A–4
Learners build words by putting the halves of plastic eggs with onsets on them together with the halves that have rimes written on them.

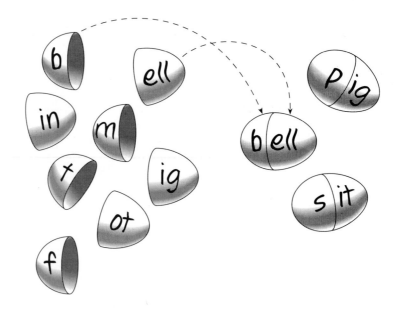

✳ Fish for Onsets

This is a version of the a fishing game in which learners fish for words in a bucket "pond" and read the words they catch. In this activity, learners exchange onsets in order to read the names of sea creatures and things found on the beach. It is suitable for first graders and second graders who need extra help learning how to exchange onsets.

Things You'll Need: A plastic bucket to serve as a pond; a pole (a ruler works well); string; paper clips; a magnet; shapes of sea creatures and beach items made of laminated construction paper; a marker. (Look in Appendix B for directions.) *The Magic School Bus on the Ocean Floor* (Cole, 1992) is an excellent source for words to use in this activity and also offers many possibilities to relate this activity to science. Examples of other books with watery themes are the following: *Big Al* (Clements, 1988); *There's a Sea in My Bedroom* (Wild, 1987); *20,000 Baseball Cards under the Sea* (Buller & Schade, 1991).

Exploration and Guided Practice: After sharing books about the ocean with learners, explain that they are to fish for creatures who live in the sea or for things that are found on the beach. Each creature or beach item has a word on one side and an onset (beginning letter[s]) on the other. When learners catch something, they figure out the creature's name (or the beach item) by reading the word on one side and exchanging the sound represented by the onset on the reverse side (Figure A–5). To demonstrate, ask a learner to catch a fish and then to read the word on the creature or item caught—**dark,** for example. Then show everyone the onset **sh** written on the reverse side. Write the word **dark** and the onset **sh** on the chalkboard. Erase the **d** and replace it with **sh** saying, "What new word is made when we take off the **d** and put the **sh** in its place?" Repeat several times.

Once learners understand how to Fish for Onsets, continue by having one learner "fish" at a time. As each fish is caught, challenge learners who are not fishing to write the name of the creature (or the item) caught on a sheet of paper. Ask learners to hold up the word as soon as they figure it out. Not only is this a good quick check to see who can and who cannot exchange consonants, but it gets everyone involved in an active way.

ACTIVITIES TO INCREASE LETTER NEIGHBORHOOD KNOWLEDGE

If learners stumble when they use the letter-sound strategy, cannot explain in their own words how letter neighborhoods contribute to pronunciation, and frequently connect the wrong letter neighborhoods with sounds, these activities will be helpful.

FIGURE A–5
Learners exchange one onset for another to discover the names of the animals and things that they catch in a "pond" made from a bucket or a pail.

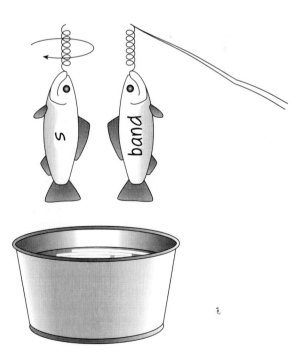

Easy-to-Do Activities

These four activities are easy ways for learners to get extra practice with letter neighborhoods:

1. Challenge second, third, and fourth graders to spot words in the dictionary that include specific neighborhoods in their spellings. Ask learners to write down the word and page number, and then to count the number of words found that include different neighborhoods.

2. Say a word and write it on the chalkboard, "**shade**" perhaps. Discuss a letter neighborhood, in this case the **VCe** letter neighborhood. Then invite learners to think of other words that have the same sound as that represented by the letter neighborhood, a long **a** sound, for instance. Write these words on the chalkboard. Discuss letter neighborhoods; explore ways in which the letters in neighborhoods represent sounds; compare and contrast neighborhoods.

3. Challenge learners to look in the books they are reading to find words spelled with letter neighborhoods that represent more than one sound. For example, learners might look for words that have an **oo** neighborhood, such as **cook** and **school**. Learners then put words into columns based on the sound(s) represented. For **oo**, learners would make two lists: (1) words in which **oo** represents the sound heard in **cook** and (2) words in which **oo** represents the sound heard in **school**. Last, learners share lists with everyone in the class and discuss the different sounds the letters in neighborhoods represent. This categorizing activity is most successful when used by third graders and up, though some end-of-year second graders may be successful, too.

4. Invite third grade and older learners to design, write, and illustrate want ads featuring a letter neighborhood they are exploring. Ads should include (1) examples of words that include the letter neighborhood and (2) an imaginative illustration. If your classroom publishes a newspaper chronicling important events, place the advertisements in the paper and have learners share them with other classrooms, friends at home, and family members. Or publish the advertisements by sprinkling them among bound volumes of learners' compositions, thus creating a class magazine.

❋ What's in a Name?

This is a variation of the party game in which players make as many words as they can from one large word, usually the name of a famous person, place, thing, or event. If words from social studies, science, math, and health are used, this game is easy to integrate with content area subjects. This activity is best used with third through sixth graders.

Things You'll Need: Letter tiles (see Appendix B); the names of famous people, places, things, or events from the content subjects learners are studying or from the books learners are reading.

Exploration and Guided Practice: Write the name of an important person, place, thing, or event on the chalkboard. Talk about why the item is important and write down what learners know about the item. Then pass out letter tiles that spell the name. Invite learners to (1) build as many different words as they can think of with tiles, (2) write down the words they build, and (3) count the number of words when building is finished. Write the words on wall charts, talk about the letter neighborhoods in words, and when finished, hang charts prominently in your classroom.

✳ Letter Neighborhood Circle

This activity uses familiar words from favorite books shared in your classroom to help learners develop code knowledge of letter neighborhoods. It is suitable for learners in first grade and up.

Things You'll Need: Wall charts with lots of words written on them; letter cards (as explained in Appendix B); colorful markebs. (This activity calls for drawing colorful circles around the words on wall charts. So, make sure that the wall charts you use are ready to be replaced or that you have, or are willing to make, duplicates.)

Exploration and Guided Practice: Talk about the words on wall charts that have a common letter neighborhood. For example, learners might discuss the words **play, black, glue,** and **flea,** which you have written on the chalkboard. Then talk about a letter neighborhood that the words have in common—the consonant blend neighborhood to which **pl, bl, gl,** and **fl** belong. Invite learners to find words on wall charts that include instances of the same letters in neighborhoods. Then ask learners to use a colored marker to circle words on wall charts that include these letter neighborhoods in their spelling. In this example, they should use a different color for each blend. For example, all words with **pl** might be circled in blue, words with **bl** in red, ones with **gl** in green, and ones with **fl** in yellow. This creates opportunities to call attention to the neighborhoods and to set words with these neighborhoods apart from other words on charts.

✳ Word Worms

Word Worms are created when learners with letter neighborhoods pinned on their shirts attach themselves to learners wearing onsets, as shown in Figure A–6. As learners form Word Worms, they blend spoken language, think analytically about the alphabetic code, and strategically use knowledge of letter neighborhoods. With its emphasis on fanciful creatures, this activity is most appealing and most appropriate for first and second graders.

Things You'll Need: Word Worms made of colored construction paper (see Appendix B); string; scissors; crayons; markers; masking tape.

Exploration and Guided Practice: Write an onset on the chalkboard, **spr** for example. Then write a word underneath it, **spray** perhaps, explaining that **spray** is formed by combining the **spr** blend neighborhood and the **ay** (**VV**) neighborhood. Encourage learners to think of other words that begin with the **spr** letter neighborhood. Write the words learners suggest underneath **spr**. Do the same with two (or three) other consonant blend (or consonant digraph) neighborhoods that serve as onsets. For example, learners might create lists for words that begin with the consonant blend neighborhoods of **spr**, **st**, and **sl**. Compare and contrast the **spr**, **st**, and **sl** neighborhoods; discuss the effect each has on pronunciation.

Now it is time to make a Word Worm for each consonant blend letter neighborhood. To do this, tape a head with an onset neighborhood written on it to the shirts of some learners (**spr**, **st**, or **sl**, for example). On other learners,

FIGURE A–6
In Word Worms, learners line up behind the onset that builds a word when joined with the letter sequence they are wearing.

tape a body section that has letter neighborhoods, such as **ain, ang, awl, age, amp, and, ide, eep,** and **ice.** Learners with body sections then decide which combinations of an onset neighborhood and the letter sequences on their shirts form a meaningful word. Learners wearing body sections with letter sequences that follow onset neighborhoods put their hands on the hips of the person wearing the proper onset (the head). For example, **spr** (the head) combines with **ain, ang, awl** (body sections) to build **sprain, sprang,** and **sprawl.** Learners with **age, amp,** and **and** line up behind **st** to from **stage, stamp,** and **stand.** The **sl** is followed by **ide, eep,** and **ice** to form **slide, sleep,** and **slice.** After word worms are created, individual learners then read the word formed by the consonant blend neighborhood at the head and the sequence of letters fastened to his or her shirt (the body section).

Next, tape each worm head to the chalkboard and invite learners to tape their body sections behind the proper head, thereby recreating Word Worms on the chalkboard (Figure A–7). Talk about letter neighborhoods; read the words in chorus. Invite learners to consider whether all the combinations make real words and whether some sequence of letters on body sections can be attached to more than one onset neighborhood. Should the sequence of letters on body sections combine to form words with more than one onset neighborhood (the **ay** in **spray** and **stay,** for example), move body sections around to create different words.

FIGURE A–7
Putting word worms on the chalkboard gives learners opportunities to decide whether all the combinations make real words and whether some sequences of letters can be attached to more than one onset.

✳ Salt Spelling

In this activity, learners read sentences and then spell words by pushing salt in a shallow container to one side as their fingers move. Salt Spelling appeals to younger and older learners, calls for movement, touch, and a thoughtful analysis of how letter neighborhoods combine to form meaningful written words.

Things You'll Need: One covered container about nine by twelve inches (or slightly larger) for each learner (see Appendix B); salt; large index cards with a sentence from a familiar story on one side and a word from that sentence on the other side.

Exploration and Guided Practice: Show learners a sentence written on a large index card. (There is writing on both sides of the cards: one has a familiar sentence, the other a single word from that sentence.) Ask learners to read the sentence and to point to a word you indicate, which they will later write in salt (this is the word on the back of the card). Now turn the card over and show learners the word written by itself. Ask learners to read the word and discuss the letter neighborhoods in spelling. Next, ask learners to look at the word and to write it in the salt, saying each letter as it is written. Gently shake containers to erase words. Then cover up the word on the card and challenge learners to write the word from memory. As soon as everyone is finished, show learners the card and check for accuracy. Now turn the card over again to show the sentence. Ask learners to read the sentence in chorus and ask one learner to point to the word they just wrote. Repeat several times with different sentences and words.

✳ Clothespin Words

This large-group activity for first grade learners gets everyone involved, is easy to do, requires minimal preparation, and gives learners lots of solid practice using letter neighborhoods.

Things You'll Need: One rope for a clothesline; an assortment of clothespins; word cards; blank cards (or pieces of construction paper) cut out in the shape of clothes; markers.

Exploration and Guided Practice: String a clothesline across a corner of the room and give several word cards to each learner. Write a word on the chalkboard, say the word, and point out a letter neighborhood in spelling. Ask learners to look at the words in their hands and to see if one (or more) is spelled with the same letter neighborhood. Learners then read words that have the same letter neighborhoods, get a clothespin, and pin word cards to the clothesline. When finished, learners read the words in chorus and discuss letter neighborhoods.

As a follow-up, make a clothesline bulletin board by zigzagging a clothesline from top to bottom. Pin a word card on the top of the clothesline and underline a letter neighborhood. Invite learners to find words in which the same letter neighborhood represents the same sound. Once words are found, learners make their own clothesline words by writing words on cards (or pieces of paper) cut in the shape of clothes and then fasten the words along the clothesline.

✳ Fly Away Words

In this activity, first and second graders read words on make-believe flies, bees, or mosquitoes and, as quickly as possible, smack the flies, bees, or mosquitoes with a swatter. This is a team game that takes a relatively short time to play, so plan on using it in the twenty minutes or so before special classes, on days when learners finish projects early, or whenever an amusing bit of practice is a welcome addition to the school day. Books like *The Giant Jam Sandwich* (Lord, 1972) and *Why Mosquitoes Buzz in People's Ears* (Aardema, 1975) are examples of stories that feature insects. Should your class be sharing these books or others like them, this game is a good way to reinforce letter neighborhood knowledge and to do so in keeping with the theme of familiar books.

Things You'll Need: Two flyswatters; tape; words written on pieces of construction paper cut to resemble flies, bees, or mosquitoes, with one word written on each. (When you make Fly Away Words, be sure to select words that appear frequently in the books learners read and that are spelled with letter neighborhoods that learners need practice identifying.)

Exploration and Guided Practice: Tape the Fly Away Words (written on the insect forms) to the chalkboard, spacing them fairly far apart. Divide players into two teams. Call one player from each team up to the chalkboard; give each a swatter. Then pronounce a word and tell players to swat a word that has a letter neighborhood represented by the sound heard at the beginning or end of a word. For instance, you might say, "Swat a Fly Away Word that has the letter neighborhood you hear at the beginning of the word 'trade.'" The first player to swat a word, perhaps **trip**, reads it aloud. Or you might say, "Swat a Fly Away Word with the letter neighborhood you hear at the end of 'low.'" If the player is correct, the swatted word is taken off the board—it "flies away"—and the team gets a point. The team with the most Fly Away Words wins. At game's end, hold up each Fly Away Word and ask learners to read words in chorus.

✸ Letter Neighborhood Bingo

An oldie but goodie for learners of any age, bingo is a favorite because it has so many variations, gets everyone involved, and effectively targets letter neighborhoods.

Things You'll Need: Bingo cards (as described in Appendix B; see "Bingo Cards"); buttons, small pieces of paper, or bottle caps.

Exploration and Guided Practice: To play, write a word on the chalkboard, read it, and underline a letter neighborhood. Players listen for the sounds that the letter neighborhood represents and look on their cards to see if a word in one of the Bingo squares has a neighborhood with the same letters in spelling and the same pronunciation. If so, players cover the square with a button, small piece of paper, or cap. Repeat with different neighborhoods. Traditional rules hold: any five consecutively covered squares lined up diagonally, horizontally, or vertically wins. Four corners or postage stamps (four squares in any corner) are fun to play, too. Coveralls are always challenging, but they take more time, so save them for days when there is plenty of flexibility in the schedule.

✸ Letter Neighborhood Word Wheels

Wheels are made of two circles, one with letter neighborhoods that come at the beginning of words (act as onsets) and one with letter neighborhoods that follow onsets (Figure A–8). Though this kind of practice is strictly rote, it pays off when learners have plenty of other opportunities to strategically use letter neighborhoods.

Things You'll Need: Colorful tagboard; a black marker; scissors; one brad for each wheel you make. (Directions for making wheels are in Appendix B.)

FIGURE A–8
Learners think about the sounds that the letters in neighborhoods represent and then turn the word wheel to form real words.

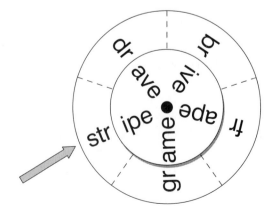

Exploration and Practice: Show learners how to spin the wheels so that the letter neighborhoods written on the inner wheel line up with those on the outer wheel, thus forming words. To check on learners' success, ask them to write down all the words they form with each word wheel. Letter Neighborhood Word Wheels are fine additions to learning centers and the word lists learners make are a permanent record of this learning activity.

✸ Code Making and Code Breaking for Fun

This activity cannot be considered practice or reinforcement because learners do not strategically use letter neighborhoods. However, this activity does give learners opportunities to gain insight into how written codes are constructed and deciphered. Added to this, it is challenging, creative and mind engaging, and particularly appealing to older elementary learners, say fourth graders and up.

Things You'll Need: No special materials are needed.

Exploration and Guided Practice: Begin with a discussion of codes: Talk about all sorts of codes learners use every day; how codes are constructed; how codes are deciphered. Then challenge learners to make up their own secret codes and to use those codes to write secret messages like the one in Figure A–9. After codes are devised and messages written, ask code makers to exchange secret messages with each other. The challenge now is to decode someone else's secret message—to figure out the code, to understand the message, and to write down a meaningful transcription. Last invite code makers to explain the codes they devised. As learners explain codes, they have opportunities to gain greater insight into their own ability to use codes and into the mechanisms codes typically use to represent meaningful messages.

ACTIVITIES TO INCREASE KNOWLEDGE OF MEANINGFUL CHUNKS IN WORDS

These activities are for learners who (1) cannot identify words when prefixes or suffixes are added, even though learners identify the same words without prefixes and suffixes, (2) cannot identify words when written as contractions, and (3) do not use Greek and Latin roots to gain insight into the meaning of the words in content area textbooks and other reading material. As with all practice and reinforcement activities, include these activities as part of the ongoing learning in your classroom and give learners lots of in-depth experiences with print.

FIGURE A–9
Creating and deciphering codes is creative and mind engaging, and it gives learners opportunities to gain insight into the ways that codes represent meaningful messages.

Coded Message: UWOOGT XCECVKQP KV EQOKP!! QPNA VYQ OQTG YGGMV! K NQXG UMOOGT!

Key:
A-C G-I M-O T-V
B-D H-J N-P U-W
C-E I-K O-Q V-X
D-F J-L P-R W-Y
E-G K-M Q-S X-Z
F-H L-N R-T Y-A
          S-U Z-B

✳ Fold-Over Contractions

This hands-on activity is beneficial for learners who find contractions bewildering. It provides quick and easy practice, can be used with any contraction, and is appropriate for groups of learners from first through third grade.

Things You'll Need: Construction paper cut into strips; markers (look in Appendix B for directions); masking tape.

Exploration and Guided Practice: Write several sentences on the chalkboard that include words that can form contractions. Select sentences from content area textbooks, familiar books learners are reading, or make up sentences that relate to learners' lives or to the subjects learners are studying. Read the sentences one at a time; point out words that can form contractions and write them on the board. Discuss contractions and invite volunteers to change each word pair on the chalkboard into a contraction. Next, reread the sentences with contractions. Now ask learners to make Fold-Over Contractions (as described in Appendix B) for words on the chalkboard. Fold-Over Contractions look like accordions in which deleted letters are simply folded out of sight and replaced by a piece of masking tape with an apostrophe on it. The tape holds the Fold-Over Contraction in place, as shown in Figure A–10. Support learners as they describe in their own words the idea behind missing letters, as well as the purpose and placement of the apostrophe.

FIGURE A–10
Fold-Over Contractions is a
hands-on activity in which
learners fold deleted letters in
contractions out of sight and
replace them with an
apostrophe.

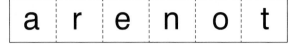

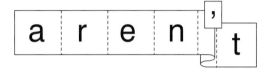

❋ Flip-up Suffixes

This is another version of the memory game in which players remember which two facedown cards of twenty (or less) match and then flip up matches. The objective is to flip up cards that are a match between a word on one card (**swim**, for example) and another card that has the same word only with a suffix added (**swimming**). This is a good group activity for learners of any age, provided that learners need extra practice with suffixes. The game can be played as a contest in which learners take the cards for the words they match; the player with the most cards when all the cards are taken wins.

Things You'll Need: Playing cards with pairs of words that do and do not have suffixes (described in Appendix B).

Exploration and Guided Practice: Nearly all learners will be familiar with this old standby, so little explanation is needed. Enjoy this activity with learners or leave it in learning centers. Flip-up Suffixes also makes a good activity for learners to enjoy during their free time. Another version of this activity is to write words that have prefixes added, such as **play** and **replay** or **lit** and **unlit**.

❋ Creative Compounds

In this activity, first through third grade learners put two everyday words together to create their own unique compounds.

Things You'll Need: Large pieces of white construction paper; pencils, crayons, or colored markers.

Exploration and Guided Practice: Explain that learners are to think of two words they use every day and then put those words together to make a brand-new compound word. Demonstrate how to coin new compounds by writing a few nouns on the chalkboard and then putting two together to form a new, imaginative compound. When learners understand what they are to do, pass out construction paper and crayons or markers. Invite learners to coin their own compounds, to define, and to illustrate the newly coined compounds, as in Figure A–11.

✹ Greek and Latin Prefix/Suffix Posters

This practice activity capitalizes on learners' enthusiasm for poster making, actively involves groups in cooperatively planning and designing posters, calls for thinking analytically about prefixes or suffixes borrowed from Greek and Latin, and provides learners with opportunities to explain and share their work with classmates. This poster making activity is most successful when learners are sixth graders and older.

FIGURE A–11
Coining new compounds gives learners opportunities to creatively use their knowledge of word meaning and to write definitions for the unusual compounds they create.

ToothCoat

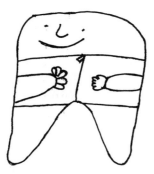

A tooth coat is a coat for your teeth

FIGURE A–11, *continued*

Things You'll Need: Small slips of paper with either a prefix or suffix written on each; tagboard; colorful markers; glue; colored construction paper; scissors; dictionaries for each cooperative group in your classroom.

Exploration and Guided Practice: Invite learners to work collaboratively and cooperatively to create their own posters for prefixes or suffixes borrowed from Greek and Latin. Begin by putting slips of papers that have either a prefix or suffix written on them into a paper sack and asking one learner from each group to randomly draw a prefix or a suffix. Once each group has a prefix or suffix, explain that posters are to be planned carefully and must include (1) a definition of the prefix or suffix; (2) the language from which the prefix or suffix was borrowed; (3) four special words (found in the dictionary or content area textbooks) that are spelled with the prefix or suffix; (4) at least one illustration; and (5) a brief sentence or two telling why this prefix or suffix is especially helpful. Allocate more than one work period for groups to make their posters. Then, when posters are complete, hold a poster-sharing session and invite groups to explain their posters to their classmates.

✳ Greek and Latin Root Roundup

This activity encourages learners to look for meaningful chunks in words, to use dictionaries, and to work together in a spirit of competition among teams. Greek and Latin Root Roundup is suitable for learners who are in the sixth grade and older and who need extra opportunities to pay attention to Greek and Latin roots.

Things You'll Need: The only thing needed is a sheet of instructions for each team that explains Root Roundup rules.

Exploration and Guided Practice: In this activity, cooperative groups find as many different Greek and Latin roots as possible over a five-day period. Greek and Latin roots are to be found in words anywhere inside the school grounds—your classroom, the library, cafeteria, art and music rooms, hallways, and so on. The rules are as follows:

1. Each team is to find as many different words as possible that include Greek or Latin roots. Any word inside the school grounds is fair game, provided that it has a Greek or Latin root in its spelling.
2. Teams are to write words with roots on a sheet of paper and to indicate where words were found. (This can be done by including a sample of the document in which the word is used or by explaining where in the school the word appears, such as on a cafeteria menu.)
3. A dictionary definition must be provided for each word.
4. Each Greek and Latin root must be defined. Teams are given one point for each different word they find that includes a Greek or Latin root. At week's end, the whole class works together to verify words with Greek and Latin roots. Each team shares the words it has found during the week, discusses the roots inside words, and explains the contribution roots make to word meaning. The team that has found the most roots by the end of the fifth day receives an appropriate prize.

REFERENCES

Aardema, V. (1975). *Why mosquitoes buzz in people's ears.* New York: Dial Books for Young Readers.

Buller, J., & Schade, S. (1991). *20,000 baseball cards under the sea.* New York: Random House.

Clements, A. (1988). *Big Al.* New York: Scholastic.

Cole, J. (1992). *The magic school bus on the ocean floor.* New York: Scholastic.

Lord, J. V. (1972). *The giant jam sandwich.* Boston: Houghton Mifflin.

Wild, M. (1987). *There's a sea in my bedroom.* Worthington, OH: Willowisp Press.

MATERIALS AND TECHNIQUES FOR LEARNING ACTIVITIES

DIRECTIONS FOR MAKING MATERIALS FOR LEARNING ACTIVITIES

The following are directions for making materials for learning activities referred to in the text. The places where the activities are mentioned in the text are given.

Bag Books

Referred to in Chapter 5
Bag books are stories written by learners in which pages are put inside plastic bags (see Figure 5–10 in Chapter 5). The bags are fastened together to make a book that is sturdy and convenient to read. To make these books, use gallon-size plastic bags that lock at the top. Place each page of the stories learners write inside a bag and then seal it. When all the pages are inside bags, use a paper punch to make two or three holes on the far left of the bags. Put colorful ribbon through holes and tie the ribbon into bows. This fastens the books together.

Bingo Cards

Referred to in Appendix A, Recommended in Chapter 7
To make bingo cards, create a prototype card by drawing a square on a piece of stiff paper and then dividing the square into five rows of five boxes each. Duplicate the paper (which serves as a bingo card) and then fill in words with letter neighborhoods as needed for the focus of instruction. You can create lots of variations. Be sure to use a variety of words with neighborhoods and place them in different boxes on the cards. Laminate cards if you plan to use

them over and over again. Otherwise, toss out the cards when they become soiled or torn.

Egg Words

Referred to in Appendix A

Egg words are formed when two halves of plastic eggs, each with an onset and a rime written on them, are locked together. (The students make words when they match onset and rimes.) To make egg words, write an onset on one half of a colorful plastic egg and a rime on the other half. (Note that the Easter season is the best time of year to purchase plastic eggs in stores. You can find them in a variety of sizes and colors.) Be sure to use a permanent black marker for writing or the ink will smear. You can make matching easy by writing an onset and rime that form a word on egg halves that are the same color or more difficult by mixing colors of egg halves. Keep the eggs in a basket when they are not being used.

Fish for Onsets

Referred to in Appendix A

This activity requires a fishing pole and fish to catch, as well as a plastic bucket. To make the fishing pole, tie a string to a ruler and fasten a small magnet to the end of the string. To make the fish, cut construction paper into the shapes of sea creatures and items found on the beach, such as shells. Write a word on one side of each creature or beach item—the word **dark** for instance. On the other side, write an onset that creates a creature name or beach item when exchanged with the onset in the word—the onset **sh** for example, which makes the word **shark** when the **d** in **dark** is exchanged for the **sh**. Last, fasten a large paper clip to each sea creature or beach item and dump all the creatures and items in the pond (the plastic bucket).

Flip-Up Suffixes

Referred to in Appendix A

Flip-Up Suffixes is a memory game. To make cards for the game in which players match words with suffixes to the same words without suffixes, cut unlined index cards in half and then divide cards into two sets of ten to twenty each. On one set of cards, write words that do not have suffixes, such as **come, slow, interest,** and **toy.** On the other set, write the same words with suffixes added, such as **coming, slowly, interested,** and **toys.** Flip-Up Suffixes is easier when all suffixes are the same, more difficult when a variety of suffixes are used. Laminate cards for longevity and store them in bags that lock. This memory game also works with prefixes, such as **seen** and **unseen; match** and **rematch; paid** and **prepaid.**

Fold-Over Contractions

Referred to in Appendix A

Fold-Over contractions are words on paper strips that fold together to make contractions. (See Figure A–10 in Appendix A.) To make fold-over contractions, give each learner a paper strip about two inches wide and six inches long, and a small piece of masking tape. Then you write two words that can form a contraction on the chalkboard; for example, **are** and **not**. First, learners count the letters (six) and fold their paper strips accordion style to make as many boxes as there are letters in the two words (six). Second, learners write the two words one after the other, putting one letter in each box. In this example, learners write six letters: **a-r-e-n-o-t**. Third, learners write an apostrophe on the small piece of masking tape. Fifth and last, learners turn the accordion into a contraction by (1) folding the square with the letter to be deleted (**o**) under the square with the preceding letter on it (**n**) and (2) putting the masking tape apostrophe at the top to hold the contraction together, thus forming **aren't**.

Letter Cards

Referred to in Chapter 5 and Appendix A

These are cards with single letters written on them. Use white unlined cards. I suggest that you cut 3" X 5" cards into thirds, which results in sections that are roughly 1½ inches. This is a nice size to put into pocket charts. Write one letter on each section. Write in black marker so that learners cannot use color as a cue. Do not use uppercase (capital) letters unless they are needed for a proper noun. Laminate cards to make them last longer.

Letter Neighborhood Word Wheels

Referred to in Appendix A

Letter Neighborhood Word Wheels are two wheels with letter neighborhoods written on them. (See Figure A–8 in Appendix A.) Words are formed when the letter neighborhoods on the two wheels are aligned. To make Letter Neighborhood Word Wheels, cut two wheels out of brightly colored tagboard. One wheel should be about nine inches wide, the other about six inches. Sizes may vary, however, depending on your personal preference, as long as one wheel is larger than the other. On the outermost portion of the large wheel, write letter neighborhoods that come at the beginning of words. On the outermost portion of the small wheel, write letter neighborhoods that come at the end of words. Poke a hole in the center of each wheel and fasten the wheels together with a brad. Now spin the wheels to align letter neighborhoods. Voilà! Words are formed.

Letter Tiles

Referred to in Chapter 5 and Appendix A, and recommended in Chapter 7
Letter tiles are one-inch tiles with letters written on them. Use a laundry marker to write the letters on tiles. Make sure that tiles are fully dry before they are used. When the writing is thoroughly dry, spray the tiles with a matte finish to help them resist smudging. (I usually give tiles two coats of spray.)

Tiles can be purchased at relatively low cost from many tile stores. I have had consistent good luck at the sort of stores that specialize in flooring and carry a good stock of inexpensive tiles. Tiles come in several sizes. You may find loose tiles, but in all likelihood you will find tiles glued to sheets of sturdy mesh. Look for smooth tiles, not rough-finish tiles. Look, too, for tiles that are easy to manage—small tiles, rather than large, heavy ones. Buy tiles the same color, such as white or beige.

For each set of letter tiles, make at least six tiles for frequently used letters such as **b, d, l, m, n, p, r, s, t,** and all of the vowels. Make three tiles for the other letters. (Depending on the words that learners build, you may want to make more or fewer than six tiles for specific letters.) With these tiles, learners build words letter by letter, thus creating letter neighborhoods as words are spelled. Store tiles in a plastic container that has a lid and is partitioned into many compartments. The container I use has twenty-four compartments, so I store the letters **x, y,** and **z** together in one compartment. Look for containers in the fishing or tool section of large discount department stores or hardware stores. Containers are inexpensive, and the lid ensures that the tiles do not spill. Or store letter tiles in bags that lock and put the bags in sturdy shoe boxes.

Mini-Chalkboards

Referred to in Chapter 4 and recommended in Chapter 7
Mini-chalkboards are lap-size chalkboards on which learners write words during whole-group activities. A helpful hint is to get lots of old socks to use as erasers. Put a piece of chalk in the toe of each and store socks right along with the mini-chalkboards. This way learners have an eraser (the sock) and chalk all rolled into one. With eraser and chalk always available, the mini-chalkboards are very convenient to use!

Movie Projectors

Referred to in Chapter 5
Homemade movie projectors are made from cardboard boxes. Learners put "homemade" movies on butcher paper and show them on the projectors. To begin, get a plain cardboard box and two dowels. Then cut a rectangle in the bottom of a box to serve as a viewing screen. Cut two sets of holes on either

side of the box: Cut one set toward the top of the box (one above the screen), the other toward the bottom (one below the screen). Make the holes large enough for a dowel to fit through. Slide each dowel through one set of holes. Now, working through the back of the box, tape the movie to the dowels. Wind the entire movie around one dowel; wind only the lead (the blank butcher paper that precedes the movie frames) around the other dowel. Turn the dowels to simulate a movie as the paper film moves from one dowel to another (Figure B–1). Adjust the tension by turning either the top or bottom dowel. Advise learners to make the pictures and text a little smaller than the actual frame. This way there is some leeway just in case the frames drawn on butcher paper are not positioned on the movie screen quite right.

Muffin Tin Words

Referred to in Appendix A and recommended in Chapter 7

Find old muffin tins (yard sales and secondhand shops are great sources). Put an assortment of onset and rime tiles (see "Onset-Rhyme Tiles" on the following page) in each compartment of the muffin tin. Tape a small label above each compartment to tell which onset or rime tile is inside. To make a paper guide for muffin words (see Figure A–3 in Appendix A), draw several circles on a sheet of blank paper to simulate a row on a muffin tin. Then write a word above the simulated muffins. Underline a rime or an onset in the word. Learners then build words that share the underlined onset or rime, and write them in the "muffins."

Onset-Rime Cards

Referred to in Chapter 4

These are unlined cards that have either onsets or rimes written on them. Use black ink, write in lowercase letters, and laminate for longevity. Store them in envelopes with labels telling the kinds of onsets and rimes that are inside.

FIGURE B–1
Movie projectors made of a cardboard box, dowels, and butcher paper are inexpensive, sturdy, and reusable.

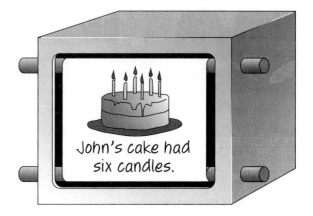

Onset-Rime Tachistoscopes

Referred to in Appendix A

Tachistoscopes are devices that reveal words one at a time. (See Figure A–2 in Appendix A.) To make a tachistoscope, write onsets on a strip of tagboard. Then cut a medium-size shape out of tagboard to serve as the body of the tachistoscope. You can use all sorts of shapes for the body—airplanes, panda bears, ice cream cones, telephones, cereal boxes, valentines, the sky's the limit. Next write a rime on the tachistoscope and cut a window (two horizontal slits) beside the rime. Make the window large enough so that the strip with onsets can be threaded through. When the strip is pulled through the tachistoscope, different words are formed.

Onset-Rime Tiles

Referred to in Chapter 4 and Appendix A

Onset-Rime tiles are ceramic tiles about 1½ inches square, with onsets and rimes written on them. See the instructions for "Letter Tiles" on page 186 for specifics about the types of tiles to purchase. Use a laundry marker to write onsets on some tiles, rimes on others. Wait until tiles are thoroughly dry and then spray them with matte finish. The matte finish will help tiles resist smudging. (I recommend two coats of matte finish for the maximum effect.) Store the onset-rime tiles in a plastic container that has a lid and is partitioned into many small compartments. Inexpensive plastic containers may be purchased at large discount stores or perhaps hardware stores. If you do not use a plastic container, store tiles in bags that lock and put the bags in a sturdy shoe box.

Pocket Charts

Referred to in Chapters 2, 4, and 5 and in Appendix A

Pocket charts are hanging charts that have rows of pockets in which cards with words, rimes, letters, and meaningful chunks are placed. The idea is to show learners how words form sentences and how letters (onsets, rimes, letters, and meaningful chunks) form words. Pocket charts can be purchased from school supply stores and from catalogs. I suggest that you order the largest pocket chart available. This way you are ensured of enough room to build words and sentences.

Rime Tic-Tac-Toe

Referred to in Appendix A

This is a version of the traditional tic-tac-toe game, in which players write words in spaces that have the same onset or rime as a word written on the top of the page instead of **X**s and **O**s as they play. To make tic-tac-toe cards, draw the traditional nine-box design on tagboard or heavy paper. Above the design, write two rimes (if the rimes are real words, such as **at** and **an**) or two words with different rimes, one rime or word with a rime for each player. For example, a tic-tac-toe card might have **bat** at the top for one player and might have **bug** at the top for the other player. If words with rimes are written at the top of cards such as **bat** and **bug**, underline the rime in each word. Laminate cards and ask learners to use erasable markers when they play. This way the same cards may be used many times. This game can be used for letter neighborhoods, prefixes, and suffixes. To do this, write two words with different letter neighborhoods, prefixes, and suffixes at the top of the cards.

Salt Spelling

Referred to in Appendix A
Salt spelling requires a shallow, covered container about nine inches by twelve inches (or slightly larger) for each learner. Put a small amount of salt in the bottom of the container. Learners spell by writing letter by letter in the salt, pushing salt to one side as their fingers move. For this reason, the salt layer must cover the bottom of the container, but not be too deep. If salt is too deep, learners will not be able to make a clear pathway with their fingers. Put covers on the containers when they are not in use and stack them to store. (Colored sand works just as well as salt, and it adds a certain pizzazz to the activity.) Additionally, you will need cards that have a sentence from a familiar book on one side and a single word from the sentence on the other side (these are to supply the words for learners to spell).

Sandpaper Words

Referred to in Appendix A
Learners can trace words made of sandpaper letters to gain experiences in blending sounds and to internalize spellings. To make sandpaper words, find fine-grade pieces of sandpaper—pieces that are not too rough. Cut out lower-case letters and sequence them to form words. Glue words (one letter at a time) to sheets of stiff tagboard or to cardboard. This way letters stay in place and learners can trace over letters one by one to form words. Put the sandpaper words in flat, covered containers and stack the containers in the closet or on a shelf.

Sound Box Cards

Referred to in Chapter 2
Sound Box Cards are cards with boxes drawn on them. Cards like these are used in Reading Recovery lessons and recommended by Clay (1985). Each box on a card represents a sound heard in a spoken word. To make sound box

cards, draw a large rectangle and then divide it into two, three, or four boxes or more. Laminate the cards to increase longevity. You may also want to color code cards. For example, all cards with two boxes could be blue, those with three boxes could be green, and so on. Learners still have to think analytically about the sounds in words in order to decide which Sound Box Card to select. So, in this instance, color does not detract from learning. If you plan to use words with different numbers of sounds in one lesson and if you are working with a group of learners, color coding works well: With color-coded cards, you will know at a mere glance whether learners have selected the card with the number of boxes that matches the number of sounds in a word. I suggest that you laminate cards. Otherwise, cards quickly become soiled.

Techniques for Reading Classroom Walls, Windows, and Doors

Referred to in Chapter 4

This activity, which is described in Chapter 4, challenges learners to read everything on the walls of the classroom. However, when reading wall charts that are tacked to windows, it is easy to lose one's place. Since it is important that learners focus their attention on the words they read in sentences and stories, I suggest that you ask learners to point to each word as it is read. This develops a good match between what is read (the voice) and what is seen (the written words). For pointing to words high on wall charts, tacked on windows, and pasted on doors, learners need a pointer. I recommend using a yardstick. Yardsticks make good pointers because they are long enough to reach words in high-up sentences, lightweight, easy to store, and, of course, usable for other purposes. It is also fun to give learners who are reading classroom words something special to wear, such as a special hat, a colored shirt, or a brightly colored pin. This serves two purposes. First, it makes reading the classroom walls special. Second, it lets you know instantly what learners are doing, which makes classroom management easier.

Tiles for Listening for Sounds Activity

Referred to in Chapter 2

Tiles are one-inch ceramic squares. You might find them glued to mesh sheets in some tile stores; in other stores, you may find loose tiles. Use many different-colored tiles. Learners move the tiles when they hear individual sounds. If you cannot find tiles, colored squares of tagboard will work.

3-D Objects

Referred to in Chapter 7

Learners who speak languages other than English at home benefit when they have opportunities to see and touch objects combined with spoken language and written language. It is much more meaningful, not to mention fun, to talk and write about things in learners' environments. A big orange pumpkin, coins from Mexico, pairs of chopsticks, a globe, a toy car, life-size plastic food, miniature farm animals—all make wonderful learning tools. Look for such items at yard sales or in the bargain section of your local variety store. For example, rather than asking learners to arrange word cards in alphabetical order, challenge learners to arrange small plastic replicas of a horse, pig, fence, and cow in alphabetical order and to match objects with word cards, cross-checking with the ABC chart. When exploring letter neighborhoods such as the **Vr** (**r-controlled**) neighborhood, you might bring to school a fork, a shirt, a toy horse, and so on. Write the words on the chalkboard, make sentences with words, and point out the **Vr** letter neighborhood in the words. Then challenge learners to look around their own homes to find things that are spelled with the **Vr** neighborhood. Use 3-D objects whenever possible as learners talk and write about various topics, and make sure to call learners' attention to the words, onsets, rimes, letter neighborhoods, and meaningful chunks in written language.

Windows for Words

Referred to in Chapter 2

Windows are pieces of tagboard with rectangles cut out of the center. The purpose of windows is to call attention to specific words, onsets, rimes, letter neighborhoods, or meaningful chunks (Clay, 1985). All you do is cut a rectangle in a piece of tagboard or plain white construction paper, and place the window over print so that only the word, onset, rime, letter neighborhood, or meaningful chunk shows. My advice is to use tagboard sentence strips for windows if you are going to highlight print on large charts. For print in books, use small pieces of plain white construction paper or tagboard. Windows make it easier to call attention to specific segments of text, whether these segments are words, onsets, rimes, letter neighborhoods, or meaningful chunks. It is important, however, to always refer to the whole sentence after calling attention to the print revealed in the window. This way learners think about our alphabetic writing system in the context of large, meaningful sentences and stories.

Word Cards

Referred to in Chapter 5 and in various activities in Appendix A

Word cards are index cards or pieces of paper with individual words written on them. Make small word cards out of 3" X 5" white unlined cards by cutting them into fourths, resulting in pieces of roughly ¾" X 1¼", or write them on small pieces of stiff paper, such as construction paper. Use 3" X 5" or 4" X 6" cards to make large word cards. Write the words in black ink; otherwise, learners may use cues based on color. Write words from wall charts, storybooks, novels, textbooks, and learners' writing. Margarine containers with lids make great places to store small word cards. Write the selection of words (or the various types of words) in masking tape on the lid of each container so that you instantly know the types of words stored inside. Store large cards in envelopes on which you have written the types of words found inside. For example, one label might read: Words spelled with the **at** rime; another might read words with **t** as an onset.

Word Worms

Referred to in Appendix A

Make Word Worms out of colorful construction paper. (See Figure A–6 in Appendix A.) Cut out as many heads as there are worms to be formed. Decorate the heads with eyes, noses, big smiles, and any other fanciful attributes. On each head, write one onset (such as **spr**). Cut out body sections from construction paper. Make the sections simple circles and on each write one or more letter neighborhoods (such as **ay** or **inkle**). When the onset neighborhood on the head is combined with the letter neighborhoods on the body, words are formed (**spray** and **sprinkle**, for example). Tape or pin the heads and body sections to learners' shirts.

REFERENCE

Clay, M. M. (1985). *The early detection of reading difficulties* (3rd ed.). Portsmouth, NH: Heinemann.

APPENDIX **C**

WORDS WITH RHYMES

Rime	Words
ab	cab, crab, drab, flab, grab, jab, lab, nab, scab, slab, stab, tab, prefab, taxicab
ace	face, brace, grace, lace, pace, place, race, space, trace, aerospace, anyplace, birthplace, boldface, carapace, commonplace, efface, embrace, fireplace, interlace, marketplace, outface, replace, shoelace
ack	back, black, pack, quack, sack, track, attack, backpack, bushwhack, cossack, cutback, drawback, haystack, hijack, horseback, knapsack, piggyback, racetrack, ransack, rickrack, setback, skyjack, tamarack, thumbtack, tieback, wisecrack, zwieback
act	act, fact, abstract, artifact, attract, cataract, compact, contact, contract, detract, distract, extract, impact, intact, interact, protract, react, subtract, transact
ad	bad, clad, dad, fad, glad, had, lad, mad, pad, sad, dyad, ironclad, keypad, nomad, triad
ade	blade, fade, grade, made, shade, trade, wade, abrade, accolade, arcade, barricade, blockade, brigade, cascade, cavalcade, charade, crusade, decade, dissuade, escapade, evade, handmade, marinade, motorcade, parade, persuade, pervade, renegade, tirade
ag	bag, brag, crag, drag, flag, gag, lag, nag, rag, sag, shag, slag, snag, stag, tag, wag, beanbag, carpetbag, handbag, mailbag, ragtag, saddlebag, scalawag, zigzag
ail	bail, fail, grail, hail, jail, mail, nail, pail, rail, sail, snail, tail, trail, airmail, assail, bewail, bobtail, coattail, contrail, curtail, derail, detail, entail, fingernail, handrail, hangnail, hobnail, monorail, ponytail, prevail, retail, toenail, topsail, travail

ain   brain, chain, drain, gain, grain, main, plain, sprain, stain, train, abstain, appertain, ascertain, attain, complain, constrain, contain, detain, disdain, domain, entertain, eyestrain, explain, ingrain, maintain, ordain, pertain, refrain, restrain, sustain, terrain

air   air, chair, fair, flair, hair, lair, pair, stair, affair, armchair, corsair, debonair, despair, eclair, horsehair, impair, mohair, wheelchair, wirehair

ake   bake, brake, cake, fake, flake, lake, make, rake, shake, snake, stake, take, wake, awake, cheesecake, clambake, cupcake, forsake, fruitcake, grubstake, handshake, keepsake, mistake, muckrake, namesake, overtake, pancake, partake, snowflake

all   ball, call, fall, hall, mall, small, squall, stall, tall, wall, appall, baseball, befall, carryall, catchall, coverall, downfall, enthrall, eyeball, fireball, football, forestall, install, meatball, nightfall, overall, pitfall, rainfall, seawall, snowball, snowfall, stonewall

ame   blame, came, fame, flame, frame, game, lame, name, same, shame, tame, became, mainframe, nickname, overcame, surname

amp   camp, champ, clamp, cramp, damp, lamp, ramp, scamp, stamp, tramp, vamp, decamp, firedamp, revamp, sunlamp

an   bran, can, fan, man, pan, plan, ran, scan, span, tan, than, van, afghan, airman, bedpan, began, caravan, divan, dustpan, fireman, mailman, rattan, sampan, seaman, sedan, suntan, toucan, wingspan

and   band, bland, brand, gland, grand, hand, land, sand, stand, strand, ampersand, backhand, command, contraband, demand, disband, expand, farmhand, firebrand, handstand, offhand, quicksand, reprimand, understand, withstand

ane   cane, crane, lane, mane, pane, plane, sane, vane, wane, airplane, arcane, germane, humane, hurricane, inane, inhumane, insane, membrane, methane, mundane, octane, profane, propane, seaplane, sugarcane, urbane, urethane, windowpane

ang   bang, clang, fang, gang, hang, pang, rang, sang, slang, sprang, tang, twang, boomerang, mustang, overhang, shebang

ank   bank, blank, clank, crank, dank, drank, flank, frank, lank, plank, prank, rank, sank, shank, shrank, spank, stank, swank, tank, thank, yank, gangplank, outflank, outrank, riverbank, sandbank

ant   ant, cant, chant, grant, pant, plant, rant, scant, slant, decant, eggplant, enchant, extant, gallivant, houseplant, implant, supplant, sycophant, transplant

ap   cap, clap, flap, gap, lap, map, nap, scrap, slap, snap, strap, tap, trap, wrap, bootstrap, burlap, catnap, entrap, firetrap, ginger-

	snap, handicap, hubcap, kidnap, mishap, mousetrap, overlap, pinesap, stopgap, thunderclap, wiretap
are	blare, dare, fare, flare, glare, hare, mare, pare, rare, scare, share, snare, spare, square, stare, tare, ware, airfare, aware, beware, compare, declare, ensnare, fanfare, hardware, nightmare, prepare, stemware, threadbare, welfare
arm	arm, charm, farm, harm, alarm, disarm, firearm, forearm, rearm, sidearm, underarm, yardarm
art	art, cart, chart, dart, kart, mart, part, smart, start, tart, apart, counterpart, depart, impart, outsmart, pushcart, rampart, restart, upstart
at	bat, cat, chat, fat, flat, gnat, hat, mat, pat, rat, sat, scat, slat, spat, that, acrobat, autocrat, bobcat, brickbat, bureaucrat, butterfat, chitchat, combat, copycat, democrat, diplomat, doormat, format, habitat, hemostat, muskrat, nonfat, photostat, rheostat, wildcat
atch	catch, latch, match, patch, scratch, snatch, thatch, crosspatch, dispatch, outmatch, potlatch, rematch, unlatch
ate	crate, date, fate, gate, late, mate, plate, rate, sate, skate, slate, state, abate, calculate, candidate, create, debate, disintegrate, dissipate, donate, elate, elevate, estimate, excavate, inmate, irate, irritate, locate, migrate, motivate, mutate, negate, notate
ay	bay, clay, day, gay, gray, hay, lay, may, pay, play, ray, say, stay, stray, sway, tray, way, allay, anyway, ashtray, away, betray, birthday, castaway, dismay, doorway, foray, freeway, gateway, hearsay, holiday, mainstay, payday, portray, relay, someday, subway
eal	deal, heal, meal, peal, real, seal, squeal, steal, teal, veal, zeal, appeal, conceal, congeal, cornmeal, ideal, piecemeal, oatmeal, ordeal, repeal, reveal, surreal
eam	beam, cream, dream, gleam, ream, seam, scream, steam, team, airstream, daydream, inseam, midstream, moonbeam, sunbeam, upstream
ear	clear, dear, ear, fear, gear, hear, near, rear, sear, shear, smear, spear, tear, year, appear, arrear, disappear, endear
eat	beat, bleat, cheat, cleat, heat, meat, neat, peat, pleat, seat, treat, wheat, browbeat, buckwheat, defeat, downbeat, drumbeat, entreat, heartbeat, mincemeat, offbeat, overheat, repeat, retreat, upbeat
eck	check, deck, fleck, heck, neck, peck, speck, wreck, bedeck, bottleneck, breakneck, crookneck, flyspeck, henpeck, paycheck, redneck, roughneck, shipwreck
ect	aspect, bisect, collect, connect, correct, deflect, deject, detect, dialect, direct, dissect, effect, eject, infect, insect, inspect,

intersect, neglect, object, perfect, protect, reflect, respect, select, subject

eed   bleed, breed, creed, deed, feed, freed, greed, heed, need, reed, speed, steed, tweed, weed, airspeed, aniseed, birdseed, exceed, inbreed, indeed, linseed, misdeed, nosebleed, proceed, ragweed, seaweed, succeed

een   between, green, keen, queen, screen, seen, sheen, spleen, teen, canteen, careen, eighteen, evergreen, foreseen, fourteen, Halloween, overseen, sunscreen, tureen, velveteen, windscreen

eep   beep, cheep, creep, deep, jeep, keep, peep, seep, sheep, sleep, steep, sweep, weep, asleep, oversleep, upkeep

eer   cheer, deer, jeer, leer, peer, queer, sheer, sneer, steer, veer, career, commandeer, domineer, engineer, mountaineer, musketeer, pioneer, reindeer, veneer, volunteer

ell   bell, cell, dell, dwell, fell, quell, sell, shell, smell, spell, swell, tell, well, yell, barbell, befell, bluebell, bombshell, doorbell, eggshell, farewell, foretell, inkwell, nutshell, oversell, stairwell

end   bend, blend, fend, lend, mend, send, spend, tend, trend, vend, addend, amend, append, ascend, attend, commend, comprehend, condescend, contend, defend, depend, descend, dividend, expend, extend, intend, offend, portend, pretend, subtrahend, suspend, upend

ent   bent, cent, rent, scent, sent, spent, tent, went, cement, consent, event, extent, foment, intent, invent, lament, orient, percent, resent

ept   crept, kept, slept, swept, wept, accept, adept, concept, crept, except, inept, intercept, overslept, percept, precept, transept, upswept, windswept

ert   pert, alert, assert, avert, concert, controvert, covert, culvert, desert, dessert, disconcert, divert, exert, expert, extrovert, inert, insert, introvert, invert, overt, pervert, revert, subvert

est   best, chest, crest, guest, jest, lest, nest, pest, quest, rest, vest, west, wrest, zest, armrest, arrest, attest, bequest, congest, conquest, contest, detest, digest, divest, infest, ingest, invest, request, suggest

et   bet, get, jet, let, met, net, pet, set, vet, wet, yet, abet, alphabet, bayonet, cadet, dragnet, duet, egret, forget, inlet, parapet

ick   brick, chick, click, crick, flick, kick, lick, nick, pick, prick, quick, sick, slick, stick, thick, tick, trick, wick, airsick, derrick, gimmick, handpick, homesick, limerick, lipstick, maverick, sidekick, rollick, seasick, yardstick

ict	strict, addict, afflict, conflict, contradict, convict, depict, derelict, district, edict, evict, inflict, interdict, predict, restrict, verdict
id	did, grid, hid, kid, lid, skid, slid, squid, acid, arid, aphid, avid, candid, carotid, cuspid, fervid, flaccid, florid, fluid, frigid, horrid, humid, insipid, intrepid, languid, liquid, livid, rapid, rigid, solid, sordid, splendid, squalid, tepid, timid, torpid, valid, vapid, vivid
ide	bride, chide, hide, pride, ride, side, slide, stride, tide, wide, abide, aside, astride, bromide, chloride, collide, confide, decide, dioxide, divide, fireside, fluoride, outside, oxide, peroxide, preside, provide, reside, roadside, subside, suicide, sulfide
ig	big, brig, dig, fig, jig, pig, rig, sprig, swig, twig, wig, bigwig, shindig
ight	bright, fight, flight, fright, knight, light, might, night, plight, right, sight, slight, tight, airtight, alright, copyright, daylight, delight, firelight, fortnight, headlight, highlight, hindsight, limelight, midnight, skylight, spotlight, starlight, stoplight, tonight, twilight
ill	bill, chill, dill, drill, fill, frill, gill, grill, hill, kill, mill, quill, sill, skill, spill, still, swill, thrill, till, twill, anthill, distill, doorsill, downhill, fiberfill, foothill, freewill, fulfill, goodwill, handbill, instill, landfill, playbill, sawmill, treadmill, windchill, windmill
im	brim, dim, grim, him, prim, rim, shim, skim, slim, swim, trim, vim, cherubim, seraphim
ime	chime, crime, dime, grime, lime, prime, slime, time, anytime, bedtime, daytime, lifetime, lunchtime, maritime, mealtime, meantime, nighttime, noontime, overtime, pantomime, ragtime, sometime, sublime, teatime
in	chin, grin, pin, skin, spin, thin, tin, twin, win, akin, begin, chagrin, doeskin, kingpin
ind	bind, blind, find, grind, hind, kind, mind, rind, wind, behind, humankind, mankind, mastermind, rebind, remind, rewind, spellbind, unkind, unwind, womankind
ing	bring, cling, ding, fling, king, ring, sing, sling, sting, string, thing, wing, wring, zing, anything, awning, bedspring, bowstring, bullring, downswing, drawstring, earring, hamstring, handspring, latchstring, offspring, plaything, shoestring, upswing, wellspring
ink	ink, blink, brink, chink, clink, drink, fink, kink, link, mink, pink, rink, shrink, sink, slink, stink, think, wink, hoodwink
int	dint, flint, glint, hint, lint, mint, print, quint, splint, sprint, squint, stint, tint, blueprint, footprint, imprint, newsprint, peppermint, skinflint, spearmint, thumbprint, voiceprint

ip	chip, clip, dip, drip, flip, grip, hip, lip, nip, quip, rip, ship, sip, skip, slip, snip, strip, tip, trip, whip, zip, airship, catnip, equip, fingertip, flagship, kinship, outstrip
ire	dire, fire, hire, mire, shire, sire, squire, tire, wire, acquire, admire, aspire, attire, backfire, bonfire, conspire, desire, empire, entire, esquire, inquire, inspire, perspire, quagmire, require, respire, retire, sapphire, satire, shire, vampire
ish	dish, fish, swish, wish, abolish, accomplish, anguish, astonish, banish, blemish, catfish, cherish, codfish, dervish, establish, famish, fetish, finish, furbish, furnish, garish, garnish, lavish, nourish, perish, publish, punish, radish, ravish, relish, varnish
it	bit, fit, hit, kit, knit, lit, pit, quit, sit, skit, wit, acquit, admit, commit, credit, emit, omit, permit, retrofit, submit, transmit
itch	ditch, flitch, glitch, hitch, itch, pitch, snitch, stitch, switch, twitch, witch, backstitch, bewitch, hemstitch, topstitch, unhitch
ob	blob, cob, glob, gob, job, knob, lob, mob, rob, slob, snob, sob, throb, corncob, doorknob, hobnob, kabob
ock	block, clock, crock, dock, flock, frock, knock, lock, rock, shock, smock, sock, stock, bedrock, deadlock, gamecock, hemlock, livestock, o'clock, padlock, peacock, roadblock, shamrock
og*	bog, clog, cog, dog, fog, flog, frog, grog, hog, jog, log, slog, smog, analog, backlog, bulldog, bullfrog, catalog, dialogue, eggnog, epilogue, hedgehog, leapfrog, polliwog, underdog, watchdog, waterlog
oil	boil, broil, coil, foil, soil, spoil, toil, airfoil, charbroil, embroil, hydrofoil, parboil, recoil, subsoil, tinfoil, topsoil, trefoil, turmoil
oke	awoke, broke, choke, coke, joke, poke, smoke, spoke, stoke, stroke, woke, yoke, artichoke, backstroke, bespoke, cowpoke, evoke, heatstroke, invoke, keystroke, provoke, slowpoke, sunstroke
old	bold, cold, fold, gold, hold, mold, scold, sold, told, behold, billfold, blindfold, enfold, foothold, foretold, freehold, household, manifold, marigold, outsold, retold, scaffold, tenfold, threshold, toehold, undersold, unfold, uphold
ond	bond, fond, pond, abscond, beyond, blond, correspond, despond, fishpond, frond, millpond, respond, vagabond
one	bone, clone, crone, lone, prone, shone, stone, throne, tone, zone, acetone, alone, backbone, condone, cortisone, enthrone,

---

*Pronunciation of this rime may vary for learners in different regions.

	flagstone, headphone, hormone, limestone, methadone, monotone, ozone, postpone, silicone, telephone, wishbone
ong	bong, gong, long, prong, song, strong, thong, tong, wrong, along, furlong, headlong, headstrong, lifelong, oblong, prolong, sarong, sidelong, singsong, scuppernong, tagalong
op	chop, crop, drop, flop, hop, mop, pop, prop, shop, stop, top, airdrop, backdrop, bellhop, blacktop, dewdrop, doorstop, gumdrop, hardtop, hilltop, lollipop, outcrop, raindrop, rooftop, tabletop, teardrop, treetop, workshop
ope	cope, dope, grope, hope, lope, mope, rope, scope, slope, antelope, envelope, gyroscope, horoscope, interlope, isotope, microscope, periscope, telescope, tightrope
ore	chore, more, score, shore, snore, spore, store, tore, wore, adore, anymore, before, bookstore, carnivore, commodore, deplore, drugstore, encore, explore, folklore, herbivore, ignore, implore, seashore, semaphore, sophomore, therefore
orm	dorm, form, norm, storm, brainstorm, chloroform, conform, deform, hailstorm, inform, landform, outperform, perform, platform, reform, transform, uniform, windstorm
ort	fort, port, sort, tort, abort, airport, assort, carport, cavort, cohort, comport, consort, contort, davenport, deport, distort, escort, exhort, export, extort, import, passport, purport, report, resort, retort, short, snort, sport, support, transport
ot	blot, clot, cot, dot, got, hot, knot, lot, not, plot, pot, shot, spot, trot, allot, apricot, ascot, ballot, cannot, despot, earshot, feedlot, forgot, gunshot, inkblot, jackpot, mascot, ocelot, robot, shallot, sunspot, teapot
ought	ought, bought, brought, drought, fought, sought, thought, wrought, besought, bethought
ound	bound, found, ground, hound, mound, pound, round, sound, wound, abound, aground, around, astound, compound, confound, expound, impound, inbound, outbound, profound, propound, rebound, resound, runaround, snowbound, surround, wolfhound
out	bout, clout, flout, pout, scout, shout, snout, spout, sprout, trout, about, bailout, blackout, blowout, brownout, cookout, cutout, devout, dugout, fallout, flameout, handout, hideout, layout, lockout, lookout, printout, tryout, walkout, without
ow	*(long o)* blow, flow, glow, grow, know, low, row, show, slow, snow, throw, aglow, arrow, below, bestow, borrow, bungalow, burrow, elbow, escrow, follow, inflow, marrow, meadow, mellow, minnow, narrow, pillow, rainbow, shadow, shallow
ub	club, cub, grub, hub, nub, pub, rub, scrub, shrub, snub, stub, sub, tub, bathtub, cherub, washtub

uck	buck, chuck, cluck, duck, luck, pluck, snuck, struck, stuck, suck, tuck, truck, amuck, awestruck, mukluk, potluck, woodchuck
uct	duct, abduct, adduct, aqueduct, conduct, construct, deduct, destruct, induct, instruct, misconduct, obstruct, product, reconstruct, viaduct
ude	crude, dude, prude, rude, allude, attitude, collude, conclude, delude, exclude, extrude, fortitude, gratitude, include, interlude, lassitude, occlude, protrude, longitude, magnitude, multitude, platitude, plentitude, rectitude
uff	bluff, buff, cuff, fluff, gruff, muff, puff, ruff, scruff, scuff, snuff, stuff, dandruff, earmuff, foodstuff, handcuff
ug	bug, chug, dug, drug, hug, jug, lug, mug, plug, pug, rug, shrug, slug, smug, snug, thug, tug, bedbug, earplug, firebug, fireplug, humbug
ult	cult, adult, catapult, consult, difficult, excult, insult, occult, result, tumult
um	chum, drum, glum, gum, hum, plum, slum, sum, album, cadmium, calcium, cranium, decorum, eardrum, forum, fulcrum, lithium, maximum, minimum, modicum, optimum, premium, quantum, rostrum, sanctum, serum, stadium, sternum, tantrum, uranium
ump	bump, chump, clump, dump, frump, grump, hump, jump, lump, plump, slump, stump, thump, trump, mugwump
un	bun, fun, gun, nun, pun, run, shun, spun, stun, sun, begun, handgun, homespun
ung	bung, clung, dung, flung, hung, lung, rung, slung, sprung, strung, stung, sung, swung, wrung, hamstrung
unk	bunk, chunk, clunk, drunk, dunk, flunk, funk, hunk, junk, plunk, punk, shrunk, skunk, slunk, spunk, stunk, sunk, trunk, debunk, chipmunk
up	cup, pup, backup, blowup, checkup, holdup, linkup, pickup, roundup, setup, teacup, windup
ure	cure, lure, pure, allure, coiffure, demure, endure, epicure, impure, insecure, manicure, mature, obscure, pedicure, procure, secure
ust	bust, crust, dust, gust, just, lust, must, rust, thrust, trust, antitrust, disgust, distrust, encrust, entrust, sawdust
ut	but, cut, glut, gut, hut, jut, nut, rut, shut, strut, abut, catgut, coconut, crosscut, donut, haircut, halibut, peanut, rebut, shortcut, uppercut, walnut, woodcut

D

LETTER
NEIGHBORHOODS

Consonant Letter Neighborhoods

Single Consonant Neighborhood

Letters in a single consonant neighborhood represent the sounds heard in the following words:

B,b	boat	buffalo	P,p	popcorn	pineapple
C,c	cat	city	Q,q	queen	quack
D,d	dish	donkey	R,r	rabbit	raisin
F,f	fish	fox	S,s	salad	daisy
G,g	game	gem	T,t	toad	turtle
H,h	hat	hippopotamus	V,v	valentine	volcano
J,j	jet	jam	W,w	wagon	wave
K,k	kangaroo	kite	X,x	fox	exit
L,l	lamp	lollipop	Y,y	yellow	barnyard
M,m	monkey	mask	Z,z	zoo	zipper
N,n	nut	nest			

W and **y** act as consonants when they are onsets, as in **wagon**, **wafer**, **yellow**, and **barnyard**.

Though **Y,y** represents the consonant sound heard in **yellow** when it is an onset, **Y,y** also acts as a vowel in many letter neighborhoods.

X,x does not occur in many frequently used words and seldom represents the sound heard in **Xray**, a favorite example in ABC books. Though **X,x** represents several sounds, the sound of "**ks**" in **fox** (particularly at the end of words) and the sound of "**gz**" in **exit** are most common.

Consonants, such as **c**, **g**, and **s**, that represent more than the sound are explained later.

Twin Consonant Neighborhood

Formed whenever the same consonants are immediate neighbors (double letter), the sound represented is usually that of a single consonant neighborhood, as in **rabbit** and **cotton**. When there is a twin consonant in a word, the consonant sound most often goes with the preceding vowel to form a neighborhood, as in **rabbit** ("rab") and **mitten** ("mit"). The exception is when words are joined together to make compounds, in which case both sounds may be heard, as in **headdress** and **bookkeeper**. For the purpose of dividing words into syllables, the syllable division is between the double consonants (**rab-bit, mit-ten**), and the first syllable is most often the syllable that is accented.

In some words spelled with a double **c**, the first **c** represents the sound of "**k**" in **kite** and the second the "**s**" in **save**, as in **accent**, **accept**, and **accident**.

When suffixes are added to some words, such as **slam** and **wrap**, consonants are doubled, as in **slamming** and **wrapped**. Whereas it is easy to infer the pronunciation of the twin consonant neighborhood, it is challenging to learn when (and when not) to double consonants in writing suffixes.

Consonant Blend Neighborhood

The sounds represented by letters in a consonant blend neighborhood are joined together during pronunciation. Knowledge of the single consonant neighborhood transfers to the blend neighborhood, so readers need only learn how sounds are blended together during pronunciation.

Two-Letter Blends

bl Neighborhood	*cl* Neighborhood	*fl* Neighborhood
b + l = bl black	c + l = cl clam	f + l = fl flag
blame	clasp	flake
blanket	class	flame
blaze	clay	flare
bleach	clean	flat
blew	clever	flea
blight	cliff	fleet
blind	clip	flesh
blizzard	clock	flight
block	clod	fling
blond	cloth	float
blouse	cloud	flood
blossom	club	flour
blue	clump	flow
blush	cluster	fluid

gl Neighborhood	*pl* Neighborhood	*sl* Neighborhood
g + l = gl glad	p + l = pl place	s + l = sl slab
glance	plane	slant
glare	planet	slap
glass	plank	sleep
gleam	plant	slice
glen	plastic	slide
glide	play	slim
glimmer	please	slip
glimpse	pledge	slit
glitter	plenty	sliver
globe	plod	slobber
gloom	plot	slogan
glow	plow	slope
glue	plum	slouch
glutton	plus	slow

br *Neighborhood*

b + r = br bracelet
brag
brain
brake
branch
brass
brave
bread
breeze
bride
brim
broil
broom
brown
brush

cr *Neighborhood*

c + r = cr crab
cradle
craft
crash
crawl
cream
creature
crew
crib
cricket
crop
cross
crown
crush
crust

dr *Neighborhood*

d + r = dr dragon
drain
drama
drape
draw
dream
dress
drift
drill
drink
drip
drop
drown
drug
drum

fr *Neighborhood*

f + r = fr frame
frank
free
freeze
fresh
fright
fringe
frock
frog
front
frost
frown
frozen
fruit
fry

gr *Neighborhood*

g + r = gr grab
grain
grand
grape
grass
grateful
great
green
grew
grill
grip
groom
ground
grow
grump

pr *Neighborhood*

p + r = pr prefer
present
press
pretty
pride
prim
print
prize
probe
problem
proof
proud
prove
prude
prune

tr Neighborhood

t + r = tr

track	
trade	
train	
trap	
treat	
tree	
trial	
tribe	
trick	
trim	
troll	
tropic	
trout	
truck	
trunk	

sc Neighborhood

s + c = sc

scale	
scan	
scare	
scarf	
scoff	
scold	
scone	
scoop	
scope	
score	
scotch	
scour	
scout	
scowl	
scuttle	

sk Neighborhood

s + k = sk

skate	
skeleton	
sketch	
skew	
ski	
skid	
skillet	
skim	
skin	
skip	
skirt	
skit	
skull	
skunk	
sky	

sm Neighborhood

s + m = sm

smack	
small	
smart	
smash	
smear	
smell	
smelter	
smile	
smirk	
smock	
smog	
smoke	
smooth	
smudge	
smug	

sn Neighborhood

s + n = sn

snack	
snail	
snake	
snap	
snarl	
sneak	
sneeze	
snicker	
sniff	
snob	
snoop	
snout	
snow	
snub	
snuff	

sp Neighborhood

s + p = sp

space	
spade	
spaghetti	
spark	
speak	
speed	
spell	
spend	
spice	
spider	
spill	
spoon	
sport	
spout	
spun	

st Neighborhood

s + t = st

stack	
stain	
stamp	
station	
steak	
steel	
steeple	
stiff	
still	
stir	
stock	
stone	
stop	
store	
storm	

sw Neighborhood

s + w = sw

swallow	
swamp	
swan	
swarm	
sway	
sweep	
sweet	
swell	
swift	
swim	
swing	
swipe	
swish	
switch	
swoop	

tw Neighborhood

t + w = tw

tweed	
tweezers	
twelve	
twenty	
twice	
twig	
twilight	
twill	
twin	
twine	
twinkle	
twirl	
twist	
twit	
twitch	

Sk, **sm**, **sp**, and **st** occur at the beginning and the end of words, as in **mask**, **prism**, **clasp**, and **last**. All the other two-letter blends occur at the beginning of words, not the end.

The letters **wr** do not form a blend neighborhood. When they are next-door neighbors, the **w** is silent, as in **wrap**, **write**, and **wreck**.

Some letter combinations, such as **nd**, **mp**, **ld**, **nt**, **lk**, and **nk**, form a blend neighborhood at the end of words, as in **stand**, **jump**, **held**, **sent**, **talk**, and **sink**. In my experience, the blend neighborhoods at the end of words are most easily learned as rimes (see Appendix C).

Three-Letter Blends

scr Neighborhood	*spl* Neighborhood	*spr* Neighborhood
s + c + r = scr scram	s + p + l = spl splash	s + p + = spr sprain
scramble	splat	sprang
scrap	splatter	sprawl
scrape	splay	spray
scratch	spleen	spread
scrawny	splendid	spree
scream	splendor	sprig
screech	splice	spring
screen	splint	sprinkle
screw	splinter	sprint
scribe	split	sprite
script	splotch	sprout
scrod	splurge	spruce
scroll		sprung
scrub		spry

squ Neighborhood	*str* Neighborhood
s + qu = squ squabble	s + t + r = str strap
squadron	strawberry
squall	streak
squander	stream
square	street
squaw	strength
squawk	stress
squeak	stretch
squeamish	stride
squeeze	strike
squid	string
squint	stroke
squire	stroll
squirrel	strong
squirt	structure

The following letters in a three-letter blend neighborhood represent two sounds.

chr *Neighborhood*	***sch*** *Neighborhood*	***thr*** *Neighborhood*
ch + r = chr christen	s + ch = sch schedule	th + r = thr thrash
Christmas	schema	thread
chromate	schematic	threat
chromatic	scheme	three
chrome	schizoid	thresh
chromium	schizophrenia	thrift
chromosome	scholar	thrill
chromosphere	scholastic	thrive
chronic	school	throat
chronicle	schoolbag	throne
chronology	schoolhouse	throng
chronometer	schooner	through
chrysalis		throw
chrysanthemum		thrust

Except for the frequently used words **Christmas**, **school**, and **schedule**, **chr** and **sch** are not often present in the words readers and spellers encounter everyday. This is not the case for **thr**, which is part of many words authors routinely use. Young learners (kindergarteners to third graders) read more words with two-letter blends than three-letter blends. It is easier to learn the sound represented by letters in a three-letter blend neighborhood when the two-letter blend neighborhood is learned first.

Consonant Digraph Neighborhood

The letters in a consonant digraph neighborhood represent one sound that is very different from the sounds that the letters represent individually.

ch *Neighborhood*	***ph*** *Neighborhood*	***sh*** *Neighborhood*
chain	phantasy	shade
chalk	phantom	shadow
challenge	pharaoh	shady
change	pharmacy	shark
channel	phase	sheep
check	pheasant	shell
cheer	phenomenon	shelter
cheese	phenotype	ship
cherish	philander	shirt
chili	philosophy	shock
chimpanzee	phobia	shop
chip	phone	short
choose	phoneme	shot
church	photograph	show
churn	physical	shuffle

Other sounds that the **ch** digraph neighborhood represents are the "**sh**" heard in **chagrin** and the "**k**" heard in **choir**. Even though **ch** represents sounds other than that heard in **chirp**, this is the most frequent sound that **ch** represents, and so it is a good sound to try first.

The digraph **ph** commonly represents the "**f**" sound heard in **phone**. Every now and then **ph** represents the sound of "**p**," and sometimes **ph** is silent.

th Neighborhood (Voiceless)	*th* Neighborhood (Voiced)	*wh* Neighborhood
thank	than	what
theater	that	wheat
theft	the	wheel
theme	their	when
thermal	them	where
thick	then	whether
thief	there	which
thimble	these	while
thing	they	whine
think	this	whip
thirst	those	whir
thorn	though	whisk
thumb	thus	whisper
thump	thy	whistle
thunder	thyself	why

The examples show that the digraphs **ch**, **ph**, **sh**, and **th** occur at the beginning of words. These digraphs also occur in the middle of words, such as **franchise**, **dolphin**, **bishop**, and **heathen**, and at the end of words, such as **perch**, **graph**, **fish**, and **teeth**.

The letters **th** represent two sounds—the sound heard in **thank** (called voiceless) and that heard in **than** (called voiced). Advise learners to first try the voiceless "**th**" in **thank** and, if that does not form a contextually meaningful word, to try the voiced "**th**" in **than**.

When **wh** precedes **o**, it represents the "**h**" in **who**. The "**hw**" sound in **white** is much more common, so encourage readers to first try the "**hw**" sound and, if that does not form a meaningful word, to next try the "**h**" sound. However, in some American's speech, the "**h**" is not pronounced in a word such as **white**; just the "**w**" is pronounced. This reflects readers' normal pronunciation and hence should not interfere with word identification.

When the letter **e** follows the digraph **th** at the end of a word, such as in **bathe**, the **th** represents the voiced sound heard in **that**. This explains the difference in pronunciation betweeen **cloth** and **clothe**, and **teeth** and **teethe**.

tch Neighborhood

tch = tch   catch
            crutch
            ditch
            etch
            fetch
            glitch
            hitch
            itch
            latch
            match
            notch
            scotch
            stitch
            stretch
            wretch

Whereas readers should have no trouble inferring that the **t** in **tch** is silent, they must remember to include the **t** in spelling. Hence, **tch** may well be more problematic for spellers than for readers.

The **ck** neighborhood (which represents the sound of "**k**" at the end of words such as **back**) and the **ng** neighborhood are not included here because they are quicker to learn as part of the rimes **ack**, **eck**, **ick**, **ock**, and **uck**, or the rimes **ang**, **ing**, **ong**, and **ung**, as shown in Appendix C.

The letters **gh** also form a digraph neighborhood. As an onset, **gh** represents "**g**," though few English words begin with **gh**. When **gh** is not an onset, there are two options: the **gh** is silent, as in **thigh**, or it represents the "**f**" sound as in **laugh**. When words include the sequence **ght**, the **gh** is silent, as in **bought**, and **night**. Rimes with **gh** are a shortcut to word learning; look in Appendix C for examples.

The qu Neighborhood
When **Q,q** is present in spelling, its next-door neighbor is almost always **U,u**, which acts as a consonant.

Onset "kw" Sound		*Middle "kw" Sound*		*Final "k" Sound*	
q + u = qu	quack	q + u = qu	acquit	q + u + e = que	antique
	quaff		adequate		baroque
	quaint		banquet		bisque
	quake		conquest		boutique
	quality		eloquent		clique
	quantity		exquisite		critique
	quarter		frequent		grotesque
	queen		inquest		oblique
	question		liquid		opaque
	quick		request		physique
	quiet		require		plaque
	quill		sequel		statuesque
	quit		sequin		technique
	quiz		tranquil		torque
	quote		vanquish		unique

Though sometimes **u** is silent, as in **mosquito**, this occurs so seldom that it does not merit specific attention. **Q,q** occurs without **u** in a few words, as in **Iraq**, but this is so rare in English that it does not warrant special consideration either.

S,s as a Next-Door Neighbor

As an onset **S,s** represents the "**s**" heard in **sack**, never "**z**." Only two alternatives, "**s**" or "**z**," are possible when **s** is a middle or ending neighbor in spelling. **S,s** is not troublesome for most readers and spellers. Encourage readers to form a mind-set to attempt pronunciation with the "**s**" first and, if that fails, to try the "**z**."

Onset	*"s" Sound*	*"z" Sound*
sack	arson	amuse
salad	basic	arise
salt	bus	cause
satin	crisis	chisel
seal	dress	closet
seed	essay	cousin
sell	focus	daisy
sick	grass	drowsy
sift	hassle	fuse
sight	house	his
six	person	please
soap	surpass	raise
sock	tassel	resent
soft	toss	those
sun	verse	turquoise

Sure and **sugar** are exceptions, for the **s** in these words represents the sound of "**sh**." This is rare, however.

When **-es** is a suffix as in **dishes** or **washes**, the **-es** represents "**z**."

The letters c and g as the Next-Door Neighbors of a, o, and u

The **ca**, **co**, **cu** Neighborhoods

When **ca**, **co**, and **cu** are immediate neighbors, the **c** usually represents the "**k**" sound heard in **kite** (called a hard sound).

ca Neighborhood	*co* Neighborhood	*cu* Neighborhood
c + a = ca cabbage	c + o = co coach	c + u = cu cube
cabin	code	cuddle
cable	coffee	cuff
cactus	cold	culture
call	color	cunning
camel	comb	cupcake
camp	come	cupid
canary	consider	curb
candle	contest	cure
canteen	control	curious
canvas	cook	curl
cape	copy	curtain
capture	corn	curve
cartoon	cost	custom
castle	cover	cut
avocado	alcove	excuse
brocade	balcony	locust
educate	deacon	focus
placate	falcon	mercury
volcano	glucose	secure

The ga, go, gu Neighborhoods

In the **ga**, **go**, or **gu** neighborhoods, the **g** usually represents the sound associated with the "**g**" in **gate** (called a hard sound).

ga Neighborhood	*go* Neighborhood	*gu* Neighborhood
g + a = ga gable	g + o = go go	g + u = gulch
gag	goal	gulf
gain	goat	gull
galaxy	goblet	gulp
gaily	goblin	gum
gallery	golf	gumbo
gallon	gone	gun
gallop	good	guppy
game	goose	gurgle
gang	gopher	gush
gap	gossip	gust
garden	got	gutter
garlic	govern	guy
gate	gown	guzzle
began	Angora	August
legal	cargo	begun
organ	category	bogus
slogan	jargon	disgust
vulgar	lagoon	yogurt

The letters c and g as the Next-Door Neighbors of e, i, and y
The ce, ci, cy Neighborhoods
In the **ce**, **ci**, and **cy** neighborhoods, the **c** usually represents the sound associated with the "**s**" in **soap** (called a soft sound).

ce Neighborhood	*ci Neighborhood*	*cy Neighborhood*
c + e = ce cedar	c + i = ci cider	c + y = cy cyan
celebrate	cigar	cycle
celery	cinch	cyclist
cell	cinder	cyclone
cement	cinema	cyclops
censor	cinnamon	cygnet
center	circa	cylinder
centigrade	circle	cymbal
central	circuit	cynic
century	circumstance	cynical
ceramic	circus	Cynthia
cereal	citizen	cypress
ceremony	citrus	cyst
certain	city	fancy
certificate	civil	literacy
decent	decide	mercy
excel	excite	pharmacy
faucet	lucid	policy
parcel	pencil	privacy
percent	placid	vacancy

As an onset the **c** in **ci** represents "**s**," but in the middle of words **ci** represents the "**sh**" sound, as in **social**.

The ge, gi, gy Neighborhoods

When **ge**, **gi**, or **gy** are neighbors, the **g** usually represents the sound associated with the "**j**" in **jelly** (called the soft sound).

ge Neighborhood	*gi Neighborhood*	*gy Neighborhood*
g + e = ge gelatin	g + i = gi giant	g + y = gy gym
gem	gibe	gypsy
gender	gigantic	gyrate
gene	gigolo	gyroscope
general	gin	allergy
generic	ginger	analogy
generous	giraffe	apology
genial	gist	biology
genius	angina	clergy
gentle	digit	dingy
genuine	engine	ecology
geology	fragile	effigy
gerbil	frigid	energy
germ	legion	lethargy
gesture	logic	liturgy
digest	magic	orgy
diligent	margin	prodigy
halogen	origin	strategy
urgent	tragic	synergy
wage	virgin	zoology

The combinations **ge** and **gi** are not as dependable as the others. Support learners as they draw the conclusion that when **ge** and **gi** are immediate neighbors, first try the sound of "**j**" in **jelly** and, if that fails, try the sound of "**g**" in **gate**.

Vowel Letter Neighborhoods

VC/VCC Neighborhood

When letters reside in a **VC/VCC** neighborhood, the sounds generally represented by the vowel are short. Short vowel sounds are often indicated by a breve (˘), which is explained in the glossary (see Appendix H). A consonant neighborhood before the vowel forms a **CVC** (**cat**), **CCVC** (**brat**), **CVCC** (**back**), or **CCVCC** (**black**) sequence, and does not affect the sound that the vowel in the **VC/VCC** neighborhood represents.

Short Vowel Sounds

- **a** in **apple**
- **e** in **elephant**
- **i** in **igloo**
- **o** in **olive**
- **u** in **umbrella**

aC(C) Neighborhood	*eC(C) Neighborhood*	*iC(C) Neighborhood*
a + C(C) = act	e + C(C) = bent	i + C(C) = bit
bath	depth	distill
camp	hem	drip
cast	leg	fill
fact	let	lift
gas	men	limp
last	mess	miss
man	nest	mix
match	peg	picnic
pass	pen	pig
path	pet	pin
ramp	press	rib
sad	red	risk
tap	set	sick
tramp	shed	tip

oC(C) Neighborhood	*uC(C) Neighborhood*	*yC(C) Neighborhood*
o + C(C) = dot	u + C(C) = bluff	y + C(C) = abyss
drop	cut	analyst
got	dug	crypt
hot	dust	cyst
job	Dutch	Egypt
lock	fun	hymn
mob	gum	lynch
not	luck	myth
odd	lump	nymph
opt	mud	onyx
pop	mulch	polyps
posh	numb	rhythm
rock	nut	symbol
spot	shrug	syndrome
top	trunk	synergy

Though the vowel in the **VC/VCC** neighborhood generally represents a short sound, in some words the vowel represents a long sound. Advise readers to first try a short sound. This usually results in a meaningful word. Tell readers to try a long sound if the short sound does not form a word that is meaningful in the reading context.

Sometimes the vowel letter in a **VC** and **VCC** neighborhood represents a long sound, as in **cold** (**old**), **bolt** (**olt**), **find** (**ind**), **night** (**ight**), and **child** (**ild**). Additionally, this neighborhood can have more than two consonants, as in the **ulch** in **mulch** and the **ynch** in **lynch**. Considered within the context of rimes, combinations like these are quite predictable. Encourage readers to remember rimes.

VCe Neighborhood

In the **VCe** neighborhood, the **e** is silent and the preceding vowel usually has a long sound, which is often indicated by a macron (⁻) and explained in the glossary. A consonant neighborhood before the vowel forms a **CVCe** (**save**) or a **CCVCE** (**slave**) sequence and does not affect the sound that the vowel in the **VCe** neighborhood represents.

Long Vowel Sounds

- a in **cave**
- e in **gene**
- i in **bike**
- o in **code**
- u in **cube**
- y in **type**

aCe Neighborhood	*eCe* Neighborhood	*iCe* Neighborhood
a + Ce = bake	e + Ce = cede	i + Ce = bike
cage	delete	chive
chafe	effete	dime
chase	mete	hide
date	gene	jibe
face	impede	mice
flake	obese	mime
game	plebe	pile
gave	recede	pine
lane	scene	prize
made	scheme	quite
maze	secede	rile
plate	serene	ripe
tale	theme	rise
wage	these	size

o+Ce Neighborhood	*u+Ce Neighborhood*	*y+Ce Neighborhood*
o + Ce = bone	u + Ce = accuse	y + Ce = acolyte
choke	amuse	analyze
code	cube	argyle
dome	cute	enzyme
doze	demure	genotype
drove	dune	lyre
hose	execute	megabyte
mope	fume	neophyte
note	fuse	paralyze
phone	huge	pyre
probe	immune	rhyme
quote	mule	style
robe	mute	thyme
stole	plume	tyke
those	yule	type

There are some marked exceptions to the **VCe** neighborhood. For one thing, it is not conventional for English words to end in the letter **v**, so **e** is tacked on to avoid spelling **have** as **hav**, **love** as **lov**, and **live** as **liv**. Words spelled with **r** conform to the **r-controlled (Vr)** neighborhood, which explains the pronunciation of **care** and **more**. When the last syllable in a word is **ate** or **ite**, and when the syllable is not stressed in pronunciation, the **a** in **ate** and the **i** in **ite** do not represent a long sound, as in **frigate**, **climate**, **private**, **granite**, **definite**, and **opposite**. Some loan words from French, such as **cafe**, are exceptions, and are pronounced accordingly.

VCCe Neighborhood

In the **VCCe** neighborhood, the vowel generally represents a short sound and the **e** is silent. A consonant neighborhood before the vowel forms a **CVCCe** (**dance**) or **CCVCCe** (**chance**) sequence, and does not affect the sound that the vowel in the **VCCe** neighborhood represents.

ba<u>dge</u>	de<u>nse</u>	inv<u>olve</u>	pri<u>nce</u>
bala<u>nce</u>	fe<u>nce</u>	la<u>nce</u>	ri<u>nse</u>
bri<u>dge</u>	Fra<u>nce</u>	la<u>pse</u>	sa<u>lve</u>
bro<u>nze</u>	fu<u>dge</u>	lo<u>dge</u>	si<u>nce</u>
cha<u>nce</u>	hi<u>nge</u>	nu<u>rse</u>	te<u>nse</u>
da<u>nce</u>	impu<u>lse</u>	plu<u>nge</u>	we<u>dge</u>

The letters **dge** usually represent the sound of "**j**" and the final **e** is silent. Never an onset, **dge** is included in the spelling of many different words and hence readers have ample opportunities to acquire this code knowledge during reading and writing. If the short vowel sound does not result in a meaningful word with a **VCCe** neighborhood, advise readers to try the long sound.

The **VCCe** neigborhood is challenging to spellers inasmuch as the **e** is sometimes dropped when suffixes are added to words, as in **lodging** and **dancing**.

Cle Neighborhood

Ble, **cle**, **dle**, **gle**, **kle**, **ple**, **tle**, and **zle** are typically found at the end of many words and may represent intact units of pronunciation. They are usually pronounced as separate syllables.

ble Neighborhood	*cle* Neighborhood	*dle* Neighborhood
b + le = ble able	c + le = cle article	d + le = dle bridle
audible	barnacle	bundle
bubble	bicycle	candle
double	chronicle	dawdle
enable	circle	fiddle
fumble	cubicle	girdle
marble	cycle	handle
nibble	icicle	hurdle
noble	miracle	middle
pebble	obstacle	muddle
quibble	oracle	needle
ramble	particle	noodle
stable	spectacle	poodle
viable	uncle	puddle
warble	vehicle	riddle

gle Neighborhood	*kle* Neighborhood	*ple* Neighborhood
g + le = gle angle	k + le = kle ankle	p + le = ple ample
bangle	crinkle	apple
beagle	periwinkle	couple
bugle	rankle	crumple
dangle	sparkle	dimple
eagle	sprinkle	example
gargle	tinkle	people
giggle	twinkle	purple
haggle	winkle	sample
jingle	wrinkle	scruple
mingle		staple
single		supple
tangle		temple
toggle		topple
waggle		triple

tle Neighborhood	*zle* Neighborhood
t + le = tle beetle	z + le = zle bamboozle
bottle	dazzle
cattle	drizzle
chortle	embezzle
gentle	fizzle
hurtle	frazzle
little	guzzle
mantle	muzzle
startle	nozzle
subtle	nuzzle
title	puzzle
turtle	sizzle
whittle	

The letters **ble** are pronounced as "**bul**," **cle** as "**kul**," **dle** as "**dul**," **gle** as "**gul**," **kle** as "**kul**," **ple** as "**pul**," **tle** as "**tul**," and **zle** "**zul**." These neighborhoods pose challenges to spellers inasmuch as the **e** is sometimes dropped when suffixes are added to words, as in **bubbly** and **bubbling**. In words such as **whistle** and **trestle**, the **t** is silent. Exceptions are so few that they do not pose a problem and so do not merit special attention.

In words such as **stable**, **cycle**, **cradle**, **bugle**, **wrinkle**, **dimple**, **title**, and **puzzle**, the first vowel either (1) represents a long sound because it is part of a **CV/CCV** neighborhood (as the **CV/CCV** in **sta-ble**) or (2) a short sound because it is in a separate **VC/VCC** neighborhood (as the **VC/VCC** in **puz-zle** in which the twin consonant neighborhood is divided).

VV Neighborhood with an a or e

In the **VV** neighborhoods of **ai**, **oa**, **ay**, **ee**, **ey**, and **ea**, the first vowel represents a long sound and the second is silent.

ai Neighborhood	*oa Neighborhood*	*ay Neighborhood*
bait	boat	bay
brain	cloak	clay
chain	coast	day
faint	float	gay
hail	goal	hay
maid	goat	lay
maim	load	may
paint	loaf	pay
quail	loan	play
raid	oak	ray
sail	road	say
snail	roam	slay
trail	soak	stray
trait	soap	tray
waist	toast	way

ee Neighborhood	*ey Neighborhood*	*ea Neighborhood*
beef	abbey	appeal
creek	alley	beach
creep	barley	cheap
deed	cagey	defeat
feel	covey	dream
feet	donkey	heap
flee	galley	leaf
green	hockey	mean
keep	honey	ordeal
meet	jersey	reap
need	key	reveal
queen	kidney	scream
reef	medley	streak
seem	money	squeal
tree	valley	team

The letter **y** is a vowel when it follows **a** and **e**, thereby creating the **VV** neighborhood of **ay** and **ey**.

Most of the time **ai** represents long **a**, but occasionally it represents the sound heard in **said** (seldom the sound in **plaid**). Tell learners to first try the long **a** sound and, should that fail to create a meaningful word, to try the sound heard in **said**.

The letters **ey** represent the sound of long **e** heard in **key** and the sound of long **a** heard in **they**. Advise readers to first try the sound of long **e** and, if that fails to produce a meaningful word, to try the sound of long **a**.

The letters **ea** sometimes represent the short **e** heard in **head**. Infrequently, they represent a long **a** as in **great**. Advise learners to first try long **e** and, if that does not form a contextually meaningful word, to try short **e**.

When two next-door neighbors are in different syllables, then both vowels represent a separate sound, as in **trial** and **create**.

Double oo Neighborhood

The double **oo** neighborhood usually represents the sound heard in **school** or the sound heard in **book**.

oo in school	*oo in book*
broom	brook
cool	cook
food	crook
hoop	foot
moon	good
pooch	hood
proof	hook
roost	look
scoop	nook
smooth	shook
soon	soot
spook	stood
spoon	tool
tooth	wood
zoom	wool

Advise readers to try one sound and, if that does not result in a sensible word, to try the other sound.

Vowel Diphthong Neighborhood

When **ow**, **ou**, **oi**, and **oy** are immediate neighbors, these combinations often represent the following sounds in pronunciation:

ow in **cow**
oi in **oil**
ou in **out**
oy in **boy**

ow Neighborhood	*oi Neighborhood*	*ou Neighborhood*
brow	boil	bound
brown	broil	cloud
clown	coin	county
cow	doily	flour
cowl	foist	grouch
crowd	join	ground
down	moist	hour
drown	noise	loud
gown	point	mouth
growl	poise	noun
how	soil	ouch
plow	spoil	pouch
scowl	toil	pound
town	voice	scout
wow	void	shout

oy Neighborhood
boy
cloy
convoy
coy
decoy
deploy
employ
enjoy
envoy
foyer
joy
ploy
royal
soy
toy

The letters **ow** also represent the long sound of "**o**" in **crow**, so readers have two sounds from which to choose—the "**ow**" in **cow** and the "**o**" (long **o**) in **crow**. If one sound does not work, the other will.

The letters **oi** may be part of the large chunks **oise** (as in **noise**) and **oice** (as in **voice**). Encourage readers to draw these conclusions during the normal course of reading and writing.

Though the letters **ou** frequently represent the sounds heard in **out** and **cloud**, these two letters represent several other sounds in words; for example, **soul**, **tour**, **group**, **shoulder**, **encourage**, **could**, and **double**. **Your**, **pour**, and **four** are examples of other exceptions to the **ou** neighborhood. However, words such as **your**, **four**, **should**, **would**, and **could** are used with such high frequency that they do not create problems for readers inasmuch as these words are automatically recognized early. If readers cannot identify a contextually meaningful word by associating the sounds heard in **out** and **cloud** with the letters **ou**, encourage them to think of words that are in their speaking and listening vocabularies that include other letter neighborhoods in the words (as the **gr** blend and single consonant letter **p** in **group**, or the single consonant **d** and the **ble** neighborhood in **double**) and that make sense in the reading context.

Vr or r-Controlled Neighborhood

The letter **r** affects pronunciation so that vowels cannot be classified as short or long.

ar Neighborhood	*er Neighborhood*	*ir Neighborhood*
arm	alert	bird
barn	adverb	chirp
car	butter	dirt
chart	ceramic	fir
dark	clerk	firm
far	differ	flirt
farm	exert	girl
hard	fern	shirt
jar	herd	sir
mart	inert	skirt
park	perch	smirk
scar	person	stir
star	stern	third
tar	term	twirl
yard	under	whir

or Neighborhood	*ur Neighborhood*
born	blur
cord	burn
corn	burst
dorm	church
for	curl
fork	fur
horn	hurt
more	lurk
north	nurse
porch	purl
scorn	purr
sport	surf
store	turf
storm	turn
torch	urn

The letters **ar** after **w** represent the sounds heard in **war**, **warn**, and **warm**, not the sound heard in **car**. This, however, is not overly difficult for observant readers to discover.

CV/CCV Neighborhood

In the **CV/CVV** neighborhood, the vowel usually represents a long sound.

C(C)a Neighborhood

C(C) + a =   basin
             canine
             crazy
             flavor
             haven
             label
             labor
             later
             major
             nation
             paper
             sensation
             tiger
             vapor
             volcano

(C)e Neighborhood

C(C) + e =   adrenal
             decal
             decency
             feline
             female
             he
             legal
             me
             meter
             senile
             sequence
             she
             we
             zebra
             zenith

C(C)i Neighborhood

C(C) + i =   bisect
             china
             digest
             giant
             lion
             microscope
             migrant
             minus
             pilot
             primate
             silent
             spider
             tiger
             title
             trifle

C(C)o Neighborhood

C(C) + o =   also
             banjo
             bifocal
             locate
             molar
             moment
             nomad
             October
             poem
             polar
             program
             rotate
             social
             total
             vocal

C(C)u Neighborhood

C(C) + u =   bugle
             cubic
             cucumber
             fuel
             funeral
             future
             human
             humid
             menu
             museum
             music
             nucleus
             puny
             pupa
             tribunal

It is also possible to have a **CCCV** neighborhood in spelling (**strident**). Although three consonants are not included in the examples here, they are, in fact, easy to infer since they conform to the same principle as that of **CV/CCV** sequence.

There are many exceptions to the long vowel sound in **CV/CCV** neighborhoods, particularly if the neighborhood occurs in a syllable that is not accented; for example, the first syllable in **develop**.

Readers may use the following guidelines to help them decide if the sequence of letters in a word is a **CV/CCV** or a **VC/VCC** neighborhood:

1. If there is one consonant letter between two vowels (as the **l** in si<u>l</u>ent), many times the first vowel ends a **CV/CCV** neighborhood and generally is long (si<u>l</u>ent).

2. If there are two consonant letters between two vowel letters as in **crimson** (**ms** between **i** and **o**), the first consonant often goes with the preceding vowel to form a **VC/VCC** neighborhood (**crim**). The first vowel (in this case **i**) is short.

3. The consonant blend neighborhood generally stays intact, as in **se<u>cr</u>et** (se-<u>cr</u>et, where the first **e** is long as part of a **CV/CCV** neighborhood) and **mem<u>br</u>ane** (mem-<u>br</u>ane, where the first **e** is short as part of a **VC/VCC** neighborhood).

4. The consonant digraph neighborhood generally stays intact; for example, **bu<u>sh</u>el** (bu<u>sh</u>-el), **fa<u>th</u>om** (fa<u>th</u>-om), **mar<u>sh</u>al** (mar-<u>sh</u>al).

5. When words end in a **Cle** sequence, the **Cle** is usually an intact neighborhood, as in **sta<u>ble</u>** (sta-<u>ble</u>, long **a** in preceding syllable), **cy<u>cle</u>** (long **i**), **cra<u>dle</u>** (long **a**), **bu<u>gle</u>** (long **u**)—the preceding vowel is part of a **CV/CCV** neighborhood—and in **wrin<u>kle</u>** (short **i**), **dim<u>ple</u>** (short **i**), and **puz<u>zle</u>** (short **u**)—where the preceding vowel is part of a **VC/VCC** neighborhood.

6. Prefixes and suffixes are usually intact units in words, such as the **pre** in **prepaid** (**pre-paid**), and the **ly** in **slowly** (**slow-ly**).

The Letter Y,y as the Final Letter

The letter **y** at the end of words acts as a vowel. When **y** forms a separate final syllable, it generally represents the sound associated with long **e**, as in **bunny** and **silly**. Y,y at the end of words with **no other vowels** represents the sound associated with long **i**, as in **by** and **try**.

Final Syllable (long e)	Only Vowel (long i)
any	by
army	cry
baby	dry
body	fly
bunny	fry
candy	my
city	ply
funny	pry
lady	shy
melody	sky
mercy	spy
silly	spry
study	sty
taffy	try
tiny	why

Tell strategy users to try the sound of long **i** in very short words; the sound of long **e** in longer words. If one sound (long **i** or long **e**) does not work, the other one has a good chance of being correct.

When the **ly** is a suffix as in **deeply** and **cheaply**, it represents long **e**. Advise learners to try both long **e** if they think the **ly** is a suffix and to try long **i** if they think **ply** is part of the base word. If one sound does not work, the other probably will.

The au and aw Neighborhoods

When **a** and **u** are next-door neighbors, the sound they represent is generally that heard in **fault**. When **a** and **w** are adjacent in spelling, they represent the sound heard in **straw**.

au Neighborhood	*aw Neighborhood*
assault	awe
because	brawl
daunt	brawn
exhaust	claw
faun	crawl
flaunt	draw
fraud	gawk
fraught	jaw
haul	lawn
maul	prawn
saucer	shawl
staunch	spawn
taught	squaw
trauma	thaw
vault	trawl

The **au** and **aw** neighborhoods are quite reliable. The combination of **au** does not occur at the end of words. The **aw** neighborhood, on the other hand, is used as an onset (**awe**), in the middle of words (**strawberry**) and at the end of words (**draw**).

The ew and ue Neighborhoods

When **ew** and **ue** are next-door neighbors, these letter combinations usually represent the sound in **blew** and **blue**.

ew Neighborhood	*ue Neighborhood*
blew	argue
brew	avenue
chew	blue
crew	due
crewel	fondue
drew	glue
flew	issue
grew	pursue
jewel	rescue
sewage	revue
shrew	statue
shrewd	tissue
slew	true
strewn	value
threw	virtue

The **ue** neighborhood cannot be counted on to represent the sound heard in **blue** when the **ue** follows a **q** or a **g** in spelling, as in **clique**, **masque**, **mosque**, **guess**, **guest**, **league**, **morgue** and **plague**. When learners have lots of experience reading and writing words spelled with these sequences, they infer the sounds letters represent.

APPENDIX

PREFIXES

Prefix	Meaning	Examples
ab (Latin)	away, from	abscond, abnormal, absent
ad (Latin)	to, toward	advocate, admission
ambi (Latin)	both, around	ambidextrous, ambiance
ante (Latin)	before	antebellum, antechamber
anti (Greek)	against	antibody, antibiotic
circu/m (Latin)	around	circumnavigate, circumference
con, com, co (Latin)	with, jointly, together	conform, combine, coauthor, cohabited
contra (Latin)	against, opposite	contraindicate, contraband
counter (Latin)	against, opposite	counterclaim, counteract
de (Latin)	from, away	debrief, dehumidify
dis (Latin)	apart from, not	disembark, disarm
dys (Greek)	bad, difficult	dysfunctional, dyslexic
epi (Greek)	upon, in addition	epilogue, epicenter, epitaph
extra (Latin)	beyond	extrasensory, extraordinary
hyper (Greek)	excessive	hyperactive, hypercritical
hypo (Greek)	less than normal	hypotonic, hypotension
in (Latin)	not	invisible, ineffective
inter (Latin)	between, among	interact, intermingle
intra (Latin)	within, between	intramural, intracellular
non (Latin)	not	nonsmoker, nonconformist
ob (Latin)	toward, against, in the way of	obstruct, obdurate, objection
para (Greek)	beside, faulty, beyond	paralegal, parody, parachute
peri (Greek)	around, near	peripheral, period, perigee
post (Latin)	behind, after	postdate, postpone
pre (Latin)	in front of, before	predate, prepay
pro (Greek/Latin)	forward, before	pronoun, proactive
re (Latin)	back, again	realign, retell
retro (Latin)	backward, behind	retrofit, retroactive
sub (Latin)	under, inferior	submarine, substandard
super (Latin)	above, in addition	superman, supernatural
trans (Latin)	across, through	transport, transplant
ultra (Latin)	beyond, extreme	ultrasonic, ultraminiature

APPENDIX

SUFFIXES

Suffix	Meaning	Examples
able (Latin)	tending to, capable of	workable, readable
acity (Latin)	inclined to	capacity, tenacity
acy (Latin)	state of being, quality	democracy, bureaucracy
al (Greek/Latin)	relating to	personal, rehearsal, vocal
ance (Latin)	state of being	excellence, acceptance
arch (Greek)	ruler	patriarch, monarch
archy (Greek)	rule by	monarchy, oligarchy
ary (Latin)	place for or where, connected with/ related to	library, dictionary military, budgetary
ate (Latin)	acted	dictate, insulate
cracy (Greek)	kind of government	democracy, bureaucracy
crat (Greek)	one who advocates or practices	democrat, bureaucrat
er	one who more	worker, teacher faster, nicer
ery	quality of, condition place of doing	snobbery, slavery bakery, eatery
est	most	fastest, nicest
ful	quality of	beautiful, plentiful
graph (Greek)	writing	polygraph, telegraph
hood	state, condition	boyhood, neighborhood
ic (Greek/Latin)	like, pertaining to	historic, scenic
ician (Greek)	specialist in	physician, electrician
ics (Greek)	study of	mathematics, genetics
ion (Latin)	act or state of	construction, creation
ish (Latin)	like, nature of	feverish, selfish
ism (Greek)	belief or practice of	feudalism, defeatism
ist (Greek)	one who acts or believes	motorist, defeatist

Suffix	Meaning	Examples
ite (Greek)	connected with resident of	stalactite, socialite, Israelite, Wyomingite
ity (Latin)	state or quality of	alacrity, gravity
less (Latin)	without	ceaseless, fearless
logy (Greek)	science of	biology, zoology
mania (Greek)	extreme enthusiasm for	pyromania, kleptomania
ment (Latin)	result or state of	excitement, retirement
meter (Greek)	measure	diameter, barometer
metry (Greek)	science of measurement	geometry, optometry
(i)mony (Latin)	state or quality of	matrimony, acrimony
ness (Latin)	quality of	fondness, happiness
nomy (Greek)	knowledge of a field or laws governing it	astronomy, economy
oid (Greek)	having shape or form of	alkaloid, humanoid
or (Latin)	one who does, state of	actor, error
ory (Latin)	place for, serving as, characterized by	dormitory, mandatory
ous (Greek)	full of, state of, character of	numerous, nervous, amphibious, fastidious
path (Greek)	one who suffers from a disease	psychopath, sociopath
pathy (Greek)	feeling, disorder	empathy, apathy, neuropathy
phobia (Greek)	abnormal fear of	acrophobia, hydrophobia
scope (Greek)	means of viewing	telescope, horoscope
tomy (Greek)	operation on, incision	lobotomy, tonsillectomy
(i)tude (Latin)	state or quality of	latitude, servitude
ure (Latin)	act or function of	capture, puncture
y (Latin)	quality or state of full of, like	comedy, ability muddy, grassy

APPENDIX

GREEK AND LATIN ROOTS

Roots	Meaning	Examples
aer(o) (Greek)	air, atmosphere	aerial, aerospace
am(o/i) (Latin)	love	amorous, amity
anim (Latin)	mind, feeling	animal, animate
ann (Latin)	year	annual, anniversary
anthr(opo) (Greek)	human	anthropology, philanthropist
archa (Greek)	ancient, primitive	archaeology, archaic
art (Latin)	skill	artist, artifact
aqua (Latin)	water	aquatic, aquarium
ast(er) (Greek)	star	astrology, astronaut
aud (Latin)	hear	audience, auditory
aut(o) (Greek)	self	autobiography, automobile
bar(o) (Greek)	weight, pressure	barometer, barograph
bell(i) (Latin)	war	belligerent, rebellion
bene (Latin)	well, good	beneficial, benevolent
bi (Latin)	two	bicycle, bifocals
biblio (Greek)	book	bibliography, bibliotherapy
bio (Greek)	life	biology, biodegradable
cad (cas) (Latin)	fall	cadence, cascade
cap (Latin)	head	cap, captain, capital
cardi (Greek)	heart	cardiology, cardiogram
carn (Latin)	flesh	carnivorous, carnage
ced (cess) (Latin)	go, yield	concede, proceed
ceiv (Latin)	take, seize	receive, conceive
cent (Latin)	hundred	century, centipede
centr (Greek)	center	centric, centrifugal
cess (Latin)	go, yield	recess, process
chrom(at)(Greek)	color	chromatic, chromosome
chron (Greek)	time	chronicle, chronic
clam/claim (Latin)	shout	proclaim, proclamation
clud (Latin)	shut	conclude, seclude
cord (Latin)	heart	cordial, accord
corp(or,us) (Latin)	body	corporate, corpuscle
cosm (Greek)	universe, order	cosmos, microcosm
cred(it) (Latin)	believe, trust	credible, creditor
cri (Greek)	judge	critic, crisis

Roots	Meaning	Examples
culp (Latin)	blame	culpable, culprit
cycl (Greek)	circle, wheel	cycle, bicycle
deci (Latin)	ten	decimeter, decimal
dem (Greek)	people	democracy, democratic
derm (Greek)	skin	dermatology, epidermis
dic(t) (Latin)	say, speak	dictaphone, dictate
doc(t) (Latin)	teach	indoctrinate, document
dogma (Greek)	opinion, teaching	dogmatic, dogma
duc(t) (Latin)	lead	induce, conduct
dyna (Greek)	power	dynamite, dynamic
ethn (Greek)	race, cultural group	ethnology, ethnic
fac (Latin)	to make, do, see	factory, facsimile
ferv (Latin)	boil, seethe	fervent, fervor
fic (Latin)	do, make	proficient, efficient
fid (Latin)	faith, trust	fidelity, confidential
fin (Latin)	end, limit	final, finite, finish
firm (Latin)	strong, firm	confirm, affirm
flect (flex) (Latin)	bend	flexible, reflex
flor (Latin)	flower, flourish	florist, floral
flu(x) (Latin)	flow	fluid, confluent
frac(t or g) (Latin)	break	fracture, fraction, fragment
gen (Greek)	birth, race, kind	generation, genealogy
ge(o) (Greek)	earth	geography, geology
ger (Greek)	old age	geriatric
gno(s) (Greek)	know	diagnosis, prognosis
gon (Greek)	angle	polygon, hexagon
grad (gress) (Latin)	go, step	graduate, progress
grat (Latin)	pleasing, grateful	gratitude, gracious
grav (Latin)	heavy	gravity, aggravate
hol (Greek)	whole	holistic, hologram
hydr (Greek)	water	hydrant, dehydrate
ject (Latin)	throw	interject, trajectory
judic (Latin)	judge	prejudice, adjudicate
junct (Latin)	join	junction, juncture
jur (Latin)	swear	jury, perjury

Roots	Meaning	Examples
lat (Latin)	carry	relate, translate
later (Latin)	side	lateral, unilateral
liter (Latin)	letter, literature	literal, literate
loc (Latin)	place, put	locate, allocate
log (Greek)	word	dialogue, prologue
luc (Latin)	light	elucidate, lucid
lud (lus) (Latin)	play, mock	ludicrous, illusive
lumin (Latin)	light	luminescent, illuminate
magn (Latin)	great, large	magnitude, magnificent
mal (Latin)	poor, inadequate	malnourished, maladjusted
manu (Latin)	hand	manual, manicure
matr (ern) (Latin)	mother	maternal, maternity
micr (Greek)	small, one millionth	microphone microgram
mili (Latin)	soldier	military, militant
mill (Latin)	thousand	millimeter, millipede
misc (Latin)	mix, mingle	miscellaneous promiscuous
mit (Latin)	send, soften	transmit, remit, mitigate
mon(it) (Latin)	warn, advise	monitor, admonish
morph (Greek)	shape or form	endomorph, morphology
mort (Latin)	death	mortician, mortal
mov, mot (Latin)	move	move, motion, emotion
multi (Latin)	many, much	multiple, multidimensional
mut (Latin)	change	mutate, mutual
nat (Latin)	born	native, nation
neg (Latin)	deny	negative, renegade
ne(o) (Greek)	new	neonate, neophyte
omni (Latin)	all	omnivorous, omnipotent
onym (Greek)	name	synonym, pseudonym
opt (Greek)	see	option, optician
ord(in) (Latin)	order	order, ordinance
ortho (Greek)	straight	orthodontics, orthodox
pale(o) (Greek)	old	paleolith, paleontology
pater (Latin)	father	paternal, paternity

Roots	Meaning	Examples
path (Greek)	suffer or feel, disease	psychopath, sympathy
ped (Latin)	foot	pedal, pedestrian, peddler
ped (Greek)	child	pediatrician
pel (Latin)	drive, push	propel, compel
pens or pend (Latin)	hang, weigh, pay	pendulum, append
phil (Greek)	love	philanthropist, philosophy
phon (Greek)	sound	phonics, phonograph
phot (Greek)	light	photograph, photo
plen (Latin)	full	plentiful, replenish
plex or plic (Latin)	fold, interweave, tangle	complex, plexiglass
pod (Greek)	foot	tripod, podiatrist
polis (Greek)	city, state	policy, metropolis
poly (Greek)	many	polysyllabic, polynomial
pon (posit) (Latin)	place, put	postpone, deposit
port (Latin)	carry	export, porter, portable
press (Latin)	press, force	pressure, repress
prob (Latin)	test, good	problem, probation
psych (Greek)	mind	psychology, psychosis
put (Latin)	think, reckon	computer, dispute
quest (Latin)	seek, ask	question, quest
rect (Latin)	upright, straight	rectangle, resurrect
reg (Latin)	straighten, rule	regulation, regal
rupt (Latin)	break	disrupt, interrupt
sat(is) (Latin)	enough	satisfy, satiate
schiz, schisa (Greek)	split	schizophrenia, schism
sci (Latin)	know	science, conscience
scribe (Latin)	write	inscribe, subscribe
sect (Latin)	cut	bisect, section
sed (Latin)	settle, sit	sediment, sedative
sen (Latin)	old	senile, senior
sens or sent (Latin)	feel, think	sensation, sensory
serv (Latin)	serve, save	servant, preserve

Roots	Meaning	Examples
simil, simul (Latin)	like	simulate, simultaneous
sol (Latin)	alone	solitary, solitude
solv, solut (Latin)	free or loosen, solve	solution, resolve
son (Latin)	sound	sonic, resonance
soph (Greek)	wise	philosopher, sophisticated
spec (Latin)	look, see	spectator, inspect
spir (Latin)	breath	respiration, perspire
sta(t) (Greek and Latin)	stand, stop	stationary, static
strict (Latin)	draw tight	constrict, restrict
stru(ct) (Latin)	build	structure, construct
tact (Latin)	touch	tactile, contact
tain or ten (Latin)	hold	contain, maintain
tech (Greek)	art, skill, craft	technician, technocrat
tele (Greek)	far away, distant	telescope, telephone
tempor (Latin)	time	temporary, temporal
termin (Latin)	end, boundary	terminal, terminate
therm (Greek)	heat	thermometer
tort, torque (Latin)	twist	torture, distort
tract (Latin)	drag, draw	contract, protract
tri (Latin)	three	triceratops, tricycle
turb (Latin)	disturb, confuse	disturb, turbulence
typ (Greek)	stamp, model	typical, type
un (Latin)	one	unicycle, unicorn
ven (Latin)	come	convene, advent
ver (Latin)	true	verdict, verify
verb (Latin)	word	verbal, verbose
vert (Latin)	turn	subvert, revert
vict or vinc (Latin)	conquer	victory, convince
vid (Latin)	see	video, evident
voc (Latin)	voice	vocal, invoke
vol (Latin)	wish	volunteer, voluntary
vulg (Latin)	common	vulgar, vulgarity
zo (Greek)	animal	zoology

DEFINITIONS

Allophones are variations of single phonemes. For example, the **"p"** in **"pie"** is slightly different from the **"p"** heard in **"diaper"** and **"leap."** Speakers of English do not consider these slight variations to be distinct phonemes and hence treat them as a single sound, even though the sounds heard in words are not precisely alike.

Code cues are the associations among letters and sounds that are the backbone of our alphabetic writing system. When readers use code cues, they ask themselves, "Does this word sound and look right?"

Compound words are formed when words are combined to create a new word with a different meaning, such as **base + ball = baseball** or **rain + coat = raincoat**.

Configuration cues are the shapes of words formed by the overall contour of letters. For example, the word **bat** has an ascending letter, one letter on the line, and another ascending letter, which results in a configuration that looks like this:

Consonant blends are two or more consonant next-door neighbors. The sounds they represent are blended together when pronounced, as the **pl** in **pl**ant and the **str** in <u>**str**eam</u>.

Context cues are the syntactic and semantic information in the surrounding words, phrases, sentences, and paragraphs in a text. Additionally, the background knowledge readers bring to reading, readers' purposes for reading, and the conditions under which material is read all contribute to the reading context. When readers meet unfamiliar words, context cues narrow down the possible word choices, thereby making word identification more efficient.

Contractions are formed when two words are combined and one or more letters (and sounds) are deleted from words. Missing letters are replaced by an apostrophe that is a visual clue telling learners that a word is abbreviated, as in **they'll** and **let's**. Words mean exactly the same thing whether they are written as a contraction or individually. They are speaking and writing shortcuts.

Diacritical marks indicate that vowels are pronounced as either short or long. A **breve** is a u-shaped mark (˘) that signifies a short vowel as in **kit**; a **macron** is a horizontal line (¯) that denotes a long vowel as in **kite**.

Dialogue journals provide a means of two-way written communication between learners and their teachers, in which learners share their thoughts with their teachers, including personal comments and descriptions of life experiences, and the teachers, in turn, write reactions to learners' messages.

Digraphs are combinations of two letters that represent one sound. My recommendation is to use the term **digraph** to refer to adjacent consonants such as **ch** and **sh**, if this term makes learning easier. **VV** neighborhoods are digraphs, too, but the use of the term **digraph** for both the **VV** and consonant digraph neighborhood may confuse learners.

Diphthongs are two vowels that represent sounds that are glided together during pronunciation, as the **ow** in **cow**, **oi** in **oil**, **ou** in **out**, and **oy** in **boy**.

In-depth experiences with print are the continuous, ongoing activities in which learners are immersed in written language, in spoken language, and in sending and receiving a variety of meaningful messages.

Language experience stories are stories learners dictate or write that then become the material learners read. Sometimes stories are bound into published books, put in centers for sharing, kept in portfolios, or given to learners to enjoy in class and to take home to share with family and friends. The words in language experience stories are a rich source of onsets, rimes, letter neighborhoods, and meaningful chunks on which learners use word identification strategies.

Long vowels represent the sounds in words that are heard in letter names, such as the **a** in **ape**, **e** in **feet**, **i** in **ice**, **o** in **road**, and **u** in **mule**.

Onsets are the consonants that come at the beginning of syllables. Onsets can consist of one, two, or three consonants, as the **s** in **see**, the **st** in **stay**, and the **str** in **street**.

Phonological awareness is the realization that spoken language is made up of word, rhyme, syllable, and sound segments, and the ability to consciously arrange and rearrange these segments.

Single code cues are one or two letter sounds (or letter names) that learners connect with the pronunciation of a written word. These are the cues used in the single code cue strategy, as described in Chapter 3.

Phonemes are the smallest sound segments that differentiate one word from another. For example, the word **"man"** has three phonemes—**"m,"** **"a,"** and **"n."** The word **"can"** is just one phoneme different from **"man,"** having a **"c"** rather than an **"m"** at the beginning.

Phonics is the study of the relationship between the letters in written words and the sounds in spoken words.

Picture cues are the cues to meaning that learners glean from the illustrations in books.

Predictable books have the same language patterns repeated several times.

Prefixes are meaningful chunks attached to the beginning of words, such as **re + play = replay** and **un + cover = uncover**.

Rimes represent the sounds heard at the end of syllables and are made up of the vowel and any subsequent consonants. Words that share rimes, such as the **at** in **cat** and **hat**, rhyme. Examples of rimes include the **ade** in **shade**, the **ould** in **would**, and the **en** in **when**. Rimes need not have a consonant following the vowel, as in the word **be** in which **e** is the rime and the syllable **sta** in **station** in which **a** is the rime.

R-controlled vowels occur when a vowel in a syllable precedes an **r** and the vowel sound is modified, as the **ar** in **car**, the **er** in **serve**, the **ir** in **first**, the **or** in **forest**, and the **ur** in **fur**.

Rhyme awareness is the realization that spoken words contain rhyming sounds. Learners who are aware of the rhymes in words can separate rhyming sounds from words, identify rhyming sounds, and give examples of rhyming sounds and words.

Short vowels represent the sound of the **a** in **apple**, **e** in **end**, the **i** in **igloo**, the **o** in **odd**, and the **u** in **bus**. Though other combinations may also be classified as short, these five are typically considered when teachers and learners explore short vowels.

Semantic context cues are the meaningful relationships among words in phrases, sentences, and paragraphs. Semantic context cues are the basis on which readers decide if an author's message is logical and represents real world events, relationships, and phenomena. When readers use semantic context cues, they ask themselves, "Does this make sense?"

Sound awareness is the realization that spoken words are made of sounds. Learners who are aware of the individual sounds in words can separate spoken words into sounds and blend spoken sounds into meaningful words.

Suffixes are meaningful chunks attached to the end of words, such as the **play + ing = playing** and **slow + ly = slowly**.

Syllables are units of pronunciation that include a vowel sound. All words have at least one syllable. To find out how many syllables there are in any word, count the number of vowels you hear as you say the word aloud.

Syntactic context cues are the systematic arrangement of words in phrases and sentences that give readers information about authors' messages. Syntactic context cues are the basis upon which readers decide whether an author's word order is consistent with English grammar. Readers who use syntactic context cues ask themselves, "Does this seem like language?"

Word awareness is the realization that spoken language is made up of words. Learners who are aware of words can separate sentences into words and consciously rearrange words to form new messages.

QUESTIONS AND ANSWERS

1. Is becoming a good strategic code user important for learning to read?

Good readers are better able to use the alphabetic code than poor readers (Biemiller, 1977-1978; Byrne, Freebody, & Gates, 1992; Foorman & Liberman, 1989; Juel, 1983; Nicholson & Hill, 1985). This is true in the early grades (Share, Jorm, MacLean, & Matthews, 1984), as well as in the later grades (Lesgold, Resnick, & Hammond, 1985; Stanovich, Cunningham, & Feeman, 1984). Though strategic code use is not all there is to reading, its contribution to comprehension is critical (Juel, Griffith, & Gough, 1986; Perfetti, 1985).

As learners move from grade to grade, those who are poor code users become less and less able to comprehend the material they read, finally falling far behind good code users (Byrne, Freebody, & Gates, 1992; Freebody & Byrne, 1988). Poor code users have smaller reading vocabularies and hence are prevented from reading the variety of challenging books that are accessible to good code users (Juel, 1988). Rather than considering the words authors write, poor code users rely on their language and background experiences to guess at meaning because their word identification abilities are not developed well enough to support paying careful attention to the words authors write (Evans & Carr, 1985). Poor code users are relatively insensitive to the information in text, constructing inaccurate versions of meaning, perhaps unaware of their failure to comprehend. Becoming a good strategic code user is not only essential for progress in the early phases of reading, but it is necessary for fluent reading and sophisticated comprehension as well (Adams, 1990; Shankweiler, 1989).

2.   Are letter neighborhoods learned incidentally?

Wide reading and letter neighborhood knowledge have a mutually beneficial affect on one another. The relationship works like this: Learners who read widely meet many new words. Inevitably, some unfamiliar words include familiar as well as unfamiliar neighborhoods. Strategy users employ the reading context and the letter neighborhoods they know to figure out unfamiliar words and, in the process, infer the pronunciation of letter neighborhoods they do not know. Strategy users then remember the pronunciation of new letter neighborhoods, thereby increasing the number of neighborhoods in their storehouse of code knowledge.

This kind of letter neighborhood learning is incidental, a by-product of word identification while reading, not a planned outcome of instruction. Hence, you can expect good strategic code users to infer a certain amount of code information on their own and to do this without direct instruction or help from other adults (Juel & Roper-Schneider, 1985; Schworm, 1979). What's more, these learners are destined to become even better strategic code users by virtue of the insights they glean from reading a rich selection of storybooks, novels, plays, poems, and articles.

Incidental learning is not enough, however. Instruction has a significant and pervasive effect on the manner in which code users identify words (Baron, 1979). Planned, organized, and systematic instruction results in far better use of the alphabetic code than either haphazard instruction or the use of writing as the primary way to develop code knowledge alone (Tunmer & Hoover, 1993). On the one hand, when letter neighborhoods are taught, learners use code knowledge to identify words that they do not automatically recognize in print (Allington, 1984; Haskell, Foorman, & Swank, 1992). On the other hand, when letter neighborhoods are not taught, learners guess at words and their guesses quite often bear little or no resemblance to pronunciation. With a combination of incidental learning, direct instruction, and in-depth experiences with print, readers add neighborhoods to the storehouse of code information that helps them communicate with authors through our alphabetic writing system.

3.   How are words learned with the whole word strategy?

Learners who use the whole word strategy memorize each word as a complete entity (Heilman, Blair, & Rupley, 1990; Lapp & Flood, 1992; Stoodt, 1989). These readers remember the connection between the sequence of letters in a word (for example, **l-a-m-p**) and word meaning (for example, a device to provide light). The conventional view holds that words are remembered with no consideration whatsoever to the sounds that letters represent. Each word is remembered totally independently of any alphabetic code cues that might augment and enhance memory.

For learners who do not know how to read many words, whole word learning is an uncomplicated, easy strategy to apply. Because the phonological awareness needed for whole word learning is minimal, this strategy is accessible to nearly all learners. To remember connections between whole words and meanings, readers need only be aware of word-length segments in spoken language. And, of course, learners must know which letters on pages represent words and which do not. On the other hand, learners do not have to know the sounds represented by onsets, rimes, or letter neighborhoods because alphabetic code cues are not used to identify and learn words.

When readers remember arbitrary associations between one thing, say a written word, and another thing, such the meaning of a word, this is called paired associate learning. Paired associate learning depends on rote memorization and hence is a rather low level way to learn. Learners who use paired associate learning merely connect one thing with another thing without any sort of systematic analysis, synthesis, hypothesis formation, generalization, or transfer.

However, the whole word strategy may not work the way those who hold the conventional view believe. An alternative view is that readers do not ignore the alphabetic code in preference for rote learning, but combine visual memory with some code knowledge (Byrne, 1992; Ehri & Wilce, 1985). It has been proposed that both meaning and sound are stored in memory and retrieved when words are seen on a page (Ehri, 1992). So, even though learners do not sound out words, learners might not completely bypass the code either (Fox, 1991).

The word **have** is a case in point: If the pronunciation of **have** were consistent with the **CVe** neighborhood, **have** would rhyme with **cave** and **wave**. Though **have** cannot be completely sounded out by the use of code cues, the two consonant letters—the **h** and **v**—represent the spoken sounds readers normally expect. Readers could use these combinations as partial cues to pronunciation, which would, in turn, make remembering **have** easier. Should learners rely on some code cues to enhance their memory, then whole word learning is a sort of hybrid—not based solely on rote memory or solely on alphabetic code cues.

If the traditional view of whole word learning as a simple process of paired associate learning is correct, then readers ignore obvious and beneficial alphabetic code clues. This is an inordinately difficult and demanding task, given the recursive way our alphabet uses the same twenty-six letters (as in **came, cane,** and **cave,** or as in **was** and **saw**). Words that have many overlapping letters pose formidable learning challenges because they can be easily confused. Furthermore, rote memory is an inefficient way to build up an extensive reading vocabulary when words are written in an alphabet. As soon as learners have a relatively small stockpile of words in memory, the probability of confusing words increases enormously. As each new word is learned, readers find it more and more difficult to recall visually similar words. And so, while words may be learned with simple paired associate memorization, this strategy does not serve readers of an alphabet well and hence cannot be the sole strategy explored in classrooms.

4.   What are the advantages and disadvantages of learning to read the English alphabet?

Advantages

Our alphabetic writing system has four important advantages: First, with a finite amount of code knowledge, readers can identify a great many words. Second, knowledge of the alphabetic code enhances and advances the independence of readers. This is so because readers who use their knowledge of alphabetic code cues can teach themselves new words without depending on their teacher or another reader to pronounce a new word (Jorm & Share, 1983). Third, alphabetic code cues are a good backup to identify unfamiliar words when context alone does not narrow down the field of possible choices. As it turns out, the easiest words to predict from context are likely to be the ones readers already know how to read, while the words readers cannot infer from context are likely to be the very ones learners do not recognize (Gough & Hillinger, 1980). Fourth and last, knowing how the alphabet acts as a code for sound contributes to automatic word recognition (Stahl, 1992). As a consequence of strategic code use, the sight and sounds of words are so firmly cemented in memory that readers recognize words on sight (Ehri, 1992). Automatic recognition is extremely important because this frees readers to concentrate on meaning, not word identification.

Disadvantages

If all words were spelled the way they sound, the four advantages would make an airtight rationale for why everyone should be taught to understand and apply code knowledge. However, the relationship between print and speech is complex, not simple. Our alphabetic code does not always represent each speech sound, or phoneme, with one and only one letter. Added to this, written English is not an absolutely perfect phonetic transcription of speech. This means that the pronunciation of some English words cannot be unlocked by relying on the alphabetic code alone. Many words that are exceptions to common sound-symbol correspondence appear frequently in written language, such as **come** and **said**; other words are obviously borrowed from foreign languages, such as **chaise lounge** (French), **mesa** (Spanish), and **sauerkraut** (German). This is a disadvantage because variation and complexity lengthen the time and increase the energy readers invest in learning to read.

A second major disadvantage is that strategic use of the alphabetic code requires relatively sophisticated phonological awareness. To use the letter-sound strategy, readers must be able to separate spoken sentences into words, words into rhymes, and words into sounds. These skills do not come automatically with exposure to print: Not all kindergartners and first graders have developed the phonological awareness needed to separate spoken words into sounds. These learners have little grasp of the way that letter neighborhoods represent sounds because they are not aware of which written language segments are associated with which spoken language segments

(Chapter 2). Consequently, learners are confused by our alphabetic principle and, if our alphabetic code continues to elude them, make little progress learning to read. Thus, the strategic use of the alphabetic code is not equally accessible to all beginning readers. Only those learners who have developed, or are able to develop, phonological awareness find the code a useful tool.

The Bottom Line

The bottom line is that children who learn to read an alphabet such as ours must at some time in their development as readers (and as writers) come to understand the manner in which the letters in neighborhoods represent speech. While our English alphabet represents spoken words imperfectly, the connections between print and speech are sufficiently regular to provide readers with a useful and productive tool to identify unfamiliar words. Children who learn to read an alphabet have at their disposal a tremendous time and labor saver, a means of independence, a pathway to automatic word recognition, and a backup when context is inadequate. These advantages support and sustain comprehension, for our alphabetic writing system best serves readers when it helps them identify words that are essential to comprehension of a text.

5.   Is onset-rime a new idea?

Thirty years ago the words in some of the material for beginning readers were grouped into word families in which every family member shared a common letter pattern. The recurring letter patterns in words included a vowel and one or more consonants. Patterns were called phonograms and, in most instances, phonograms corresponded to rimes. Phonograms were the basis for family membership. Reading materials that capitalized on phonograms were called linguistic. The sentences in these materials were jam-packed with rhyming words, like **The man has a tan pan in the van.** It was hoped that with much experience reading words from the same word families, learners would eventually memorize phonograms. Then, with even more print experiences, learners would look inside phonograms, gain insight into letter neighborhoods, and then use this information to unlock the pronunciation of unfamiliar words.

Though we appreciate the value of the phonograms that make up word families, no one today suggests that learners read sentences cluttered with words that share the same rimes. Teachers now understand how onset-rime contributes to strategic word identification and hence encourage learners to observe onset-rime in words and to strategically use this information in a variety of reading and writing contexts. All things considered, onset-rime is not a new idea. Yet, our understanding of why onset-rime is important and how onset-rime contributes to strategic word identification is new. As a result, today's teachers are better able to provide opportunities for readers to develop the analogy strategy.

6. What are the advantages and disadvantage of using rimes rather than letter neighborhoods?

Advantages

While there are many advantages for using rimes rather than letter neighborhoods, the two most prominent are these: (1) the use of rimes places fewer demands on phonological awareness than does the use of letter neighborhoods and (2) rimes are relatively dependable maps for sound. As for the first advantage, when words are separated into an onset and a rime, the rime is treated as a single entity and hence need not be divided into parts. Whereas readers must know that **"amp"** comes at the end of **"lamp"** and **"stamp,"** they do not have to be able to separate **"amp"** into three individual sounds represented by the **VC/VCC** neighborhood as would be necessary to use the letter-sound strategy. Added to this, blending onsets and rimes (**"l"** + **"amp"**) is far easier than blending the individual sounds associated with neighborhoods (**"l"** + **"a"** + **"m"** + **"p"**). Fewer demands on phonological awareness make word identification with rimes more accessible to young, inexperienced, and less phonologically aware readers.

The second advantage is that rimes are reasonably dependable routes to word identification. When readers learn rimes, they do not have to figure out the sound represented by the vowel. Instead, the sound represented by the **VC/VCC** neighborhood in **lamp** is bypassed in favor of remembering the whole rime. Hence, using complete rimes short-circuits the need to remember exceptions to our alphabetic writing code. For example, if readers consider letter neighborhoods, the sound represented by the **o** in **told** should be the same as the **o** in **clock**, which results in mispronunciations and confusion. However, when remembered as part of the rime **old**, the sound represented by the vowel **o** is not at all difficult. Readers who know the rime in **told** have a code cue to the identification of **gold, behold, scold,** and **enfold**. The net effect is that even vowels whose sounds do not conform to the conventions of our alphabetic writing code are easily remembered and decoded when embedded in frequently recurring rimes.

Disadvantages

There is one major disadvantage to relying a great deal on the use of rimes in words. Beginning readers who use rimes to make analogies are not as proficient at decoding as are beginning readers who consider the letter neighborhoods in words (Bruck & Treiman, 1992). The most likely explanation for this difference is that readers who concentrate on rimes do not pay attention to letter neighborhoods. This seems to be especially true when learners are taught to read a great many words that share rimes. It is far less challenging to learn many words with the same rime (**sat, fat, cat, rat,** for instance) than to learn words that do not share rimes (words like **sat, pan, wet, fed, dig,** and **rim,** for example).

When words are easy to learn, readers spend less mental energy trying to make sense of our alphabetic code. Learners who rely primarily on the rime in words are not forced to think carefully about the letter neighborhood structure of our alphabet. These learners do not examine the letter neighborhoods inside words as closely as learners who read lots of words that do not share the same rimes. Learners who rely on the rime in words are therefore limited in their ability to use the alphabetic code when unfamiliar words do not share familiar rimes.

A Trade-Off

There is an interesting trade-off for readers who rely heavily on rimes: It is easier to identify words with the use of rimes than to identify words with the use of letter neighborhoods. Yet readers who rely heavily on rimes to identify words are shortchanged in that their decoding expertise is limited by a lack of in-depth code knowledge. A combination of lots of print experiences that include **both** rimes and letter neighborhoods holds the most promise for success.

7. What are prefixes and suffixes?

Prefixes

Experts disagree on the criteria for prefixes. Some experts believe that prefixes are not legitimate unless prefixes can be removed from the words to which they are attached. They say that, when the prefix is taken away, the word must stand alone as a recognizable English word, as with **untold** (**un + told**) and **replay** (**re + play**) (White, Sowell, & Yanagihara, 1989). Other experts take the position that prefixes can be parts of words that are not easily recognized and cannot stand alone, as with the prefix **bene** (meaning "well" or "good") in the words **beneficial** and **benevolent** (Harris & Sipay, 1990; Ives, Bursuk, & Ives, 1979). Removing **bene** leaves **ficial** and **volent**, which do not mean anything at all. Obviously, garden variety prefixes like **un-**, **re-**, **dis-**, and **semi-** are easier to recognize in words than prefixes like **bene-**. Still, some of the more challenging prefixes offer insight into word meaning, provided that they are learned and used in reading contexts.

Suffixes

Suffixes are divided into two categories: derivational and inflectional. Derivational suffixes change word meaning and grammatical function. For instance, **fear + less = fearless** changes meaning and changes a noun to an adjective; **watch + ful = watchful** alters grammatical function from a verb to an adjective. Inflectional suffixes consist of **-s** (and **-es**), **-ed**, **-ing**, **-er**, **-est**, and **-ly** (Heilman, 1989). Though these word endings contribute to grammar, they do not substantially change the meaning of the base word. For example, **cat + s = cats** indicates a plural; **jump + ed = jumped** denotes past tense; **jump + ing = jumping** indicates a present participle. In the same way, attaching **-er** and **-est** to **small** changes an adjective (**small**) to a comparative form (**small + er = smaller**) and a superlative form (**small + est = smallest**). In each instance, meaning changes, but not in any fundamental way.

Generally speaking, the more accomplished the reader, the more prefixes and suffixes in memory.

8.   *How do chunks help readers gain insight into word meaning?*

The meaningful chunks borrowed from Latin are remarkably consistent in their letter-sound associations, and the spelling of chunks borrowed from Greek are also fairly predicable (Henry, 1993). All this is important because the Greek and Latin chunks that were borrowed with such abandon long ago form a sizeable and significant portion of the words learners read. As readers move into higher grades they meet more and more technical words, not to mention nontechnical words, that include Greek or Latin roots, prefixes, and suffixes. Readers who understand the contribution that these chunks make to word meaning have access to a multitude of words.

The more readers know about prefixes, suffixes, Greek roots, and Latin roots, the better equipped they are to learn words on their own. For instance, knowing the meaning of the chunk **sta(t)** (meaning "to stand" or "to stop") suggests something about the definition of the word **geostationary,** as well as many other words, such as **station, static, stature,** and **statue.** Indeed, one of the hallmarks of mature readers is that they are independent learners, learners who are capable of looking after themselves when it comes to understanding the vocabulary used by authors of textbooks, novels, plays, poems, and articles.

Knowledge of meaningful chunks provides readers with insight into word meaning, and this, in turn, enhances word identification, vocabulary learning, and reading comprehension. This is particularly important when unfamiliar words are technical terms, such as those found in science, health, mathematics, and social studies textbooks in the upper grades and high school. Many technical terms are inventions coined to label or describe a process, compound, or situation. These coined words are often a combination of Greek or Latin roots, prefixes, and suffixes. Science is chock full of words whose origins lie in Greek or Latin roots, as we see in the words **astronaut, biology, laboratory, aquarium, geophysics, hydrometer, germinate, cryogenics, chlorophyll, seismograph, stratosphere,** and **subterranean.** Hence, meaningful chunks give readers insight into the definition of new technical terms, thereby making the information in content subject textbooks more accessible.

Since more complex and conceptually demanding words appear with greater and greater frequency in the upper grades, knowledge of meaningful chunks makes a greater and greater contribution as readers mature. Readers need a deep-seated understanding of the contribution of meaningful chunks, not just rote-memorized definitions that are easy to parrot but not necessarily applied to reading text. An appreciation of the contribution that meaningful chunks make to English words must be part of readers' basic fabric of knowledge, an indispensable aspect of their understanding of our language, its words, and its heritage. Readers who have code knowledge of meaningful chunks understand the language of learning and are undaunted by technical vocabulary. The effect of developing a deep-seated appreciation of meaningful chunks transcends the elementary school, the middle school, the high school and even college, for this knowledge is multiplicative over a lifetime.

REFERENCES

Adams, M. J. (1990). *Beginning to read: Thinking and learning about print.* Cambridge, MA: The MIT Press.

Allington, R. (1984). Oral reading. In P. D. Pearson (Ed.), *Handbook of reading research* (pp. 829–864). New York: Longman.

Baron, J. (1979). Orthographic and word-specific mechanisms in children's reading of words. *Child Development, 50,* 60–72.

Biemiller, A. (1977–1978). Relationships between oral reading rates for letters, words, and simple text in the development of reading achievement. *Reading Research Quarterly, 13,* 223–253.

Bruck, M., & Treiman, R. (1992). Learning to pronounce words: The limitations of analogies. *Reading Research Quarterly, 4,* 374–388.

Byrne, B. (1992). Studies in the acquisition procedure for reading: Rationale, hypotheses, and data. In P. B. Gough, L. C. Ehri, & R. Treiman (Eds.), *Reading acquisition* (pp. 1–34). Hillsdale, NJ: Lawrence Erlbaum Associates.

Byrne, B., Freebody, P., & Gates, A. (1992). Longitudinal data on the relations of word-reading strategies to comprehension, reading time, and phonemic awareness. *Reading Research Quarterly, 27,* 141–151.

Ehri, L. C. (1992). Reconceptualizing the development of sight word reading and its relationship to recoding. In P. B. Gough, L. C. Ehri, & R. Treiman (Eds.), *Reading acquisition* (pp. 107–143). Hillsdale, NY: Lawrence Erlbaum Associates.

Ehri, L. C., & Wilce, L. S. (1985). Movement into reading: Is the first stage of printed word learning visual or phonetic? *Reading Research Quarterly, 20,* 163-179.

Evans, M. A., & Carr, T. H. (1985). Cognitive abilities, conditions of learning, and the early development of reading skill. *Reading Research Quarterly, 20,* 327–350.

Foorman, B. R., & Liberman, D. (1989). Visual and phonological processing of words: A comparison of good and poor readers. *Journal of Learning Disabilities, 22,* 349–355.

Fox, B. J. (1991). Acquiring recoding competence: Toward a meaning driven interactive model. In D. J. Sawyer & B. J. Fox (Eds.), *Phonological awareness in reading: The evolution of current perspectives* (pp. 127–158). New York: Springer-Verlag.

Freebody, P., & Byrne, B. (1988). Word-reading strategies in elementary school children: Relations to comprehension, reading time, and phonemic awareness. *Reading Research Quarterly, 23,* 441-453.

Gough, P. B., & Hillinger, M. L. (1980). Learning to read: An unnatural act. *Bulletin of the Orton Society, 30,* 179–196.

Harris, A. J., & Sipay, E. R. (1990). *How to increase reading ability* (9th ed.). New York: Longman.

Haskell, D. W., Foorman, B. R., & Swank, P. R. (1992). Effects of three orthographic/phonological units on first-grade reading. *Remedial and Special Education, 13,* 40–49.

Heilman, A. W. (1989). *Phonics in proper perspective* (6th ed.). Englewood Cliffs, NJ: Merrill/Prentice Hall.

Heilman, A. W., Blair, T. R., & Rupley, W. H. (1990). *Principles and practices of teaching reading* (7th ed.). Englewood Cliffs, NJ: Merrill/Prentice Hall.

Henry, M. K. (1993). Morphological structure: Latin and Greek roots and affixes as upper grade code strategies. *Reading and Writing: An Interdisciplinary Journal, 5,* 227–241.

Ives, J. P., Bursuk, L. Z., & Ives, S. A. (1979). *Word identification techniques.* Chicago: Rand McNally.

Jorm, A. F., & Share, D. L. (1983). Phonological recoding and reading acquisition. *Applied Psycholinguistics, 4,* 103–147.

Juel, C. (1983). The development and use of mediated word identification. *Reading Research Quarterly, 18,* 306–327.

Juel, C. (1988). Learning to read and write: A longitudinal study of 54 children from first through fourth grades. *Journal of Educational Psychology, 80,* 437–447.

Juel, C., Griffith, P. L., & Gough, P. B. (1986). Acquisition of literacy: A longitudinal study of children in first and second grade. *Journal of Educational Psychology, 78,* 243–255.

Juel, C., & Roper-Schneider, D. (1985). The influence of basal readers on first grade reading. *Reading Research Quarterly, 20,* 134–152.

Lapp, D., & Flood, J. (1992). *Teaching reading to every child* (3rd ed.). New York: Macmillan.

Lesgold, A., Resnick, L. B., & Hammond, K. (1985). Learning to read: A longitudinal study of work skill development in two curricula. In G. E. MacKinnon & T. G. Waller (Eds.), *Reading research: Advances in theory and practice* (Vol. 4, pp. 107–138). New York: Academic Press.

Nicholson, T., & Hill, D. (1985). Good readers don't guess: Taking another look at the issue of whether children read words better in context or in isolation. *Reading Psychology, 6,* 181–198.

Perfetti, C. A. (1985). *Reading ability.* New York: Oxford University Press.

Schworm, R.W. (1979). Word mediation and generalization in beginning readers. *Journal of Reading Behavior, 11,* 139–151.

Shankweiler, D. (1989). How problems in comprehension are related to difficulties in decoding. In D. Shankweiler & I. Y. Liberman (Eds.), *Phonology and reading disability: Solving the reading puzzle* (pp. 35-68). Ann Arbor, MI: The University of Michigan Press.

Share, D. L., Jorm, A. F., Maclean, R., & Matthews, R. (1984). Sources of individual differences in reading acquisition. *Journal of Educational Psychology, 76,* 1309–1324.

Stahl, S.A. (1992). Saying the "p" word: Nine guidelines for exemplary phonics instruction. *The Reading Teacher, 45,* 618–625.

Stanovich, K. E., Cunningham, A. E., & Feeman, D. J. (1984). Intelligence, cognitive skills, and early reading progress. *Reading Research Quarterly, 19,* 278–303.

Stoodt, B. D. (1989). *Reading instruction* (2nd ed.). New York: Harper & Row.

Tunmer, W. E., & Hoover, W. A. (1993). Phonological recoding skill and beginning reading. *Reading and Writing: An Interdisciplinary Journal, 5,* 161–179.

White, T. G., Sowell, J., & Yanagihara, A. (1989). Teaching elementary students to use word-part clues. *The Reading Teacher, 42,* 302–308.

EPILOGUE

TO THE READER: SOME CLOSING THOUGHTS

In this day of video games, fast-paced television programs, and action-packed movies, books still offer readers a wonderful world of imagination and discovery. The value of word identification strategies is that they give readers pathways to figure out the unfamiliar words they see in text. The reason to understand how our alphabet represents spoken language is that the alphabetic code is the code in which authors write. Learners who know how to strategically use this code to support comprehension are well on their way to becoming accomplished readers. This, after all, is the ultimate goal and the reason that learners become expert in using word identification strategies in the first place.

When opportunities to develop word identification strategies are part of the print experiences in your classroom, learners become better strategy users. As a consequence, the learners whom you teach become better readers. Though the word identification strategies you have learned about in this book are an important part of learning to read, focusing single-mindedly on strategies without meaningful experiences with print is not enough. Likewise, giving readers opportunities to read and write without supporting strategy development is not enough, either. Readers need opportunities to develop word identification strategies and readers also need continuous, indepth experiences with written language. One without the other will not work.

Now that you have come to the end of this book, you know when word identification strategies develop, what strategies entail, how to create opportunities for readers to develop and use strategies, and ways to give readers extra practice, should they need it. You are aware of the implications for teaching, and you have a host of successful learning activities at your fingertips. Taken together, you now have the information, ideas, and learning activities you need to make strategy development part of the everyday literacy experiences in your classroom. You can, if you choose, be a teacher who makes the development of word identification strategies an integral part of the in-depth experiences with spoken and written language that go on in your classroom every day.

INDEX